# Weird

# Weird

THE POWER OF BEING
AN OUTSIDER
IN AN INSIDER WORLD

## Olga Khazan

hachette
BOOKS

*New York*

Hachette Go, an imprint of Hachette Books
Hachette Book Group
1290 Avenue of the Americas
New York, NY 10104
HachetteGo.com
Twitter.com/HachetteGo
Instagram.com/HachetteGo

First Edition: April 2020

Hachette Books is a division of Hachette Book Group, Inc.

The Hachette Go and Hachette Books names and logos are trademarks of Hachette Book Group, Inc.

The publisher is not responsible for websites (or their content) that are not owned by the publisher.

The Hachette Speakers Bureau provides a wide range of authors for speaking events. To find out more, go to www.hachettespeakersbureau.com or call (866) 376-6591.

Print book interior design by Marie Mundaca

Library of Congress Cataloging-in-Publication Data has been applied for.

ISBNs: 978-0-316-41848-5 (hardcover), 978-0-316-41849-2 (e-book)

Printed in the United States of America

LSC-C

10 9 8 7 6 5 4 3 2 1

*To my parents, the original weirdos*

# Contents

## PART FOUR: TO STAY DIFFERENT, OR TO FIND YOUR OWN KIND?

# PART ONE
# BEING WEIRD

# CHAPTER 1

# Weird

The origin of my weirdness is that I grew up a Russian-Jewish immigrant in a town called Midland in West Texas, in a region whose biggest claims to fame are being the onetime home of George W. Bush and serving as the inspiration for *Friday Night Lights*. A Chicagoan once asked me what the nearest big city to my childhood home was. When I matter-of-factly responded that it was El Paso, he burst out laughing.

My father, who had been an electrical engineer and black-market TV repairman in Russia, had secured a job at a Midland petroleum engineering company by offering to provide Russian translations for the company's oil deals with Siberians. (Siberia having had, along with the rest of Russia, recently discovered capitalism.) My mom did accounting for a small company, and sometimes she pitched in with the translating. My parents would often take me along to their translating jobs, so I spent much of my childhood asleep on white tablecloths, waiting for the adults to wrap up their schmoozing.

"Culture clash" implies a bold interplay of contrasting patterns; what we experienced could more accurately be described as a culture transplant. We were sewn into this new place and hoped it took. Almost everyone we met was an evangelical Christian who believed they would live eternally in a celestial paradise— and many felt obligated to let us know about it. My babysitter considered glossolalia to be a fun afternoon activity. The only kids' activity at our apartment complex was an improvised Sunday school, whose organizers prayed with me that my parents would become Christians. A boy called me a "wetback" in the middle of class, and I thought seriously about changing my name. When we watched the *Addams Family* movies, I developed a strong kinship with pale, dour Wednesday Addams.

Midland was a town mostly populated by white Americans and Mexicans, and both groups largely kept to themselves. Besides us, there were at most a handful of non-Spanish-speaking immigrants in town. (We did not, however, know each other, only *of* each other. As in, my dad once mentioned that he thought he saw a Ghanaian at the grocery store.)

West Texans exhibit an easy dominance of their inhospitable natural environment, which is something I never did master. They are a group of people who are simply not messed with, whereas I constantly was. Much of the grass there is not grass, but rather "stickers" that will gouge holes in your skin. Once, my father saw a man shoot a rattlesnake in his front yard with a rifle, then pick it up by the neck and present it to his children with a smile. At a treacherous desert day camp, I was stung by so many fire ants that my feet no longer fit in my shoes. As I cried, the camp counselor scolded me for not being tough.

In fourth grade, I changed schools halfway through the year because my family moved across town. Unsurprisingly, I did not take well to the new environs. A short list of things I had issues with: Going outside on field day. (Due to allergies, which my teachers took as a sign of sneaky insubordination.) In science class, making "birth announcements" for a baby dinosaur of our choosing. (Birth announcements were not a custom in Russia.) Being in the same math group as the class pretty girl. (Obvious reasons.)

At the new school, lunch was eaten in shifts, like in a Dickensian workhouse. Before lunch, our class would file out of the room and line up outside the cafeteria. We would sit down on the concrete walkway and wait for the first wave of eaters to leave so we could take their still-warm seats.

My parents grew alarmed when they learned about this system.

Not the staggered lunches—the part about the sitting on the concrete.

"You do this even in winter?" they asked.

This practice, of course, violated the iron law of Russian medicine: sitting on cold things allows pneumonia to enter the body through its most vulnerable access point, the anus.

They decided to spend their parental-concern capital on making it so that I was no longer allowed to sit on the ground with the other kids. Instead, I spent my pre-lunch minutes loitering by the teachers, attempting to make adult conversation. *"Nice brooch. Did you get that at Dillard's?"*

My exemption raised questions among my classmates, who mashed together my eccentricities to formulate a theory as to why I couldn't sit with them. One day, curiosity got the best of them, and the boldest among them asked, "Is it true you're allergic to concrete?"

---

The "holidays" at my house consist of the fake Soviet Christmas known as New Year's Eve. When you're a kid, this is the night you meet Soviet Santa, aka Grandfather Frost, who will only give you presents if you recite him some poems. (From each according to his ability...) It's the night when my mom makes eggs stuffed with caviar and puts on her finest new sweater so that we will be rich in the New Year. Then she turns on the TV and shushes us so she can hear the traditional New Year's address delivered by Vladimir Putin.

When I was in middle school, we left Midland for the relatively cosmopolitan cul-de-sacs of the Dallas suburbs, about a six-hour drive east.

Neither my parents nor I made many friends. Instead, my parents subscribed to a service that would deliver Russian television to our house. Gradually, it became practically the only TV they watched. That's still true. They also only eat Russian food, and they almost exclusively read Russian news sites. They essentially live in Russia, in the U.S.

Of course, one's native culture is always going to feel cozier. But I can't help but notice that they are missing out on the golden age of American television for a series of increasingly complex Russian ice-skating-based reality shows. I imagine this retreat to their homeland is, in part, a reaction to the alienation we experienced in Texas. In the Dallas suburbs, we had few negative experiences on account of our ethnicity, but we didn't have many especially positive ones, either. I think this ennui soured my parents on American culture slightly, and prompted them to look elsewhere for connection. You see a similar phenomenon with people who spend all their time LARPing. Yes, it's a reclusive, looked-down-upon subculture, but at least it's *their* subculture. When you find yourself in constant disagreement with the world, you withdraw into yourself. You re-watch old movies, wear your broken-in pajamas. You move back, mentally, to a country you fled. When you are the only one of your kind, you just want to find your kind again.

If "weird" has a feeling, it is at once energizing and maddening, like trying to squeeze into a space where you might plausibly fit, but don't quite. (In fact, weird people are sometimes literally told they are not a "good fit.") Being weird feels like showing up alone to a party where you only know the host, except the host is in the bathroom, and *Oh God, are you even in the right house?* Except the party is your life.

You might know what it's like to be considered weird if you have few friends, or if you have an unusual hobby or lifestyle, or if you struggle socially. Or, you might be otherwise well-adjusted but are one of the few people of your ethnicity or gender or physical appearance doing whatever it is you do or living wherever it is you live. Sometimes, weirdness hinges on identity: women who have little interest in caring for children are considered strange by society, but so are men who *do* enjoy childcare—in fact, we'll meet one such man soon.

This book is for those who have spent their lives feeling different, as well as for those who only feel different by dint of circumstance—perhaps because of a job or move. Maybe you attribute your personal or professional struggles to this difference, and the fact that you didn't choose to be different makes them all the more hurtful. As the psychologist Sharon Lamb, who grew up poor, wrote after she didn't get tenure, "That year of job hunting consolidated my suspicion that my upbringing in apartment buildings and playing in back alleys and empty lots meant that I would never be able to have a foundation among old stone buildings and those phony 'traditions.'" When you're locked outside something, it's hard to know whether it's because of something about *you*.

Weirdness affects us all, in one way or another. Maybe you aren't weird, or at least not at the moment. Maybe you simply live with social anxiety or impostor syndrome—two of the common side effects of weirdness that can gnaw at the psyche for no particular reason. Maybe you are trying to understand why your neighborhood, school, office, or social circle is so homogenous, or why so many people are uncomfortable living alongside people who are different. What is it about unusual people and ideas that makes us so uneasy? And why do so many free-thinking adults all end up living in very similar ways?

Or perhaps you're in charge, trying to help a diverse team of individuals do their best work. You hope to use their distinctiveness to fuel success, like many of the people I've interviewed for this book have done. Or maybe you're just trying to spur the team you're a part of to come up with the best, most creative solutions possible. Weirdness might be an asset, in that case.

You might be relieved to find, as I was, that it's actually advantageous to be different, and that there are ways to turn your weirdness into a superpower. The stories of the individuals in this book hold valuable lessons for people facing all of these weird situations, and more.

It can be hard to visualize "weird." (Like that other thing, you know it when you see it…or at least when you don't get the baby-shower invitation all your coworkers got.) For me, the peculiar nature of my family's immigration journey was what lodged me between identities and caused me, until very recently, to feel deeply uncomfortable in my own skin. It was what made me, for lack of a better word, weird.

Every year during my middle school years, my family moved to a different Dallas suburb right as school was letting out for the summer. The initial move was for my dad's new job, but that threw us into a prolonged house-hunting slog that I still struggle to understand. Each house we hunted happened to be in a different school district of the sprawling metroplex. This meant I never knew any of the other kids in my neighborhood before embarking on a long stretch of unscheduled, summer sitting-around time. I had to take care of my toddler brother anyway, so entire months would pass in which I wouldn't talk to any kids my own age. We had a small collection of DVDs that my mom got for free from work, including the little-seen Matthew Perry vehicle *Fools Rush In* and the movie adaptation of *Get Shorty.* I would carefully ration them out so that I had one new one to watch every week until school started.

When the school year began, I found there were usually other outcast-type kids—think intense manga fans—but they seemed able to join forces, creating their own mini-society of oddballs. I, meanwhile, never encountered another Russian immigrant kid like me. I rode the bus alone. I spent almost every evening alone. Since I didn't have an iPod yet, I spent a lot of time talking to myself—a habit that unfortunately has stuck.

For a while in high school, I decided to see what I was missing and joined a rural, evangelical Christian youth group. I began to spend hours each week scouring the Bible in search of loopholes that if read a certain way, allowed for sex before marriage. I would highlight all of these potential provisos and drag the Bible to my pastor's house, whose wife would sit me down with a plate of underdone brownies and explain why no ma'am, Jesus never did say you can have sex just 'cause you're *super* in love. To be clear: not a single human being alive on earth had expressed even a passing interest, at that point, in having sex with me. But I wanted to have my argument airtight just in case.

One day, someone toilet-papered our house, and I had to explain to my parents that this is what American kids do to losers.

Undeterred, my dad eagerly raked the toilet paper into a garbage bag and put it in his bathroom for future use. "Free toilet paper!" he said happily over dinner.

The day in high school we were supposed to have sex ed, we had instead what I can only describe as Prejudice Happy Hour. We were told to shout out qualities that we wanted in a friend, and the teacher would write them on the board. This was intended to build self-esteem, the key to avoiding pregnancy. (The belief at the time seemed to be that self-confident people never have sexual intercourse.)

"Christian," someone said. The teacher dutifully wrote it on the board.

"Straight," someone else ventured. The teacher wrote it down.

A couple kids raised their hands in protest. I'd like to think I was among them, but the embarrassing truth is I don't remember if I was.

What I do remember is the teacher defending the list's inclusion of "straight." If a gay person stood next to him, he explained, he would feel uncomfortable. But personally, he added, he had no problem with gay people.

I would go home and log on to our enormous, shared family PC. I had maybe visited ten websites at that point, all of them for school papers. The one exception was sfgate.com, where I could read columns by Mark Morford.

In my teenage disgruntlement, I had begun painting Texans with too broad a brush. Kind, open-minded Christians got lumped in with fundamentalists who beat their children in front of strangers. I wrote off apolitical popular kids, by virtue of their likability, as ignorant and unsophisticated. I mentally ignored the English teacher who was fond of saying, with a twinkle in her eye, "Candy is dandy, but sex don't rot your teeth," and instead focused on my classmate who said she was confident we would win the Iraq War, because God was on our side. (As psychology poetically tells us, other people are all alike; people within our own tribe are dazzlingly unique.) Years later, I learned through Facebook that a lot of my classmates had grown up to be politically moderate yuppies who were not so different from me.

At the time, though, I relished the escape Mark Morford provided. Each week, Mark dedicated his column to skewering the war hawks and Bible thumpers that I had come to feel surrounded by—even if wrongly. Despite Mark's probable veganism, he was one of the few American writers my dad loved, and one of the few interests he and I shared. Mark was unlike anyone I knew: He hated homophobes; he loved yoga. He is how I first learned about soy milk. I was amazed that he inhabited the same physical world that I did, yet he could voice these incendiary opinions, which almost everyone I knew opposed. He was like a portal to a parallel universe, one where weirdos ruled.

I developed something between a crush and a cult member's devotion to him, which was only consummated by a long email of appreciation I drafted circa 2004, but never sent. I must have gushed extensively about Mark around my dad, because one day he tried to temper my expectations.

"He look gayish," he warned.

All of this did little to prepare me for college at American University, an East Coast school that was approximately 110 percent Jewish and liberal. After a lifetime of having *maybe* three friends, I was to live in a dorm room with another girl—one who had, no less, premarital sex.

In the first few weeks at AU, we had a very different type of sex ed class—one that didn't make me any more comfortable than the Texan one did. We gathered in a small study room and were told to write down as many synonyms for penises and vaginas as we could think of. By the time someone shouted "cum bucket," I was rending my garments. Then they showed us dental dams, and I did not know what they were for, and someone saying "oral sex" did not get me any closer to figuring it out. A few years prior, at my high school, a girl had gotten in trouble for acting "unladylike."

That first year of college was so disorienting. At one point, a guy friend of mine opened his mail to find *The New Yorker*—a gift subscription from a doting, learned aunt. Someone joked that the articles are so long he'd probably never get through an issue, and everyone laughed and said that was sooo true. I laughed too because it seemed better than admitting I had never heard of *The New Yorker.*

I had also never met so many male Democrats, which thank goodness, because if I had I might have tied a lasso and roped them, just like they taught us they do with errant calves back in grade school. It wasn't so much their views on NAFTA or solar panels that I craved as the fact that Democrats, in my mind, meant *different.* A *different* guy, I thought, would understand me.

Except I now had an ideological panoply of males before me, but I had no idea where to begin. One specific problem was that I didn't know how to end conversations. No boy-of-interest had ever started a conversation with me. And I, in turn, had never started a conversation with one. So naturally, I had no idea how or when one was finished.

I went with my best guess: just swiveling on my heels and walking away abruptly, whenever there seemed to be a lull. I tried this in my first week, in the cafeteria, with a cute guy who had expressed an interest in me.

Sauntering away, I remember thinking, *Yes, this was the right thing to do,* which is something people never think when it actually was.

I wish it had been a phase. I wish I was the nerd who became hot by taking off my glasses. But social skills are *skills.* At my first party in college, I felt inept and imperiled, the way people feel the very first time they try to strike a match.

Well into my job at the *Washington Post,* I was hounded by a feeling that my employer shouldn't have taken a chance on someone like me, who didn't grow up reading her hometown newspaper and penning precocious letters to the editor. I was someone who had instead spent all her time watching *Saved by the Bell* and falling even further behind the coterie of well-read ideators.

Having been weird for so long still haunts me in so many ways:

Like when I feel like I can't socialize without a glass of wine oiling me up from the inside—and how often I replay those conversations after the fact. Or the time my therapist held out one hand parallel to the floor to show me where everyone else is, mood-wise, and then held out another hand, about six inches lower than the other one, as though her hands were two trains about to pass each other, and I was on the lower train, going in the wrong direction. "Your affect is kind of, *here*," she said, jiggling the bottom, depressive hand. Sometimes, strangers ask me if I'm lost.

A few years ago, I was interviewing a man named Michael Ain, and in the middle of our conversation I started to feel unusually, well, insecure about my inability to get over my insecurities. This is what he told me:

In the early 1980s, Michael was wrapping up his junior year at Brown University. He had excellent grades, a record of volunteer work, and a stack of awards from his elite high school, Phillips Academy. He was determined to pursue a career in medicine, so he made an appointment with the adviser in charge of students who were med-school bound.

The moment Michael walked in the door, the counselor bristled. "You check all the boxes, and your grades are good," Michael remembered him saying. "But you're going to have a hard time."

Michael asked what he meant by that.

"Look," the counselor said, walking over to a paper thermometer taped to his wall. The temperature reading was supposed to represent the percentage of med-school applicants who had gained admittance to their top-choice school. The counselor pointed to the 95-degree mark.

"That's my average," he said. "You're gonna be bad for my average."

"I don't give a shit," Michael said, using what would become a go-to phrase for him in situations like these.

The counselor thought for a minute. "Well, in that case I guess you have two options," Michael recalled. "Either tell them about it ahead of time, or . . . just go to the interview and see what they say."

The "it" the counselor was referring to was that Michael, an adult man, was just 4 feet, 3 inches tall. If he stood toe-to-toe with an average nine year-old, their eyes would meet. That's a standard height for someone with his condition: achondroplasia, or dwarfism.

Michael's interest in medicine took root during his regular childhood trips to various medical specialists, who worked on his painful joints and ligaments. He admired how some doctors treated Little People with respect, giving them a little more time to take their pants off, for example, but not doing it for them. He imagined how great it would feel for a kid with dwarfism to have a doctor who knows exactly what it's like.

Michael excelled in school, and even sports, but when he was preparing to graduate from college, society had not yet progressed sufficiently to allow Little People to be considered capable doctors. At the time, people like him were still derisively called "midgets." Still, after the counselor's appointment, Michael decided he wasn't going to back down. He figured he'd just leave his height off his application. He applied to thirty medical schools in all.

Being short has, for centuries, been associated with not just physical but mental frailty. Little People have long been laughed at and exploited, enlisted as court jesters or circus performers. A medical textbook from 1959 speculated that many dwarfs are "backward for their age," adding, "Because of their deformed bodies they...are emotionally immature and are often vain, boastful, excitable, fond of drink and sometimes lascivious." Even today, bias against people of short stature is one of the last acceptable prejudices in the world. Short men are still joked about and discriminated against in the labor market.

When Michael arrived for his med-school interviews, he was looked down upon in more ways than one. Some admissions officers would go through the motions. Others stared awkwardly, then dismissed him from the meeting. "Patients won't respect you," one said. "They want tall doctors with long, white coats." He was rejected from every single school.

Many rational people—even very dedicated ones—would have

given up at this point. Michael's reaction could not have been more different. "I wasn't going to let these fuckers stop me," he said.

He applied to thirty more schools. Only one accepted him, and only because the admissions officer loved baseball, the sport Michael played in college.

When Michael finished up med school, he decided to pursue a residency in neurosurgery. But when he sent out his residency applications, he once again faced a slew of rejections because of his height. He resigned to work in pediatrics for a year. "It was good, but I missed surgery really badly," he told me.

He applied to dozens of orthopedic surgery programs, managing to land at Albany Medical College, where the head of the orthopedic surgery program didn't care what anyone else thought. Michael assured his colleagues all he needed to do his job was a step stool. He excelled at the program and was even chosen to lead grand rounds in orthopedics.

Eventually, Michael became a professor of orthopedic surgery at Johns Hopkins Hospital in Baltimore, one of the country's top medical institutions. He specialized in children with dwarfism and developed new techniques to help people with spinal deformities.

When I reached this point in my conversation with Michael, I was as awed by his accomplishments as I was by his easy acceptance of his physical difference. I also felt that—there's no other way to say this—by comparison, I sound really whiny.

Yes, I had a rough time in childhood and adolescence. But I'm virtually indistinguishable from all the other mid-career office drones in Washington, D.C., where I now live. Even if I weren't, there are plenty of immigrants here, and it's considered politically incorrect to probe too deeply into anyone's ethnicity. In short, I can pretty much glide through life pretending that I've always been a middle-class, East Coast white girl. When people learn I'm from Texas, they're often surprised.

So, I thought, why am I in therapy, but Michael Ain is at Johns Hopkins, saying "fuck you," literally, to the naysayers? How do you write your sixtieth medical-school application when everyone is telling you that short people can't be doctors?

Michael knew he was an outsider. Yet he seemed certain he belonged among the insiders. I was curious whether people could cultivate an attitude like his. How can people who are different embrace whatever it is that makes them unusual and, just like Michael did, use it to power them?

At the same time that I wanted to feel more accepted, I wanted it to be for reasons other than my ethnic origin. Outside of D.C., the questions from strangers tend to follow a similar progression: "That's an interesting name…where are you from?" "Were you born there?" "Why did your parents move here?" How nice it must be, I sometimes think, to describe your passion for surfing or Krav Maga to new acquaintances instead of the visa processes of the former U.S.S.R.

I was always jealous of people who were able to move through the world unencumbered by assumptions about them. There must be something so blissful about an identity you picked, rather than were arranged to marry.

When you're the only one of your kind, you're rarely just "yourself." Instead, you're an ambassador for a country you never chose. In my case, it was an actual country, but for Michael Ain, it was being short. For the other people in this book, it was some other identity marker they never quite chose to be yoked to.

I was surprised to find that I am not alone in feeling simultaneously overly conspicuous and under-included: We are a nation of accidental outsiders. A lot of us, in essence, feel weird. Nearly one in eight Americans experience social anxiety, defined as a persistent fear of talking to or being scrutinized by strangers. And *most* Americans report feeling lonely and misunderstood. In a 2018 survey of 20,000 American adults, 54 percent of the respondents said that they "always or sometimes feel that no one knows them well," and 47 percent sometimes or always feel "left out." "Most Americans," the report concluded, "are considered lonely."

Feeling understood is important for more than just kumbaya reasons. For example, women are less likely than men to finish traditionally male PhD programs, in subjects like computer science or physics, if they have no other women in their cohort. "More female peers," the authors of that study write, "create a female-friendly environment that encourages women to persist in doctoral programs." Being the only one of your kind is doable, but wearying.

Lacking connection with other people carries steep health consequences, too. As Robert Putnam prophesied in his book at the turn of the millennium, Americans are increasingly *Bowling Alone,* and it's killing us. One researcher found that lacking social connections is as harmful as smoking fifteen cigarettes a day. Loneliness is deadlier than obesity, and it increases the risk of dementia.

And yet, the way we live now seems destined to cause more and more people to feel like lonely outliers. Workplaces are actually becoming *more* segregated by race. Residential income segregation is also on the rise, which means neighborhoods are increasingly all-rich or all-poor. Wealthy people tend to socialize more with self-selected friends than with their neighbors, further pruning their social circles to people who match them perfectly. Nearly a quarter of Americans now say they seldom or never interact with someone from a different political party, and nearly a third rarely interact with someone who has a different sexual orientation. Crossing any of these rigid identity boundaries can feel very anxiety provoking, indeed.

This feeling of estrangement can be especially pronounced for people who didn't grow up around the "rules" of elite jobs and social circles. For example, the sociologist Daniel Laurison examined one television-production firm where there was a "studied informality" to the style of dress. "People were wearing sneakers and all kinds of casual, fashionable clothes," Laurison told *The Atlantic.* "There was a sort of 'right' way to do it and a 'wrong' way to do it." One man, who was black and from a working-class background, didn't quite match the aesthetic, opting for tracksuits instead of the more acceptable hip hoodies. Eventually, the man left. Everything from how to dress to whether it's okay to swear in the office can keep people barred from unfamiliar worlds.

America has also grown profoundly politically polarized—so

much so that actual political partisans are writing books about how we need to put an end to all the partisanship. A person's political party now says more about them than simply who they voted for. Democrats, as the political scientists Shanto Iyengar and Masha Krupenkin write, have become "the party of non-Whites, women, city dwellers, the young, and 'highbrow' culture." Meanwhile, "the Republican electorate consists disproportionately of older White males, evangelicals, southerners, and people more interested in NASCAR than the NBA." These crystallized identities cause fault lines to deepen and foster us-versus-them thinking. It's now common for people to ask me what my political affiliation is before they agree to talk with me for a story. Being the only Republican in a liberal workplace or social circle—or vice versa—would feel especially awkward these days.

At the same time, it is becoming more important to get along well with other people. Since 1980, jobs requiring lots of social interaction increased by 12 percentage points as a share of the overall labor force, and high-paying jobs increasingly require social skills. As the researcher David Deming writes, "employers routinely list teamwork, collaboration and oral communication skills as among the most valuable yet hard-to-find qualities of workers." Conjuring an image of a frustrated office worker trying and failing to get a robot to fist-bump him, Deming writes that this is because "social interaction has—at least so far—proven difficult to automate."

That is, just as we're becoming more alienated from one another, splintering into tribes and escaping to our screens and echo chambers, our livelihoods increasingly depend on being smooth and capable collaborators. Everyone is feeling weirder, and we're all supposed to be fine with it.

## TODD, PART I

Even seemingly normal, average people can struggle to make or keep friends. At first glance, Todd, a white man in his forties who works in tech, seems like he could perch atop any social pyramid if he so desired. (Todd is a pseudonym, for reasons that will become clear later.) I first met him several years ago at a conference in a hotel ballroom, and if there was anything remarkable about him, it's that there was nothing remarkable about him. He looked like he sprang from an infomercial, dusted himself off, and could at any minute begin ShamWowing the banquet chairs.

Despite his everyman-ness—he's married with children—he explained to me by phone later, he's never had any close friends. As we talked, the similarities between Todd and myself became more and more evident. We both seem to lack the friendship gene. Small talk, for people like us, feels like tap dancing while frosting a cake.

As a kid, Todd attended a predominantly Christian elementary school where, like me, he didn't quite fit in because he's half Jewish. He was an only child, and he remembers trying to play board games against himself a lot, trying to beat the other four versions of himself. He would add extra rules to Monopoly, trying to stretch it to four or eight hours. He watched how his scholarly parents interacted with their friends, and he tried to spar intellectually like that with his own classmates. The only problem was that Todd and his friends were eight years old.

Having failed to get in with the popular crowd, Todd never developed the social skills that seem to come so easily to well-liked kids. Before long, what had been a small difference in social aptitude between him and his elementary school classmates yawned into an unbridgeable gap. In college, he did finally make a few friends, but they lost touch after graduation, leaving Todd, once again, alone.

He admitted that he put less effort into developing friendships than other people do. He's not hard to get along with, but he had a tendency to speak to people like an anthropologist, not a friend. He'd ask, "What do you do? What are you interested in?" After building a full psychological profile of his interlocutor, he wouldn't reveal even a morsel about himself.

He described the following thought process whenever he was in conversation with a group of people at a party: *"I wish I could come up with something to say… why didn't I think of that thing that person just said?* Then I'm so far behind and I realize I haven't said anything for ten or fifteen minutes, and now I might as well just pay attention to other people."

When he did meet people, Todd didn't follow up about getting together. He seemed befuddled about whether he should be texting people more often or sending out more birthday cards.

Fortunately, Todd was happy to be alone most of the time. His propensity to look inward, he felt, helped him understand the technology he used for work in a deeper way. But, even in our first phone call, he wondered, ever so tech-ily, if this lifestyle "scales." He was worried that he didn't really have any guy friends to talk with about married life or fatherhood. He had been on his own socially for so long, it was starting to wear away at him. He was beginning to experience the downsides of his own weirdness.

It would turn out that his long game of solo Monopoly was quickly coming to an end, in a disastrous way.

While working on this book, I realized that sometimes my weirdness was someone else's fault, but sometimes it was actually mine. Sometimes it was no one's fault, but the wound from all the previous times was still so raw that I reacted three or four or forty times as strongly as I needed to. Later, experts would tell me this is called "inflammation." Either way, my weirdness was the defining experience of my life. Both my pathologies and strengths flow from it.

At some point several years ago, I decided to start interviewing people who also seem like misfits, but who for the most part handle it well. It was an attempt, I later realized, to answer the question: Why are they so comfortable with themselves, and I'm not? (Later, experts would tell me this feeling is called "impostor syndrome.") For this book, I've interviewed more than three dozen people who are unique in their environments: they live or work in situations where—because of their ideology, gender, race, background, or some other factor—almost no one else is like them.

Their stories, though wildly different, tended to follow similar trajectories. Each person I met faced an acute realization of their outsider status, followed by a period of reckoning with their difference. In most cases, they experienced a change—of mindset, of setting, or even personality—that enabled them to find happiness, or at least contentment. Some of them ended up seeking out people just like them, while others were happy to be eternal sore thumbs. But all of them have found some measure of success, despite being no less unusual than when they started. What they learned in the process may prove helpful to anyone who's felt they can't quite break through to the "in" crowd, regardless of what's keeping them out.

As I met with and learned from my interviewees, I attempted to cure my own insecurities by putting into practice some of their strategies. I also dug deep into the psychological research on social anxiety and nonconformity, and, because it was 2019, I used an app. These measures have all helped, as I'll describe, to varying degrees.

Here is the conclusion I came to: It's good to be a weirdo. Being different from other people around you confers hidden advantages that can help you in life and in work. It also behooves you to live and work among weirdos: Groups are smarter and more powerful when their members hold a diversity of views. If standing out makes you uncomfortable, as it did me for many years, there are ways to smooth your reentry into Normville while still staying true to your weird roots. These strategies and life hacks, which I learned from the people I interviewed, can be applied by those facing a wide array of social challenges, even if they're otherwise perfectly normal. Many of us might want to lead a group of people in an unconventional direction, gain a new perspective on our problems, or simply make more friends. My interviewees—people who have had to do all of those and more in the most extreme of circumstances—are the ideal teachers.

---

Before we set off on our journey, I have a few notes to readers:

All of the people I feature are unique because of some combination of their identity and where they happen to live or work. (A Muslim may be considered "weird" in certain parts of America, but would not be in Pakistan.) Because I focus on this binding tie—the condition of being an outsider—in some cases I will discuss people who have suffered different levels of adversity within the same chapter.

I don't mean for this grouping, however, to imply that I consider the low-level unease of, say, a white immigrant to be equivalent to the obstacles faced by people of color or those living with rare medical conditions. Being laughed at by preteens and being discriminated against for centuries are simply not comparable experiences.

There are systemic, horrific problems in our society that the tools of psychology are not equipped to address. The fact that marginalized people have learned to cope with some of them does not mean the fight for equality should ebb.

However, in other, more subtle ways, social exclusion affects a broad swath of humanity. We can learn how to overcome it from those who have dealt with it best. We can look to people who have battled stigma, coped with social anxiety, and smashed stereotypes in order to learn more about those phenomena—and what we can do about them.

Finally, a word on "weird." I have several reasons for using a word that's sometimes considered offensive, or at least negative.

First, I hope to reclaim it. People who have different beliefs, appearances, or identities are often written off as just plain weird. In the worst cases, we're actually called weird under people's breaths or to our faces. But I've come to view weirdness as a strength rather than a hindrance—even if aspirationally. Maybe in becoming comfortable with applying the word to people who are successful, we'll start to see difference as less of a negative trait.

Second, it surprised me to learn, in the course of my research, that the word has not always had a negative connotation. "Weird" has had, frankly, a weird history. The word's usage gained popularity after the 1850s and fell again after the 1920s, only to reemerge, with spandex and big hair, in the 1980s.

"Weird" developed its more positive, quirky meaning in these more recent decades. Travel books came out urging you to explore "weird and wonderful" something. A book called *Weird Maryland,* for instance, promised to show you the state's best-kept secrets. In 2000, when Austin Community College librarian Red Wassenich coined the phrase "Keep Austin Weird," he meant we should preserve its one-of-a-kind culture. (In a *Washington Post* interview, he even used "weirdo" the way I mean it here: "You've got underpaid, highly educated people, and that makes for a breeding ground for weirdos," he said, attempting to explain the city's urban-Western *je ne sais quoi.*)

But it was an earlier definition of "weird" that captured my interest. Before the 1800s, weird was more likely to mean supernatural, or fantastical. Shakespeare, for instance, called the witches in *Macbeth* the "weyard sisters." Wyrd is the Old English word for "fate," and by the eighth century, a form of it, wyrde, was used to refer to the three Roman mythical, goddess-like Fates. The first one, Nona, spun the thread of life; the second, Decima, measured it; and the third, Morta, cut it as she saw fit. The three Fates represented the idea that our futures are determined, in part, by our circumstances.

In that case, wyrde—weird—could be considered a kind of prediction, a destiny. Much like what psychology suggests, your unusualness is a fabric woven from the thread of your life. Your identity, your environment, and your experiences all combine to make you who you are. But your weirdness is also a hint at what you might live to see and do, at what hidden powers you possess. "Weird," then, is your potential.

CHAPTER 2

# The Realization

Your middle school teacher was wrong. Like it or not, it matters what other people think of you. Again and again, research has shown that our opinions about what's right are shaped by the people around us. And usually, what we consider "right" is whatever everyone else is doing.

Psychologists in labs have changed individuals' perception of how much a dot of light moved, how long a line is, or even how much it's appropriate to hurt someone, simply by surrounding them with the opinions of other people. In group-discussion experiments, people rate those who agree with the average sentiment of a group highly; they reject those who disagree with the group. To encourage people to use less energy, the Sacramento Municipal Utility District sent residents report cards revealing how their energy use compared with that of their neighbors. The utility set the norm, and people used less energy as a result. All these findings point to roughly the same conclusion: we like to fit in with the group; we like people who fit in with the group; we dislike those who don't. These norms, or unwritten rules about what we "ought" to be doing, determine what's weird or isn't.

Michael Ain broke norms because most doctors weren't short. My family broke norms in Texas with every facet of our being, from our language to our religion, or lack thereof.

On an individual level, how much we care what society thinks of us might be influenced by our biology. In a 2014 study, the psychologist Shinobu Kitayama found the degree to which we uphold cultural norms is related to the type of variation we have on one gene, the dopamine D4 receptor gene.

The gene doesn't change how we behave; instead, it influences how much we endorse the prevailing norms of our environments. Asians who carried certain variations of this gene became more interdependent. They were more likely to endorse values related to social harmony, collectivism, and modesty. Meanwhile, European Americans who carried the same gene variants became more individualistic—a traditionally white American norm. The gene makes you more of a rule follower, whatever the rules happen to be.

People with borderline personality disorder and certain other conditions, such as autism, have trouble comprehending social norms. People with borderline, or BPD, as it's abbreviated, struggle with mentalizing, or guessing what other people are thinking. They tend to be hypermentalizers—they interpret people's intentions in the worst way possible, and they don't react, well, *norm*ally. People with BPD sometimes come from difficult homes, or they have unusually sensitive temperaments.

"Your first laboratory to learn how to read the minds of other people is your family environment," explained Carla Sharp, a professor at the University of Houston who has studied the disorder. It's where you learn "that it's okay to ask someone what you're thinking, that it's okay to change your mind." For some people with BPD, this laboratory failed. They didn't get to practice "the literacy of interaction," as she puts it. Social norms are the first book we all learn to read.

Norms, though, are fickle friends. On the positive side, the tipping norm pays waiters' salary and the "don't walk into traffic" norm prevents chaos and carnage in the streets. Most people like following norms, and they like people who do, because we don't like to be surprised by every single thing that happens. The rhythms of small talk and office speak steady us with their predictability.

In her masterful study of social norms, *The Age of Innocence,* Edith Wharton describes a "hieroglyphic world" of Gilded-Age

New York. At first, the couple at the center of the story—Newland Archer and his fiancée, May—happily follow these rigid formulas. "Nothing about his betrothed pleased him more than her resolute determination to carry to its utmost limit that ritual of ignoring the 'unpleasant' in which they had both been brought up," Wharton writes of Archer early in the book.

But later, Archer leaps to the defense of May's cousin, Ellen Olenska, saying her "unhappy life"—a scandalous and very norm-violating separation from her husband—"doesn't make her an outcast," despite what those around him claim.

As Archer found, norms can also hold us back. They give us structure, but they punish anyone who dares break free of them. "Norms are inherently conservative," says Chris Crandall, a psychology professor at the University of Kansas. "We tend to persist in doing what the people before us did."

Countless interracial couples suffered, for example, when there were strong norms against so-called miscegenation. In maintaining social order, norms can make things too tidy. Norms freeze our lives in amber, a process that can be beautiful, but also deadening. To return to our fictional example, because of the norm that one should marry "well" and stick with one's partner, Newland Archer is never able to be with Ellen, even though he realizes he loves her more than May.

Émile Durkheim, the nineteenth-century French father of sociology, described the importance of having a balance between societal rules that are too strong or too weak. Without norms, he wrote, we enter *anomie,* a lawless state in which groups don't cooperate and the goals of society and the individual begin to diverge. Lacking any guideposts for how to feel or what to do with their lives, people in a state of anomie are likely to commit anomic suicide, he speculated.

But when we break social norms, Durkheim explained, we are often punished socially as harshly as we would be under the law:

> If I do not conform to ordinary conventions, if in my mode of dress I pay no heed to what is customary in my country and

in my social class, the laughter I provoke, the social distance at which I am kept, produce, even though in a more mitigated form, the same results as any real penalty.

When norms are too harsh, when society is too strict, Durkheim speculated that people feel "choked by oppressive discipline" and instead commit "fatalistic" suicide. (This idea of rampant suicide may sound very Victorian and melodramatic, but the fact that suicide rates are higher when society is either too libertine or too oppressive was found in a study just a few years ago.)

Many social norms don't necessarily make sense—what is the purpose of a necktie, for example, or of asking "How are you?" when you don't really care—they just exist. Those who break them, even in benign ways, are known in the scientific literature as "deviants." They bear all the baggage that word suggests.

There is, perhaps, no better representation of the randomness of social norms than swimwear. The entire process, from purchasing the bikini to donning the bikini to moistening the bikini to covertly picking the bikini out of your butt, entails specific, unwritten requirements that are hard to figure out yet unthinkable to violate. Forget literature; future anthropologists will study our pool selfies to gain knowledge of our ways.

Swimwear, if you think about it, is nearly identical to underwear. Consider the horror you would feel if someone walked in on you changing. Now consider the fact that all the women at the pool are wearing roughly the same amount of—or even slightly less—material than comprises their typical bras and briefs.

Yet we encourage this because…swimming.

Despite their skimpiness, there are elaborate rules women must adhere to when it comes to swimsuit shopping:

1. It can't be an actual one-piece racing suit, like the kind Olympians wear. If you are fit enough to be a professional swimmer, the thinking seems to be, you should dress like you aren't one.

2. The swimsuit must be revealing enough to perform your gender, yet modest enough to perform your age.
3. It must look like it *could* slip off very easily, while being unlikely to actually do so.

The one-piece swimsuit is back in vogue, but for most of my life it was the aquatic equivalent of pleated khakis. One summer at my church youth group, it came from on high, Pastor Kyle's office, that we would be having a mixed-gender field trip to the local water park.

There was a swell of excitement. Many of us girls, I suspect, yearned to parade our nubile bodies around like a bunch of Pearberry-scented Jezebels. But then came a very unfortunate caveat: all the girls would have to wear one-piece bathing suits, and those who didn't wear one-pieces would have to wear a t-shirt to cover themselves. In the end, it would be many years before a man would see my navel.

A few summers ago, I bought a new swimsuit from a hip young people's store. When I put it on, I realized the top violated rule 3 from above—it started sliding down my chest just as soon as it was on me. In hopes of salvaging the situation, I ordered a new top from a more grown-up store, since I have also heard that "mixing it up" is an acceptable thing to do with the two halves of a bikini these days.

As soon as the new top arrived and I tried it on, I knew I had only made the problem worse. It was neon yellow. It looked cheap and hastily made, like a sexy banana Halloween costume. I returned to the store website to read the online reviews: "BEWARE. The seams on this make it look like there are ARROWS pointing at your nipples."

This is a common complaint among female bathing-suit reviewers: that a bathing suit clearly designed to showcase your breasts makes it too obvious that you have breasts. The ladies' swimsuit sweet spot seems to lie on the smudgy line between confidence and modesty, originality and conformity, body shame and unabashed celebration.

"This 'elephant in the room' is perhaps the strangest paradox of the pool: everyone is nearly naked, yet nobody refers to the fact," writes the sociologist Susie Scott in *Reclothing the Emperor: The Swimming Pool as a Negotiated Order*, her study of the norms of swimming pools. "Male swimmers wear trunks or boxer shorts and women wear swimsuits or bikinis, in both cases to cover the sexualized parts of the body, though actually accentuating them."

But ignoring this is necessary so that we can maintain the notion that sprawling out in two square feet of polyester is just what respectable career women do on weekends.

"To openly acknowledge the potential for sexual contact between people would disturb the polite fiction that this is just a place of exercise, inviting embarrassment and making normal swimming impossible," Scott adds.

My pool employs a rotating cast of dreamy lifeguards hailing from faraway countries. When you first walk in, their deep accents beckon you to sign a form that indemnifies them in case you drown in the three feet of water. Most people, including me, stay fully clothed for this part. I usually strip down to my swimsuit later, huddled under a towel.

Scott compares pool lifeguards to wardens in Foucault's Panopticon tower, set apart from the nearly naked riffraff:

> Lifeguards...must maintain a delicate balance between appearing vigilant in watching over the swimmers and demonstrating that their gaze is nonsexual....Lifeguards wear a uniform that strips them of their individuality and defines them by their role: like doctors wearing white coats, they show that they are present in a professional capacity and have no other interest in the proceedings.

Then there are the norms related to actually submerging oneself. At my pool, few people go in the water, despite wearing outfits designed expressly for this purpose. Meanwhile, some women do go in the water, but they keep their shorts on, even though they billow up around them like Ursula's tentacles.

One day, a woman at my pool was wearing a slinky bikini top, which, as the day wore on, strained against the weight of its cargo. As she embarked on a mission toward the beer cooler, one of her agents, perhaps expectedly, went rogue. Everyone stopped and stared at it, even the heretofore-disinterested lifeguard. We then quickly whipped our heads away and pretended to examine the pool water. (To stare longer, as Scott points out, would be to bring "the discreditable stigma of nudity to bear on the individual's social face.")

The woman stopped, tucked her boob back in, shrugged, and kept walking. Janet Jackson was pilloried for less, but the pool's norms are singular, and they contain nipples.

One day recently, my friend got a Groupon for a Korean spa that's in a local strip mall among karaoke joints and dim sum. The spa is a hidden gem of Asian Northern Virginia, a place where forty dollars buys you up to twelve hours of sweating near strangers.

The thing about this spa is that you are fully naked for part of it. I texted my friend to make sure she knew this, since if this information is sprung on you, it can be jarring. My only experience with public nudity at that point had been in middle school, when I changed in the locker room without a bra on, since I didn't wear a bra, since I didn't grow breasts until well into my third decade. Middle school opprobrium ensued, and I haven't quite felt free to let it all hang out since. I was worried my friend of fifteen years with whom I've talked at length about the virtues of the male form would suddenly think I was a lesbian.

My friend was not similarly concerned. "So?" she texted back.

In the line to get into the spa, we saw a crestfallen couple who were apparently expecting something more like a resort, rather than a cross between a gulag and a nude beach.

My friend was, apparently, fine with it. "Ready to get naked?" she asked me cheerily as we tucked our phones and shoes into our lockers.

After my friend and I had stripped, a random stranger, her

nipple rings glinting in the fluorescent light, showed us the way to the "bade pool." The pool, with its cerulean water, mushroom-shaped fountains, and gobs of nude flesh, looked like something out of an adolescent rococo painter's wet dream. Best friends gossiped while their bare asses got kneaded by underwater jets. The only safe place to gaze was somewhere in the middle distance. One woman stood under a very open-facing showerhead, closed her eyes, and scrubbed her crotch diligently. The Koreans seemed to take it in stride, but at least for the awkward white people, there was a suspension of social norms to a degree that was alarming.

What's interesting about the spa is that it's not like people suddenly began to celebrate nudity. Instead, it was proof that social norms can change *without* people changing their actual attitudes—toward naked butts, in this case. It's enough simply to plant the idea that something is normal and suggest that it's the right thing to do. How you, personally, feel about it doesn't matter; you'll do it anyway.

Princeton University professor Betsy Levy Paluck discovered a similar phenomenon in a study on a far more tragic topic a few years ago. For her work, she focused on Rwanda, where a genocide against the Tutsi ethnic group by the Hutu-majority government in 1994 resulted in the death of three-quarters of the Tutsi population.

After the genocide ended, but trauma remained, Paluck traveled to the country to examine the effects of a radio program called, in English, *New Dawn*. It was produced by a nonviolence nonprofit, and it aimed to ease ethnic tensions. The program portrayed two ethnic groups who worked together and spoke out against violence, and even included a Romeo-and-Juliet-like story line about two lovers from different communities. Over the course of a year, Paluck studied groups of Rwandans who were exposed either to the *New Dawn* program or to a control program about an unrelated topic.

Her results were either disappointing or uplifting, depending on how you look at it. The *New Dawn* program didn't change the community's beliefs about violence, trauma, or war. The people who had listened to the "correct" messages about violence were still just as likely to believe that "evil people" cause violence, rather than more practical factors like passive bystanders or a lack of open dissent and intergroup connections. They still thought traumatized people are just crazy and can't recover.

But surprisingly, the *New Dawn* listeners' norms shifted anyway. They became less likely to advise their children to marry only within their own ethnic group. They grew more tolerant of dissent, and were more likely to say trauma survivors should talk about their struggles with someone. Her experiment showed, in essence, that we will often uphold whatever we perceive the norm to be, even if our minds don't change accordingly. People will endorse a norm even when their personal beliefs completely contradict it. Just ask any "cool boss" who has ever drug-tested an employee.

To root us back in our far, far less important example: Our fellow spa-goers still thought being naked was shameful. But they did it anyway because the teenage clerks in the lobby told them to.

After our naked time, my friend and I donned the spa-provided orange uniforms to go to a coed area, where we would sit in a variety of gem-encrusted rooms. There's an amethyst room, a charcoal room, and a room that has thousands of tiny clay balls rolling around the floor. They provide a range of healing properties, as long as what you need to be healed from is not having enough strange smells in your life.

In the "cold" room, whose walls are covered in ice, a group of twenty-something guys sat on little stone stools. Three were bearded, one clean-shaven. The Beards talked jovially among themselves, while No Beard, who seemed to have been dragged to the spa by the others, gazed sullenly at the tile floor.

The Beards talked about how funny it was that everyone was naked. (If you break the norms, you have to make fun of yourself for doing so, thus neutralizing your original infraction and making yourself, once again, a norm follower.)

"Let's go to the clay ball room next!" one of the Beards yelped.

"I think," No Beard said, "I've seen enough balls today already."

Compare all of this to the experience of Annette Kellerman, one of the first women to attempt to swim the English Channel. In 1907, she appeared on Revere Beach near Boston wearing a one-piece bathing costume with short sleeves and pant legs that ended two inches above her knees. To us, she would have looked like a woman dressed in modest shorts and a tank top.

And yet, "a shocked howl went up and down the land," the *New York Times* wrote in 1951.

At the time, most women swam in wool dresses over bloomers and stockings, along with knitted caps, often with tassels on top, and "bathing coats" to wear over the whole getup. This was a norm mandated from above, but which had mass buy-in. One British official was quoted as saying, around this time, "mixed bathing stops more marriages than any other cause [and] much of the unrest in the country is due to the barbarous license in women's dress." (Today, there are still rigid norms around women's bathing outfits. More recently, in Italy, where ten-year-olds roam beaches topless, women in burqinis have been banned from swimming pools because, according to critics, they look improper.)

All Annette Kellerman wanted to do was swim freely. Instead, she was arrested. The judge took pity on her and told her she could wear her suit—but only if she wore a cape covering it to the water's edge.

Annette later launched her own one-piece swimwear line and wrote about the importance of letting women swim unencumbered. "Not only in matters of swimming but in all forms of activity woman's [*sic*] natural development is seriously restricted and impaired by social customs and costumes and all sorts of prudish and Puritanical ideas," she wrote in *How to Swim* in 1918.

But when the bikini was unveiled decades later, she didn't sound quite so progressive. "The bikini shows too much," she said, according to the *Boston Sunday Globe*. "Only two women in a million can wear it. And it's a very big mistake to try."

Annette Kellerman was willing to create an avant-garde new rule, one saying people should be, in some contexts, free to escape the confines of culture. But social norms are as strong as they are arbitrary. The female navel was too much, even for a radical like her.

## DANIEL, PART I

In 2007, Daniel, a young man living in Ottawa, had recently dropped out of college after a long illness. He was bumming around, unsure what to do with himself. His family was urging him to pick a career. Any career.

He considered teaching high school history, but he found Canada's bureaucratic teacher-certification program daunting. He figured getting an early-childhood education certificate would be easier than becoming a licensed teacher, so he took early-childhood development classes at night through a local college. He had always loved working with little kids, and he was awed by how important the first five years of life are, in terms of human development. At worst, he thought, it would be a fast track into teaching elementary school.

His family was relieved Daniel had finally settled on a path toward adulthood, but privately, they hoped preschool was just a starting point to a proper teaching job. Daniel's father was especially unimpressed, calling early-childhood education Daniel's "Mickey Mouse" degree.

When Daniel arrived for one job interview, he walked up to the school secretary's desk and told her he was the job candidate. "Are you Danielle?" the woman said.

"Daniel," he answered.

The first thing that happens when we encounter a norm violator, says Chris Crandall, is to subtly communicate that they have strayed. *What kind of hair is that? Where did you get that outfit? Are you Danielle?* The idea is to give you a chance to prove your normalcy after all.

On a tour of one center, preschool administrators showed

Daniel the men's bathroom. It was being used as a storage closet. "We've never had a man work here before," they explained.

For Daniel, it was moments like these—grasping that he would need to alert people not to refill their office supplies whenever he needed to urinate—it really hit him that he was not going to blend in effortlessly. Almost all my interview subjects had a moment like this, one where they personified the *Sesame Street* song, "One of these things is not like the others." They felt like a skydiver as the first rush of open atmosphere whips past. They were on their own.

There might be more men finding themselves in Daniel's position soon. Traditionally manly jobs in factories are disappearing, and some of the jobs with the greatest projected growth, like home health aides and nurse practitioners, are historically and overwhelmingly female.

Laid-off, male coal miners and factory-floor workers have been reluctant to take these jobs. Part of it has to do with hang-ups around gender stereotypes: "I've always seen a woman in the position of a nurse or some kind of health care worker. I see it as more of a woman's touch," is how one laid-off welder put it to the *New York Times* in 2017.

Although some research suggests men who enter traditionally female professions are put on a fast track to supervisory positions—a phenomenon called the "glass escalator"—there's also evidence that men are just not as respected when they're in roles like nursing or elementary school teaching. In one survey, half of men thought women make better nurses than men, and 16 percent of women thought so, too. Only male patients preferred male nurses, and only when the task the nurse would be doing was something intimate, like giving them a bath or shaving their genitals.

Some male teachers of young children are similarly stigmatized. A 2002 sociological study of male elementary school teachers found they were afraid to let children sit on their laps, something female teachers often allowed. Even when parents were happy their children had male teachers, they sometimes projected stereotypes onto the men. As the sociologist Paul Sargent wrote, one single mom was happy her son would have a male teacher, Javier, because she was concerned her son was getting too interested in art and poetry. Javier, as it happened, loved art and poetry.

Daniel, who is rotund, with dark hair and glasses, enjoys people and thrives on a certain amount of bedlam. I met him and his boyfriend, Patrick, for lunch one summer at a popular Toronto Thai spot called Salad King.

Daniel explained that as he worked his way up through various preschools in Toronto, he occasionally faced judgment from parents. One mom asked the principal not to leave Daniel alone with her kids. At one job, if he was the first to arrive to work, a mom would wait in the room awkwardly with him until a female staffer arrived. More typically, moms would second-guess his opinions. "Mum knows and that's it," he told me. "Upon giving birth, there's a beam of light that imbues you with knowledge."

Perhaps it was no wonder moms were so skeptical of male early-childhood experts: they are vanishingly rare. In the U.S., men make up just over 2 percent of all preschool and kindergarten teachers, and the numbers are similar in Canada. Most of the men Daniel studied early-childhood development with had left the field almost immediately. Kids, apparently also unsure what to make of him, tended to call him "Miss Daniel."

When Daniel did an Ask Me Anything interview with Reddit, the social network, it attracted the attention of so-called men's rights activists. They wrote things like, "What is this stupid man doing? Why is he working with kids, he's gonna get himself accused, and his life is over," Daniel recalled.

At the time, he laughed it off.

When we reached this point in the interview, Patrick interjected, trying to sum up how people think of his partner: "He's either a unicorn or the scary penis."

In 2017, Daniel became the supervisor of a daycare center in Toronto. The role put him in charge of hiring, training, billing, and otherwise running a center for children aged nine months to four years.

The new job was fun and rewarding, but stressful. The entire staff was new, so there was a lot of turnover at first. There were cameras in all the classrooms, and in one case, Daniel had to fire a male teacher because he saw him yelling at a child.

The sudden disappearance of a male teacher clearly rattled the parents. "Ooooh, I'm so sorry about Mr. Michael," the moms said. Then, more hesitantly, they'd add, "Did anything happen? Is there anything we should be...concerned about?" Daniel estimates he reassured about forty moms that day that essentially, no, Mr. Michael did not molest their children.

That's on top of the more run-of-the-mill disasters, like the toilets exploding or the virus that mowed down all the teachers in one week. Out of forty-five children, eleven had anaphylactic allergies. One girl was allergic to cold (yes, in Canada). One boy, unbeknownst to his parents, was allergic to legumes. One child's parents claimed he was allergic to "anything red."

A few months into Daniel's tenure, it became clear that one of the teachers on staff was "not working out." She was an older woman who seemed rather set in her ways. Her room was often messy, Daniel and a coworker told me. She would, for example, leave moldy chickpeas in the cupboards or ignore some of the kids while they climbed on top of tables. When Daniel gave her instructions on how to improve, she would say, according to Daniel, "How do you know? You've never had kids."

After a string of problems, Daniel sat the woman down and told her she was fired. He had expected her to be sad, but instead, she grew enraged.

"This is racism," he remembers the woman, who was not a native English speaker, saying. Then she said, "I feel so blessed to be leaving here."

Shortly after that, a review appeared on the daycare's Facebook page purporting to be from a parent of one of the children. It called the daycare center "racist" and made references to the person being "blessed." It seemed like it was written by someone who speaks English as a second language. Toward the end, as though in a throwaway line, it claimed Daniel touched kids inappropriately.

Daniel suspects the post was written by a relative of the fired employee. (When I contacted the fired employee, she denied that either she or a relative had written the post. She also said Daniel had never behaved inappropriately with a child.)

Everyone doubted Daniel would do such a thing. The daycare center's cameras meant all the employees' actions were visible. And as a supervisor, Daniel wasn't in the classrooms much.

The owner of the daycare called the former employee and told her that the review needed to come down immediately or lawyers would get involved. The post was down within minutes, Daniel says. The timing added to his suspicion that the former employee did, indeed, have something to do with it.

However, since an allegation of child abuse counts as a "serious occurrence," the owner had to contact the local Children's Aid Society to report the incident. The idea of being tarred as one of "those" male preschool teachers who hurts kids terrified Daniel. The very thing that made Daniel different looked like it was about to bring about his downfall. That afternoon, Daniel paced the halls, crying. He figured his career was over.

## JULIA, PART I

The mirror image of Daniel is an American NASCAR driver named Julia Landauer. Like Daniel, she pursued the vocation she's most passionate about, even though few people of her gender do.

The top two series of NASCAR are called the Monster Energy Cup series and the Xfinity series. (As I would learn, everything in NASCAR is about branding.) The women currently racing in those series number in the single digits. The winner of each of the 2,546 races in the history of the top NASCAR series has been a man. Just below that level, trying to break through to the top, is twenty-eight-year-old Julia.

I wanted to see what goes into racing while female, so one day

Julia invited me to come watch her as she did her workout—one that would prepare her to wrangle a 3,400-pound machine with, I'm guessing, a size 2 frame.

Julia is brunette and slight, but with squared-off shoulders and sinewy limbs, like a ballerina who could probably kick your ass. I was expecting a tomboy, but she's more like a cool nerd. She's exceedingly polite and doesn't like fighting or roughhousing. She wears makeup, and though she told me she's not starting a family anytime soon, when she sees babies her ovaries go "into overdrive," as she puts it. In case you're wondering, she dates men.

At the gym, she sprang between the elliptical, rowing machine, and sets of planks, push-ups, and what she calls "leopard crawls" across the room on her toes and hands. She grabbed a 15-pound weight and tipped it back and forth like a steering wheel. She laid back on a bench and lifted her head up and down. Racers—including the famed Dale Earnhardt Jr.—get concussions, and this exercise builds neck strength to help protect against them.

Before we left, Julia sat on the edge of a sit-up bench, closed her eyes, and moved her hands through the air like she was turning a wheel—first gently right, then gently left, her feet cocked on invisible pedals. She was visualizing the track, coaxing her muscles to learn its shape. She did this for one dry lap, and, just in case, for one lap in the rain.

Later that day, she stretched out in front of her silver MacBook to study videos of past races. The key was to learn the track, to find out where her car should be, where she should pass, and what she should look out for. On one video, when the camera zoomed in, you could see the drivers shake from the sheer force of the speed, like astronauts during liftoff.

Silently, I worried for them.

"Super slow," Julia, at one point, muttered.

Julia is a woman of relatively few words, given all she could talk endlessly about if she wanted to. She went to Stanford, gives motivational speeches all around the country, and has been racing cars since she was thirteen years old. When she does speak, it's in a low patrician rumble, a cross between Jodie Foster and Candice Bergen. Whatever the opposite of "shrill" is, she's that.

She was raised by a lawyer mother and an anesthesiologist father on the Upper West Side of Manhattan. Julia and her two siblings all raced go-karts, and they were roughly evenly skilled, but Julia was the one who most wanted to go pro. Strangers began coming up at the go-kart races and telling Julia's father, Steve, how good she was. At first, she was intimidated at the track, casting her gaze downward, but her father and her coach, Glenn, reminded her that she had just as much a right to be out there as anyone.

From there, her career resembles a typical wunderkind montage of "firsts" and "onlys." At fourteen, she became the youngest female champion of a racing series called the Skip Barber. She was the first female champion of a 2015 NASCAR racing series in Virginia. The following year, she placed fourth at K&N, another racing series, which was the highest finish ever for a woman. In 2016 she became the only woman in her class of NASCAR Next, a program meant to develop young drivers. Overall, she has won 27 of the 150-some car races she's entered.

This success has come despite the fact that people at the track have called her a bitch. They have called her the next Danica Patrick, the one famous female NASCAR driver, when she'd rather be the next Jimmie Johnson. One time a racing official said "good luck" to every contestant, then came up to Julia and just asked if she had her safety equipment. Some men race her harder because she's a woman: they block her or push her to the side. "Emotionally," her father explained to me, "they can't be beaten by a woman."

The winner of the race we watched on Julia's laptop was a driver with the consummate French-Canadian name of Kevin Lacroix. His car bears the logo of Bumper to Bumper, an auto-parts company of which his family owns a franchise. A few people I spoke with enviously speculated that because of this sponsorship, when someone like Kevin blows a $40,000 engine, his sponsors can just write a check for another one. (Kevin, in an email, told me his budget is fixed, so it wouldn't exactly work that way.)

Perhaps more so than in many sports, money and sponsors are the lifeblood of NASCAR, covering the car's absurdly expensive "heart"—its drivetrain, engine, transmission, and chassis. The seatbelts alone can cost $500. Sponsors pay for the cars' shops and the men (it's mostly men) who staff them. They pay for the racing suits and the gas and the giant trailers that drag the cars from the shops to the tracks and back again. They cover travel, repairs, tires, backup equipment, and entry fees.

Without these sponsors, drivers can't race. One team, Furniture Row Racing, which won the NASCAR Cup championship in 2017, decided to close down the following year when one of its key sponsors pulled out. One journalist, Bob Pockrass, compared this to the "Philadelphia Eagles shutting down a year after winning the Super Bowl."

It's easier to get into good races and win often when you have a consistent sponsor, or when your family runs a business or knows someone who does, or when your parents are willing to pay millions for you to race, or when you're otherwise financially blessed in a way Julia, for the most part, hasn't been so far. I, personally, found it ironic that a sport so synonymous with the blue-collar average joe is so reliant on deep-pocketed relatives and corporations.

Fewer people watch NASCAR on TV these days, so companies are less willing to buy what Julia calls the 200-mile-an-hour billboard—their logo on the car itself. Besides, if they do, there's always the chance the car will crash, and "Allstate" will end up scrawled on a hunk of crumpled-up metal, which would be even worse optics than not sponsoring anything in the first place. The thinking among would-be sponsors seems to be, why pay to attach your name to a driver with unknown prospects when you could just throw a few grand at a Kardashian to make an Instagram post that will be seen by millions?

People tell Julia that if she had gotten into NASCAR a decade earlier, before the bottom fell out of the business model, she'd be wildly successful. "Yep," she quips. "And if my aunt had balls, she'd be my uncle."

These financial struggles may be hitting female drivers especially hard. Because it's so expensive, families might devote their racing resources to only one child—typically a boy, since boys are also more likely to be nudged toward masculine and aggressive sports like racing. Because there are fewer younger women in the NASCAR pipeline, there are then fewer women in the sport's professional ranks. Jeff Pappone, a Canada-based motorsport journalist, told me that it's getting harder to sell "being a woman" to prospective racing sponsors. The first woman to show real marketing savvy, Danica Patrick, was buzzy and new. Now, female drivers are still extremely rare, but sponsors see each new one as less of a marvel.

And even if a female driver *can* woo sponsors, as Pappone recalls hearing from one female racer, "You have to decide if you want to be a racer or a *woman* racer. Do you want to be a girly-girl or one of the guys?" In other words, do you want to be seductively eating a cheeseburger in an ad, or racing cars? Sex still sells, and it's not something female racers are always comfortable selling.

Julia does chase after whatever money is left in the sport. She gives pretty much whatever speeches people ask of her, including, once, a forty-five-minute talk on asphalt. She got really close on a big deal with a large tech company, but her contact there left.

Both Julia and Danica Patrick have suggested that it's harder to find racing teams that will throw their support behind female drivers. "Teams are more likely to assume a guy will do well until he proves he won't," Julia says, while a woman isn't assumed to do well "until she proves over and over again that she will."

Because of how difficult it was to raise funds, when I emailed Julia in the summer of 2018 to try to arrange a visit, she had no races set up. "It's a huge bummer but my unfortunate reality right now," she wrote.

She was staring down a long season without getting into a car.

One reason it's hard to be "the different one" is that to our brains, there's something intoxicating about the familiar. American actors are more likely to win Oscars than BAFTAs, the U.K.'s film award, while British actors are more likely to win the British award. ("A creation is most likely to be regarded as outstanding when artists are seen by perceivers to be 'one of us,'" the researchers behind that study concluded.) In fact, perhaps the biggest psychological myth in pop culture is that opposites attract. While this would be good news for the attractively challenged, it's unfortunately not true. Research has consistently shown that instead, in both friendships and romantic relationships, people seek out people who are almost exactly like themselves. Spouses and friends may very well become more similar to each other over time, but they start out resembling each other, too. People try to find others with the same backgrounds and beliefs in order to befriend or date them. One study found that pairs of friends even exhibited similar neural activity when watching videos, especially in regions of the brain that are associated with emotions, attention, and reasoning.

When Chris Crandall, the University of Kansas professor, discovered that friends are similar on about 86 percent of hundreds of different variables, including personality, beliefs, and behaviors, he acknowledged in a news release that this is not necessarily a good thing:

"Friends are for comfort, taking it easy, relaxing, not being challenged—and those are good things," he said. "But...you also need new ideas, people to correct you when you're loony. If you hang out only with people who are loony like you, you can be out of touch with the big, beautiful diverse world."

Because of this tendency for people to cluster with others like them, it is more difficult to find acceptance and friendship in an environment where you're the different one. No one, unfortunately, sees themselves in you.

"Khazan...is that? What nationality is that?"

My interviewee and I were sitting on a stage, about to get microphoned for a live interview I was conducting as part of an event at work. We had run out of prep material, so the conversation turned to where I'm from—I told him Midland, Texas—and eventually, to my heritage.

"I'm Russian," I responded. "The last name is Hebrew."

I learned this in a grade school genealogy project, when we had to look up the origin of our last name and then draw it. Mine was Hebrew, and as if that wasn't weird enough, the genealogy book said it meant "cantor." I didn't know what that was and had to look it up separately, only to learn that it was some sort of singer in a synagogue. I didn't know what a synagogue was either. I was jealous of the girl whose last name was Welsh for "stone."

Back onstage, my interviewee pressed me further.

"So you're Jewish?" he asked.

"My dad is," I answered truthfully, hoping we would run out of bullshitting time soon.

"So," he said, smiling slightly. I can only imagine what he was thinking: *There are so few ways to make a genuine connection in this cruel world! Let's try to make one now.* "Did you have enough Jews in Midland for a *minyan*?"

For a solid three seconds I thought he was asking me if my West Texas hometown was populated by yellow animated creatures, the Minions.

"I'm sorry," I said weakly. "I don't know what that is."

"What?" he said. *"Minyan? Minyan!"* (*Surely she'll get it, daughter of a Jew after all!*)

"I . . . I don't."

*"Minyan! Minyan!"*

"MOST RUSSIAN JEWS ARE ATHEISTS!" I cried, a millisecond before our mics went live.

I turned to the audience and smiled. "Thank you all for joining us!"

The journey of my weirdness, I suppose, begins with my family and others like it being cast aside as weirdos in our own homeland.

Jews like my father were considered a separate race in the Soviet Union, determined by blood and denoted in a person's passport. Jews ranked prominently among the many peoples ethnic Russians historically disliked.

Under the czars, my ancestors were forced to live in far-flung villages beyond the "Pale of Settlement." My great-great-grandfather was only allowed to move to Saint Petersburg because he had grown wealthy off the lumber business—then as now, money talked in Russia. Employers avoided hiring Jews, and the best universities were generally out of reach to them, as well. My father's alma mater— a strong technical university in Leningrad, as Saint Petersburg was then known—was a "Jewish school." Its director was a gentile, but because he was a war hero, he was impervious to the political pressure aimed at keeping out Jews and other minorities. Word spread that Jews would be accepted there, so an atheist yeshiva formed in the heart of Russia's second-largest city.

My mom and dad met at a party in Estonia, where my mom— a native Finn—was living at the time. After my parents began dating, my mom brought my dad home to meet her parents, a pair of Lutheran farmers with elementary school educations. They liked my dad. But they wanted their daughter to be sure she knew what she was signing up for. "People don't like the Jews," my grandma warned her.

But my mom was already taken by my dad's charm and wit. She soon moved to Leningrad to be with him. After they married, she kept her Finnish maiden name to avoid causing problems for herself.

My dad's Jewish friends were young, ambitious, and growing tired of being second-rate people in a second-rate place. The West was better, they were sure of it. Whenever they gathered, the conversation inevitably coiled back to the prospect of leaving Russia for good.

"It was, 'This one left, this one is about to leave,'" said Victor, a college classmate of my dad's, who now lives in Massachusetts. "Are you going to leave? To where? When? It's almost like if you're sixty-five and in New York, you're talking about Florida. Boca Raton or Miami?"

American Jewish organizations and their political allies considered the U.S.S.R.'s mandatory atheism and persecution of Jewish dissidents to be a sort of cultural genocide against the Jews. They began to pressure Soviet authorities to release Jews from the U.S.S.R., from which emigration was essentially forbidden. The effort came to a head in December of 1987, when more than two hundred thousand people representing three hundred synagogues, youth groups, and other Jewish organizations marched on the National Mall the day before Russian president Mikhail Gorbachev's scheduled visit with President Reagan. In talks with Gorbachev that week, Reagan brought up the situation of the Soviet Jews before he even mentioned arms control.

The doors creaked open. Tens of thousands of Soviet Jews began to flee the U.S.S.R. each year. American Jewish organizations hurried to line up Jewish communities across the U.S. to sponsor the immigrants.

The Soviet Jews folded their bedsheets and East German suits into their single allowed suitcase. They boarded planes for Austria, then Italy, where they would interview with the American authorities and be processed by a refugee agency called HIAS. In 1989, my family packed up and left, too.

American Jews, most of whom have family roots in Eastern Europe, awaited them eagerly. To them, as Fred Lazin, a scholar of Jews in America, described it, it felt like "our families are coming back."

It was only upon the Russian Jews' arrival that the Americans discovered they weren't like family at all. They were, in fact, quite weird.

The problem was, the U.S.S.R. had no religion. Having had no exposure to Judaism throughout their lives, Soviet Jews were largely ignorant of the religious traditions American Jews had always embraced. Here's how the American Jewish Committee's Russian-Jewish affairs director Sam Kliger described it in a research report several years ago:

Oral reports and publications indicate that some American Jews depict Russian Jews as not "Jewish enough" who not only are ignorant of and indifferent to Jewish religion and tradition, but also are insensitive to American Jewish culture... Explicit forms of personal religious practice or communal identification, such as wearing a kippah, and a Jewish communal life separate from the general population is [sic] unfamiliar to them and difficult to accept. Being Jewish, for them, is less about action and community and more about relaxing with friends and talking about God or about Israel's flaws and successes. For most Russian-speaking Jews, Jewish identity is not a matter of choice or religious practice, but rather a sociological fact, prescribed at birth and known to the individual and his or her family, not to be casually announced to everyone who wants to know. A Russian Jew may know he or she is Jewish, may be proud of it, may feel, think or even believe as a Jew, but rarely will act as one.

Now that we were in a place where we could act Jewish, we had no desire to. According to a 2004 survey by the AJC, only 6 percent of Russian-speaking Jews considered religion "very important."

There would be hardly any Jews in the place my family would end up next, but even if there were lots, I doubt we would have fit in well with them anyway.

A year into our new American life, my dad was persuaded to move our family from Los Angeles to Midland when, during a short visit to Midland on business, he stopped in to a random apartment complex and asked the management office how much they charged for a one-bedroom.

"Two fifty," said the woman behind the desk.

"Two hundred fifty?" my dad replied. "A week? This is not bad."

"A month, sir."

It was done. We had no money, and this arid place seemed to require very little.

My dad returned to Los Angeles and shared the good news with my mom: "You can't imagine what a hole it is. It's hideous. But we have to move there."

To be sure, we were so poor that my mom, the former head of finance at her company in Leningrad, had been working as a cashier at McDonald's, and the prospect of saving up some money was appealing. But my mom was vehemently opposed. Los Angeles had beaches, sunshine, and immigrants from all over. Just a few months after we immigrated, she had already made friends. And where the hell was Midland, Texas?

My dad promised her that Texas would only be a two-year interlude, a chance to save up some cash before we could move somewhere with a more life-sustaining climate. (Thirty years later, they still live in Texas.)

The comparatively minuscule cost of living did improve certain aspects of our lives. For me, it meant no more sleeping on a pull-out couch in the living room. I lived in water wings and a little blue bathing suit, and I could generally be found submerged in the tepid waters of our apartment complex's swimming pool. (Including, at one point, for a shallow-end baptism organized by the apartment's Sunday school.) Little indulgences, like trips to Pizza Hut, were made to gloss over the fact that we had traded palm trees for oil derricks.

Financially, things were better in Midland, but not by much. So when the phone rang with a part-time job offer, my dad was intrigued. It was a woman who said she taught Russian at the local college. The only problem was that she didn't speak it—or at least, not well enough to teach an hour-long class twice a week. In a moment of leaning in, she had convinced the college administrators that she was practically Pushkin, and they had neglected to verify her skills. Now she was coming to loathe this harsh, toilsome language and the people who wanted to learn it. There were no other Russians in town. Would my dad be interested in taking the class over?

He had never taught before, but he said yes. Every Tuesday and Thursday night, my dad would leave his day job and drive his Mazda to Midland College, a cluster of squat brown buildings across from Tumbleweed Park.

The Russian class was popular, but several people only came to the first lesson. This was before the Internet, so people saw in my father a type of Russian Google. These one-and-done people would, invariably, be most interested in one of three questions:

1. What does *Spetsnaz* stand for? ("Special Purpose Forces" is the closest English translation.)
2. How easy is it to obtain a *Kalashnikov*? (the Soviet automatic rifle also known as an AK)
3. Why did the Soviet Union end? ("That moron Gorbachev," according to my dad)

My dad had his realization: he was weird, and the Texans wanted to demystify him. They wanted to probe this strange creature, who had been swept into their land like a butterfly in a dust storm, and through him, to learn about a side of the world they had never seen. It was convenient that the town weirdo had office hours.

One day, a man with a weather-beaten face raised his hand and asked, "Are there horses in Russia?"

He got his answer (yes, e.g., the Cossacks, Russia's horse-mounted warriors) and never returned. To this day, we wonder what purpose this knowledge served, and imagine the man living out his days operating a small rodeo near Krasnoyarsk.

Another man came to the first class, then came back a second time and wordlessly handed my dad an enormous American flag. He had folded it, as if to honor my dad for a great service. My dad still has it. "I kind of cherish it," he told me.

A week into the semester, the dilettantes would largely be shaken off, and my dad would be left with a far smaller, core group, many of whom had been sent to his class by their church mission-trip organizers or by globalization-minded employers. When you're weird, people might be drawn to you out of curiosity. But there's a point at which curiosity is no match for Russian's six different noun forms.

Word of our ethnic origins spread through Sunday potlucks and Super Bowl parties. Midland was a God-loving oil town, and the locals were increasingly interested in forming bonds with resource-rich and Jesus-poor Russia. Local tycoons began hiring my dad as a sort of cultural attaché. His job on many of these gigs was not just to translate the dialogue of business deals and conversion missions, but to serve as a mediator, a kind of Slavic Boutros Boutros-Ghali. It fell to him to explain the ways of these historically godless, frequently intoxicated, newly entrepreneurial former Communists to the Midlanders, who were just their opposite in every way.

One day, an oil man named Bobby asked my dad to translate for a group of visiting Russian businessmen, to whom Bobby was trying to sell some equipment. (My dad calls Bobby a "big-jawed Anglo," which I think just means he wasn't Jewish.)

Bobby offered my dad a hundred dollars for the day, which my dad thought was going to be the easiest money he ever made. When my dad walked into the Russians-and-Bobby summit, Bobby was presiding before the room, his large mandible hovering over some blueprints that were spread across the conference table. The Russians sat around it, morose, or perhaps just hungover— it was hard to tell which. Bobby began whipping his index finger around the blueprint and firing a stream of equipment terms at them—words like "scrubber" and "pump" and "valve." My dad, who trained as an electrical engineer and had never encountered such words before in either language, started translating them for the Russians the only way he knew how: in English but with an exaggerated Russian accent.

After two hours, my dad was drenched in sweat and the Russians had still not cracked a smile. Bobby said that next, they would all be going to Outback Steakhouse because he wanted to show them a real nice time.

The Russians anticipated a celebratory *beez-ness* lunch punctuated by brimming cups of vodka. This was not, alas, the scene at the Outback Steakhouse in Midland. The Russians' faces deflated once again.

It fell to my dad to explain the situation to both his countrymen and to his host, who was increasingly feeling like perhaps this surly nation wasn't worth dealing valves with after all. "They say, 'I can eat meat at home,'" my dad explained, apologetically, to Bobby.

The week was saved with a trip to Walmart, whose bright aisles and bargain prices dazzled the Russians more than the wettest of *beez-ness* lunches could have.

However, the next time the Russians came, everyone went to a strip club instead.

While they worked, my parents put me in a series of Baptist day-cares, which were the cheapest and most abundant option in our town. I was never asked by my new overseers whether I was Christian, nor was the theological element ever really explained. We learned every Christian children's song in existence, and I thought it was just because Americans are really into this "Jesus" character, much like they revere Barney or Big Bird.

It was there that I began to realize how weird I already was.

At the daycare, we prayed before every meal and snack. These meager snacks were never enough for me, a beefy four-year-old with cheeks like skillets and a height in the 90th percentile for my age group. My parents decided to supplement the snacks with small boxes of raisins from home, for me to eat as a sort of snack-between-snacks.

One day I got busy playing, realized that snack time was nearly upon us, and decided to just quietly sit in my chair and eat my raisins before the daycare-provided snack had been distributed. A daycare worker saw me, asked, "Are you eatin' without prayin'!?," and punished me on the spot.

I didn't know how to tell them that I'm from somewhere else, that I don't believe what they do, and that this whole thing—my whole life thus far, really—was just a big misunderstanding.

When my mom came to pick me up, the daycare instructor complained to her about my misbehavior. My mom said nothing. ("We were afraid. We were new," she says now. "It was a small town. Everyone knows each other. We were trying to play by their rules.")

Someone told me, around this time, that I was an "alien," like E.T. That day, it felt more true than ever: like I had traveled to a new planet, and I'd never learn to breathe its air or speak its tongues.

## ALINA

In 2013, Russia passed its so-called "gay propaganda" law, which made holding gay-pride events or even defending gay rights punishable by fines and jail time. The country's policymakers weren't out of step with their constituents: at the time, only 16 percent of Russians considered homosexuality acceptable.

However, unlike in many countries with laws against homosexuality, the policy didn't appear to be connected to religion. Very few Russians attend church regularly. Instead, the policy seemed like it was meant to emphasize the difference between traditional Russia and the permissive West. As Russia expert Masha Lipman told me for an *Atlantic* article, "Russia is an illiberal country, and [President Vladimir] Putin's government capitalizes on illiberal sentiments."

At the time, Alina Anderson was a Russian teenager who was bothered by how illiberal her country was becoming. Alina was born in a small Russian town called Lermontov, after the poet who was banished to the Caucasus for writing a controversial poem. She was mostly raised in Moscow, but some of the attitudes there seemed just as provincial to her. She hated overhearing racist criticisms of foreign tourists. When she would mention gay rights to adults in her life, some would respond, "What are you talking about? Gay people are just trying to molest kids."

Russia's anti-gay law is an interesting example of the psychological phenomenon in which, when our self-esteem is threatened, we start to desire surroundings that are more homogeneous. The idea is that when all else fails to give us a self-esteem boost, we can shore up our identity through sameness. (In fact, just doing the opposite, reminding people of their own self-worth, can make

them more tolerant toward difference. One study found that after people wrote essays about their own positive traits, they were
more likely to offer concessions to people who disagreed with them
about abortion.) Russia has long been the punching bag of the
Western world, with the goofy accents and the goofy hats and
the goofy rusted-over Soviet architecture that Americans love to
mock. Of course Russians feel insulted. And some Russian leaders
have reacted to those insults by shutting down the borders of their
minds.

All of this helps explain why Alina loved Marilyn, her teacher
at an English-language after-school program. Marilyn was named
after Marilyn Monroe, and she was just as pretty. She was a twen-
tysomething New Yorker who wore a lot of athleisure, and Alina
thought she was just the coolest. Marilyn showed her students
documentaries like *Good Hair*, about the pressures many African
American women face to make their hair resemble that of whites.
She told them about all sorts of new ideas—government corrup-
tion, environmentalism, sexism—and Alina would look them up
later online. "There's a whole different world out there," Marilyn
would say.

It was so different from what Alina experienced at school, where
it seemed like her classmates all shared one point of view, and
dissent was discouraged. Alina and her parents used to get in arguments almost every week. Alina would tell her mom that she didn't
want to wear makeup, and Alina says her mom would say, "What,
you think women should dress like men?" At the worst moments,
her mother would weep and ask her daughter, "Who are you turning into?" (Now, she says, they get along better.)

Alina felt disappointed that so many good people around her
had views she disagreed with so profoundly. It just seemed to be
the way of things. "Russia is very infamous for having a consensus
that people come to," she told me, "and no one can challenge it."

Russia might be illiberal, as Lipman put it, but it is also more "culturally tight" than neighboring countries like Finland or Sweden, or
even than the U.S. Tight cultures are those in which social norms

are strict and formal, and the punishments for breaking them are severe. In tight cultures, people are more in step with one another, but loose cultures permit a wider range of behaviors. Tight cultures are the military, the Amish, or Singapore, where a nineteen-year-old American named Michael Fay was caned in 1994 for vandalism. Meanwhile, tech startups are loose, as is the Netherlands, where parents and teachers allow little kids to play "doctor" with one another in the spirit of positive bodily exploration. It's easier to be weird in a loose culture than in a tight one.

The idea of tight and loose nations had been circulating in the cultural-psychology world for decades, but it was scientifically firmed up by the psychologist Michele Gelfand in a major 2011 study. Gelfand and her colleagues asked people from thirty-three countries how much they agree with statements like, "In this country, if someone acts in an inappropriate way, others will strongly disapprove." She also asked them how acceptable it would be to, say, kiss in a public park. (In tight societies, it's inappropriate.)

Gelfand found a number of interesting associations between different elements of day-to-day life in these societies, all of which point to their willingness (or not) to break social norms. Tight countries were more likely to be autocratic and to have a less free media. People in tight countries are more religious, less likely to protest, and less likely to commit crimes. They're also less fat— they literally keep it tight. Loose countries have more crime, but they're also more tolerant of change or of people with facial scars. Essentially, cultures trade orderliness for creativity as they go from tighter to looser.

Tightness and looseness even show up in whether kids wear school uniforms (they do in tight countries) or in whether there are a lot of left-handed writers (there are in loose countries), as Gelfand writes in her book *Rule Makers, Rule Breakers*. Korean (tighter) magazine ads are more likely to emphasize conformity than uniqueness, while American (looser) magazine ads do the opposite. Agricultural societies, where people must carefully coordinate so the community does not starve, tend to be tight, while hunting and fishing societies tend to be loose.

The United States flipped from almost entirely rural to pre-dominantly urban between 1800 and 2000, and the psychologist Patricia M. Greenfield found that American authors' use of indi-vidualistic words went up, as well. She found American writers began to use "obliged" less but "choose" more, "give" less and "get" more. "Unique," which was almost nonexistent in 1800, was all over Barnes & Noble in 2000. Meanwhile, "obedience" had de-clined precipitously. Americans were moving to cities, where life is loose.

Within each country, tightness can vary depending on the sit-uation. Privacy is an important value in the U.S., so the normally loose Americans tighten up in that realm—they don't drop by each other's homes unannounced. Meanwhile, in the more cultur-ally tight Japan, people crowd into bars after work to let loose—literally. Overall, Gelfand has found that people in modern-day tight societies tend to be more cautious and dutiful, and they have a greater need for structure. East Germany was tighter than West Germany; Texas is tight and Hawaii is loose.

Though it might seem like loose cultures have more fun, the psychologists who study this phenomenon insist the two styles are just different, and one is not worse than the other. People trav-eling from tight to loose cultures would be just as disoriented as those migrating in the opposite direction. Tight cultures, after all, can provide order and predictability in hostile environments. One study found that people from tight cultures were less receptive to foreign ideas and less likely than people from loose countries to succeed at creative competitions, like designing a new type of water bottle, geared toward foreign markets. However, people from tight cultures performed excellently at creative tasks in their own cultures or in cultures similar to their own.

It's possible, wrote the anthropologist Pertti J. Pelto, one of the first to study tightness and looseness, "that tight and loose societies simply produce different kinds of comforts and anxieties in their people."

Alina was a loose person born into a tight culture. She admits there was an element of rebellion to her views: she wanted to zig when her countrymen zagged. Alina felt she was Russian by nationality only, and there was little else she had in common with her classmates and neighbors. To be with her own kind, Alina decided she would study abroad after high school—something Marilyn encouraged.

After she had taught Alina and her classmates for several years, Marilyn was fired, supposedly for "brainwashing" her students, Alina told me. Alina still seems bitter about it—she instantly jumped to Marilyn's defense during our Skype call—and it hardened Alina's resolve to leave Russia as soon as she could.

Right after graduation, Alina took the entrance exam to study in Finland. It was what she considered to be a looser, more liberal nation, where education also happens to be free—and where more people agree with Alina's views. She's now a student at a university in Lappeenranta, a Finnish town not far from the Russian border.

For Alina, having weird beliefs was just too distressing. "For me, you either stay and try to change the society," she explained, "or you just move out and you go to a country that's more accepting and where you're going to fit in." No doubt many other loose people living in tight cultures—or vice versa—would feel the same way.


BEVERLY, PART I

It was when she began her job as a sociology professor at a small research university in Texas that Beverly Stiles had her weirdness realization: she was informed by some of her students that she was "the liberal one." And she, meanwhile, was shocked by how conservative her surroundings were. The combination of where Beverly was teaching and her particular research focus sharpened the differences between her and her neighbors.

Beverly's university, Midwestern State, is, officially, in the most Republican place in America. The Cook Political Report's "Partisan Voting Index" measures how far each congressional district leans to the left or right. The most Democratic congressional district is in the Bronx, in New York, with an index of D+44—

meaning it votes Democratic by 44 percentage points more than the country as a whole.

The most Republican, as of this writing, is Texas's 13th district, at R+33. Texas's 13th encompasses a northern, barren stretch of the Lone Star state—the panhandle plus the top rim of the pan. The district gallops around Dallas, dances with Oklahoma along the jagged border, and swallows up a 105,000-person town called Wichita Falls.

The place was never exactly the crown jewel of Texas, even according to its native sons. *Lonesome Dove* author Larry McMurtry once had a character call Wichita Falls "the ugliest place on earth." In the late seventies, *Texas Monthly* ranked "full-time resident of Wichita Falls" sixth on its list of "worst jobs in Texas," after handling dead animals.

Still, Wichita Falls has always been big enough to matter. As the writer William Hauptman, also a native, described in a 1988 *New York Times Magazine* story, the area's oil industry made it the inspiration for *Boom Town*, a 1940 film starring Clark Gable and Spencer Tracy, and it was, perhaps out of broiling necessity, the site of the first hotel in the country that had air-conditioning.

Wichita Falls lacks natural waterfalls—they were washed away in a nineteenth-century flood, then rebuilt to drive tourism a hundred years later. But it is home to a four-story building called the "world's littlest skyscraper," as well as the sort of people who say "littlest."

It's also home to the somewhat erroneously named Midwestern State University, as well as its four-person sociology department, led by fifty-eight-year-old Beverly Stiles. And, therefore, Wichita Falls also encompasses Beverly's research, which is on all kinds of social deviance. Including the sexual kind.

The university building where Beverly works resembles an old Spanish mission. She invited me to join her and her research collaborators to parse some data she was reviewing about the university students' views toward people with disabilities and physician-assisted suicide.

The study was being performed as part of a small class that Beverly teaches so that students can learn to do research and get their name on published results. She doesn't get paid for this time, and at a larger university, she suspects she wouldn't be able to do this kind of work.

To be sure, the data was not a random sample of the student body. But some of the responses were a little grim. Of the ninety-two students who were asked, more than half agreed that it's not possible to have a normal relationship with someone with AIDS; two-thirds said it would be difficult to trust someone with AIDS; and 62 percent said there are no effective treatments for AIDS.

Still, Beverly was surprised by a couple of the statistics: nearly a third of the respondents said they don't have a religious community, and the most prevalent political orientation was "moderate."

Beverly seemed enthralled. "I can't believe I get paid to do this," she exclaimed—meaning she's overjoyed to have her dream job.

We later met up to talk in Beverly's office, which is crammed with papers and books, one of which had a spine that read, simply, "ABORTION."

When you speak to Beverly, she immediately ceases talking, leans way in, and listens like you're about to issue a critical pronouncement. I told her that it was in a gender-studies class in college that I first encountered a woman who didn't shave her legs. I became immediately and deeply afraid.

"Like, 'What is this all about?!'" Beverly said excitedly. In her gender-studies class, they discuss how leg-shaving originated.

Each semester, she throws herself into her work, teaching an overload of classes while keeping up with her research. I've seen ecstatic superfans at rock concerts, and I've seen Beverly speculating about gender norms, and the two affects are strikingly similar. She likes to do one exercise with her freshman classes in which she asks them to free-associate what they think of when she says the word "feminist" or "member of the National Organization for Women." After the students offer up all the horrible stereotypes—man-hater, etc.—comes the big reveal: "You know, when I was a student here, I was a member of the National Organization of Women!" she says, pealing with laughter.

"It's just fun to make them question what they think," she tells me. "It's fun stuff."

Beverly's journey to the academy was not that unusual. Growing up in Ohio, she was the kind of nerd who loves people. Her father was a Democrat and a truck driver, and her mother's side was all Republican. Her father mostly raised her, and as so often happens, Beverly began to see politics from his point of view.

After she graduated high school, she followed her first husband, who was in the military, to Texas to study sociology, also at Midwestern State University. She would be the first in her family to attend college. She didn't always know very much about gender issues. During her graduate training, she traveled to a workshop with students from all over North America. When one Canadian student mentioned the "glass ceiling," Beverly had no idea what the term meant.

I told her this reminded me of that same gender-studies class I took in college, which I thought was going to be a cakewalk but was instead a daily reminder of how little I knew. I told her a story about how my professor, in one of the first lectures, talked about "canonical bodies." I was so bewildered, not least because I didn't even know what "canonical" meant.

"Did you ask?" Beverly said.

It had never occurred to me to do that.

I told her I had decided to google it later, but then I realized I couldn't, because I wrote down "conical" instead of "canonical."

"But you didn't ask anyone?" Beverly asked again.

"I was very petrified that everyone else knew something that I didn't know," I explained, "because they were all from New Jersey or wherever and I was from Texas, and I was gonna look like this redneck if I asked my questions."

"That was my experience in the workshop," she said. "Oh my gosh, there's a knowledge out there that I'm supposed to know, and I don't have any idea about gender."

Suddenly I felt a deep desire to have spent all my life thus far by her side, so she could have reassured me at the million other moments like this one.

Texas colleges were also a culture shock to Beverly. When she was in graduate school at another Texas university she asked me not to name, she said there were no women teaching any of her classes. In one class, a student said every person on welfare should be mandatorily sterilized. When the professor asked Beverly what she thought of that idea, Beverly brought in data on fertility rates among people on welfare that disproved the other student's point. *I'm not like these people,* she'd think to herself.

Still, she told me, "It was good for me to have gone there, because I needed to know that there are people in the world that think like that."

When, in 1999, Midwestern State offered her a job as a sociology professor, Beverly moved back to Wichita Falls, determined to broaden her students' horizons and to reveal how society forges our notions of masculinity and femininity. For many students in Beverly's gender-studies class, the existence of gender inequality was an entirely new concept. In the early years, when Beverly brought up gender norms, some students would respond with teachings from the Bible. They denied that gender inequality existed, and a few would drop the class. Some students believed feminism was harmful to families. Once, in an introductory sociology class, a student yelled out something like, "You're a liberal, aren't you?"

Not all the students attending the college are from Wichita Falls, of course, or even from Texas. This being college, it was not entirely devoid of liberals, either. One group of students asked her to be an advisor to their feminist student group. And even a quinoa-munching Berkeleyite might find Beverly's research topics a little edgy. Beverly studies cheating, rape myths, and the business models of sex workers—a line of research for which she's interviewing women who "cam," or perform sex acts on web cameras for money. Once, a colleague jokingly made a spanking motion in reference to her research. Another colleague, upon learning that she researches BDSM, sent her newspaper clips about a woman who had been kidnapped and forced to be a sex slave. "This is not my population," she responded.

But in her first few years of teaching the gender class, getting through to the students was a more pressing problem. She heard from a few of her students that some refused to take her class because she's a feminist. A rumor spread that Beverly's a lesbian, which was helped along by the fact that she wears no makeup and that her ex-husband's name was "Dana." ("I'm not a lesbian," Beverly told me. "Not that there's anything wrong with that.")

There are things Beverly liked about Wichita Falls. On a sociologist's salary, she could afford a nice life and a four-bedroom house. She lived fifteen minutes from her office, and parking was cheap. She's just a few hours from either Dallas or Oklahoma City.

But a few years into her job in Wichita Falls, before she had earned tenure, Beverly and her husband had divorced, and there wasn't much keeping her in Texas. She felt like she wasn't able to tear through her students' defenses against the information she was trying to convey. Thinking maybe a more liberal place might be more welcoming, she started looking at job listings in California.


JESS, PART I

Violations of gender norms have a unique ability to unnerve. As late as 1965, a Philadelphia lunch counter that was popular with LGBTQ people began refusing to serve these customers, who, as one newspaper put it, wore "nonconformist clothing." In 1960, federal postal authorities monitored the mail of cross-dressers and prosecuted them for exchanging racy letters.

In more recent years, President Donald Trump has sought to ban transgender people from the military, and lawmakers in several states have introduced "bathroom bills," which would require transgender people to use the bathroom corresponding with the sex assigned to them at birth in public buildings. This would, presumably, mean a trans man who had a full beard, a flat chest, and a penis would be compelled to use the women's restroom.

The very idea of gender-segregated bathrooms came about because of gender norms, and what policymakers believed to be the
intrinsic, immutable differences between men and women. Gendered bathrooms arose in the late 1800s, during the industrial
revolution, when legislators in some states decided they could no
longer tolerate having men and women who worked in factories
side by side relieving themselves in the same place, as well. Women
were considered weaker, delicate. Ideally, the thinking was, they
should be at home, in their own sphere. But since they insisted
on working, wrote the law professor Terry Stuart Kogan, "legislators opted instead to create a protective, home-like haven in the
workplace for women by requiring separate restrooms, along with
separate dressing rooms and resting rooms." The new restrooms
went perfectly with the female-only cars on trains in those days
and the female-only reading rooms in public libraries. *We have to
protect the women,* the thinking seemed to be. Or, in the words
of North Carolina lawmakers more than a century later, bathroom bills were meant to protect women's "right to basic safety and
privacy."

In 2017, Jess Herbst, the mayor of New Hope, Texas, traveled
four hours south to Austin to testify against Texas's version of this
kind of bathroom bill.

Jess is transgender, but she didn't focus on her gender identity in
her remarks. Instead, she appealed to the state legislators as a fellow public official.

"I am the mayor of a town and oftentimes I do the things that
you do, just for a little smaller constituency," she said in her quick
twang.

There are already laws against voyeurism and assault, she said in
her testimony, so there is simply no need for a bill to protect people specifically in bathrooms.

"So I'm a little bit confused as to why we are doing these things,
because they are already covered," she said.

This was typical Jess style, to not dwell on the splashiest thing
in the room: the fact that she is transgender and, if I'm being bru-
tally honest, recognizably so. Instead, she addressed her opponents

logically, rationally, patiently. As a fellow public official, she is oftentimes in their shoes. Won't they put themselves in hers?

One recent summer, I drove past acres of pastureland and trees
that look as though they're reclining. I pulled up to Jess Herbst's
ranch-style house in New Hope, a town that's about fifteen minutes away from McKinney, where I went to high school. It's
more rural and less hopping than my hometown, to the extent
that McKinney, which was dry until recently, can be described as
"hopping" at all. Kids in my high school sometimes called it "No
Hope," because if you're from the world's most boring suburb,
you insult the second-most.

Jess answered the door looking polished, in a black blouse, red
lipstick, and gold earrings that twinkled through her long, blond
hair.

It took me a moment just to take in the scene: Jess, a gun owner,
with the large hands of the man she presented as publicly just a
few years ago, flipping her hair back and standing in the infernal
Texas heat, in an area where Jesus is most certainly the reason for
the season.

Does she feel unique? I asked right away.

Not really, she responded. According to her, there are three
other transgender people in New Hope, population 635.

In fact, Jess thought I was the strange one. When I told her I
had attended American University, her eyes bulged and she cried,
jokingly, "Are you a spy?!" (I know, it sounds fake.)

Jess was born "Jeff" in 1958 in Greenville, Texas, a small town
fifty miles northeast of Dallas. She's known she was transgender
since she was a toddler. That's also when she was first informed
that being transgender was considered weird. She would try on her
mother's dresses until her parents caught her and told her to stop.
When she was twelve, her father caught Jess hoarding her mother's
undergarments in her room and took her to a special therapist,
who recommended a strict exercise regimen to break her of the
habit. When she wouldn't do the exercises, her father paddled her.

In college, Jess met a woman named Debbie Gray, whom she

started dating after they went to a showing of *The Rocky Horror Picture Show* together. Jess was up-front with Debbie about her secret cross-dressing habit. From time to time, Jess would get dressed up, only to get so embarrassed she'd stop for six months. Debbie, though, found the cross-dressing to be kind of a turn-on. Bad boys come in all shapes and sizes, and sometimes they come in heels. Even before they were dating, "I got this vibe that Jess is like the main character," Debbie told me—the "transvestite from Transsexual, Transylvania" played by Tim Curry. "I kind of liked it."

As a teen, Jess thought she was the only person like her on earth. Anything involving gender-bending in the popular media was abhorrent and scary. Norman Bates, the *Psycho* villain, wore his mother's clothing in an effort to subsume her identity. In *The Silence of the Lambs,* Buffalo Bill is a "transsexual" who plans to make an outfit out of women's skin. Books Jess found on the topic deemed gender dysphoria a mental disorder. Sometimes, she watched *Monty Python* and, noticing that it occasionally featured men in drag, thought maybe she could find people like her in England.

After Jess and Debbie married, they lived in small towns all around North Texas and Arkansas. In 1989, they had their first daughter, Alexandria, and a second girl, Lauren Elizabeth, came eighteen months later. The girls, work, and life kept Jess too busy to sort out her soul.

When she traveled for work, she would sometimes dress up in the privacy of her hotel room. But then she'd be faced, once again, with the all-consuming shame. *Why am I doing this?* she'd think. *I should just stop.*

The feelings would linger, though, because, as she puts it, "You want to be something, and you're making yourself not be that."

Once she got the Internet at home, she found a site called Crossdressers.com and, nervously, signed up with a fake name. She was pleasantly surprised to find thousands of others like her. She suggested that maybe they should all go out in public as themselves sometime, stop hiding the pantyhose and lipstick at the bottom of their dresser drawers.

"Are you kidding?" the other members responded. "We'll get killed."

Several years went by before she found a Meetup.com group called "Dallas Feminine Expressions." The image on the home page depicts a group of middle-aged transgender women smiling in a bar with football-helmet decals on the walls. They could only look more "Texas" if one of them was stirring a pot of chili. It occurred to Jess that this is what she was. *This* is what she had been looking for all along.

The site required applicants to fill out a form about themselves, but Jess was too mortified to do it. She closed the browser window.

Eventually, she gathered enough courage to submit her application to the group. Within hours, she was accepted.

It was Wednesday. The next gathering was on a Saturday at a lesbian bar in Dallas called Sue Ellen's. There were fifty others there, and they were, indeed, her kind of people: bold and beautiful. Jess began going every week. They made her feel normal. Maybe there wasn't anything wrong with her, after all. Trans people weren't girl-suit-makers or serial killers. They were regular North Texans just like Jess.

Before long, she herself was organizing gatherings for transgender women at Sue Ellen's. Later, there were Christmas parties that transgender women from all over Texas attended. For two of the attendees, friends from deep-red Lubbock, Texas, it was their only chance to dress as women all year. They told their wives they were going deer hunting.

Jess began dressing up in her female clothes at home regularly. Debbie would call on the way home, and by the sound of Jess's voice Debbie could tell if she would be having dinner with Jeff or Jess.

When the reality of the transition loomed, it was Debbie's turn to struggle. She had always had an image in her mind of growing old with a man, and now she would be seen as a lesbian in public. But Jess was the love of her life. She decided to stay.

Jess came out to her daughter Alexandria at a two-week treatment session for sufferers of obsessive-compulsive disorder in

Austin in 2009. Alexandria was feeling bad about having the condition, so Jess went into her hotel room and came out forty minutes later dressed as a woman. "She needed to understand that everyone has something," Jess explained.

In 2015, Jess came home from the endocrinologist with patches of estrogen, which would begin to feminize her face, voice, and body. Her daughters coached her on how to do her hair and makeup. They call her "she," "her," "Jess," and "Dad." Because that's who she is.

When Jess grew tired of having to rip off her nails and long hair before meetings, she told her boss.

"I'm transgender," she said.

"Oh, well, that's okay," her boss responded.

Human resources changed her badge the following day.

(Perhaps this is because Jess worked as an IT consultant, and Michele Gelfand has found that well-paying professions have looser norms than blue-collar jobs.)

With that, Jess had told her employer; she had told her family; she had told everyone but the city of New Hope.

The Herbsts had been living in New Hope for several years when Jess, who had been a regular at council meetings, was elected alderman—another name for city council member—in 2003. Over the years, she also served as road commissioner and mayor pro-tem, a kind of backup mayor. When the sudden death of the mayor of New Hope left the town without a leader in 2016, the council appointed Jess, as Jeff, as mayor until the next election. Once a month, for city council meetings, she would wipe off her makeup, take off her wig, and dress up as a man again so no one would know.

In January of 2017, she revealed her true gender identity in a letter on the town's website. "I'm not especially sensitive to the pronoun I'm called, and I expect people to take time to make the change," she wrote. (The understanding attitude was probably a good thing, since at least one news article I found misgendered her in the very first sentence.)

Right away, the story was picked up by national and international media. People wrote letters and emails of support to the transgender woman in the middle of nowhere. People who didn't know her address simply wrote "Jess Herbst, New Hope, Texas" on an envelope, and it would somehow reach her anyway.

Around town, most people were accepting. Once, Jess was out with a trans friend who thought some women at a neighboring table were staring at her because the pair looked different. It turned out the women just wanted to know where Jess got her nails done. The chair of the planning and zoning commission from the nearby town of Anna met Jess for coffee to get her advice on coming out as transgender—then she came out, too.

Of course, there was also hate. She appeared on an Internet show whose hosts insisted that gender transition wasn't possible. When online trolls came after her, Jess responded to their questions until they had nothing left to say but "thank you." A good sense of humor, a positive outlook, and a whopping dose of mood-soothing hormones kept her from getting angry in such moments.

Some people were just nervous. One man misgendered Jess by accident during a meeting, but Jess didn't expect him to apologize as much as he did—she had known him for twenty-five years, after all. (She's only been misgendered purposefully twice, she says.)

As a consultant who had worked internationally, Jess was accustomed to switching up her speech to make people more comfortable. She describes one man, a friend of hers, who stopped coming to council meetings after she came out. When she approached him at a town picnic, he mumbled awkwardly and avoided eye contact. But she stuck by him, changing tactics slightly.

She asked him about the pergola—a wooden awning over the picnic benches. The man had worked on the park's landscaping. "What's wrong with this?" Jess asked him, pointing at the structure. "This is not matching up."

"Well, when they were building that," he said, "I told them they should have done this...."

With that, she was able to rewire their connection. "He completely forgot that I was me now," she told me happily.

She sensed the man's discomfort, and like a politician, or maybe like a parent, she offered a way to make him feel better. Along with the hair and makeup, putting people at ease was another new form of labor that came with this life.

Maybe it was because Caitlyn Jenner had come out, showing everyone that trans people could not only be normal, but extremely accomplished, but people listened to Jess in council meetings. Everything settled back into the sleepy routine of small-town life.

At a town council meeting not long after she came out, a *D Magazine* reporter described the scene: "To my right, a man is making a list of restaurants on a white legal pad, so far only writing down Buca di Beppo and Fadi's. In front of me, a man named Duke plays solitaire on his phone. A man to my left in a Vietnam veteran cap softly complains about people shooting off fireworks inside the city limits...It is boring. It is normal. It is exactly what Jess Herbst has always wanted."

Still, Jess wanted to be elected, not simply appointed because of a past mayor's death, so in 2018, she ran for mayor officially. She wanted to be the first transgender elected official in the state.

It would be, in part, a test of whether people in psychologically tight, rural Texas would be willing to loosen their norms enough to elect a trans person.

Jess took a class in campaigning, which advised her to find the people who had voted in the past two elections and target them. And that's exactly what she set out to do.

# CHAPTER 3

# The Exclusion

## JESS, PART II

Jess Herbst lost her election by forty votes, to the former mayor's widow. (The loss is not as narrow as it seems: there are only 476 registered voters in New Hope.) Jess partly blames herself, saying she focused too much on likely voters and didn't think about the people who never vote. The mayor's widow, she suspects, targeted extremely conservative never-voters by emphasizing Jess's gender identity.

"She knocked on all their doors and got them all riled up about me," Jess told me. People who supported Jess told her that some people were saying they couldn't vote for her because it was against their religion. (The new mayor did not respond to requests for comment.)

To be sure, people might have simply preferred the former mayor's widow to Jess. But if people were, in fact, turned off by her gender identity, Jess has a theory for why it might have cost her the election. People are, at their core, good, or at least decent. Even the most ardent transphobe doesn't want to confront a trans individual with their hatred face-to-face. But, put those same people behind a keyboard, or send them to the privacy of a voting booth, where they don't have to talk to or look at anyone different, where it's just them and their worst thoughts, "that's when the ugly comes out," she said.

In psychology, "wanting things to be the way they've always been" is called "system justification," and in studies, people who are more prone to system justification are more likely to oppose affirmative action and other equality-promoting policies. In Jess's case, some voters might have noticed that there are not many transgender people leading Texas, and concluded that Jess shouldn't be, either. Norms trap us in the status quo, even when the status quo is irrational.

What's more, norm violations bother us more when they affect us personally. Someone throwing trash in an entryway of an apartment building would irritate the building's residents more than someone littering on a street across town. Perhaps some people thought Jess could be transgender if she wanted, but she couldn't represent the entire town while doing it.

One burly man who rode a Harley Davidson came to a city council meeting and told Jess, "I don't care what you do on your own time. Just keep doing your job." She was happy to hear it—until she found he had written "nasty stuff" about her later online.

"Most of the time that people do that kind of thing, it's because they're afraid, because they don't understand, they don't know me, and I'm different, and different scares people," she told me.

There might be other reasons Jess lost. Unlike many people here, she supports gun control and is pro-choice. Though she's not a vocal Democrat, in our interview she referred to the 2016 election as a "disaster." She was on the news a lot, which is not really a good thing in New Hope. She was a norm violator in more ways than one.

Despite the recent election loss, Jess remained upbeat throughout the evening we spent together. She was about to leave for a leadership course at Harvard, and she planned to run for public office again.

I asked her a question that I had been suppressing since I first walked through her door and took in this incredible, cheery, Southern fish out of water: Why not move somewhere else? If she had moved to San Francisco in the '90s, I pointed out, she could have come out much sooner. Hell, she might have been governor of California by now.

She reminded me that she didn't know what transgender people were in the 1990s, or that they might live in San Francisco. Besides, there's no use crying over what happened or didn't.

"Things just had to work out the way they did, I guess," she said.

What a perfectly normal, Texan thing to say.

While it's impossible to know for certain if prejudice played a role in Jess's loss, it certainly played a role in the marginalization of trans people like her throughout history. But where does prejudice itself come from? For that, we turn to a psychologist named Henri Tajfel.

Tajfel, whose birth name was Hersz Mordche, was born Jewish in Poland in 1919. As a young man, he moved to France to study, and when World War II broke out, he joined the French army. A year later, he was captured by German soldiers. Seeking to be sent to a prisoner-of-war camp rather than a concentration camp, he somehow convinced the Germans he was French, rather than a Polish Jew. The prisoner-of-war camps, though harsh, were at least not as deadly. Being sent to a series of POW camps was probably what saved him, and it underscored for Tajfel how a person's group membership can have enormous consequences. When the war ended in 1945, Tajfel took a train crammed with other freed prisoners to the Gare d'Orsay in Paris. There, he learned his entire family had died.

The trauma of World War II seemed seared into Tajfel: he dedicated his life to understanding the animosity and mistrust that drive rifts between people. He would go on to develop the study of social identity theory, or how groups relate to one another.

When the extent of the Nazis' atrocities was revealed, it was thought that it would take a nation of very disturbed personalities to commit such violence. At the time, some psychologists thought Nazism arose in Germany because of the strict style of parenting that was popular there at the time. Authoritarian child-rearing, writes Michael Hogg, a professor of social psychology at Claremont Graduate University, was thought by these psychologists to foment "a love-hate relationship between children and their parents that produced people with authoritarian personalities who worshipped power, authority and conformity and redirected their hatred onto those who were weak and different."

Tajfel, who by this point had become a professor at the University of Bristol in the U.K., thought explanations like these were too simplistic. He believed the mere existence of groups was enough to stir intergroup conflict. In a telling set of experiments in the early 1970s, he divided British schoolboys up into two arbitrary groups—sometimes as basic as "group X" and "group W." He then had the boys distribute money among all their classmates, but leave themselves out of the deal. No matter what, the boys gave their own group members more money—even though this would not benefit them in any way and they had no expectation of interacting with this group in the future. They preferred their own tribe, even if they had only been assigned to it moments before. Seeing our group win matters, even if the group itself doesn't matter at all.

The question of how ordinary people could so easily turn on one another seemed to be on Tajfel's mind as he did this work. Studies like these helped affirm Tajfel's belief that prejudice was not an inborn personality trait, specific to one nationality or another. Instead, it's a reflection of the dynamics between groups. Prejudice, to him, was more about group-think than gut-feel. "It is therefore important and useful," Tajfel wrote in his 1981 book, *Human Groups & Social Categories*, that we consider prejudice to be "in the minds, rather than in the guts of people..."

As it would turn out, it's in both.

The Shiwiar, a remote Amazonian people in eastern Ecuador and northeastern Peru, live somewhat like humans lived before modernity. The men hunt and fish, and the women tend two to four gardens of manioc, plantains, and yams. They live according to a value called *shiir waras,* which means to do what's expected of your age and gender. For the most part, each Shiwiar household grows and obtains its own food; they don't pool their resources. One of the main situations in which they do give each other resources for prolonged periods is when they're sick.

And they do get sick. The Shiwiar have hard lives. They are stung by bees, bitten by bats and snakes, and come down with malaria and measles. They fall off of things and get struck by machetes. Lawrence Sugiyama, an anthropologist at the University of Oregon who interviewed some Shiwiar in the 1990s, found that almost everyone in his sample was disabled for a week or more, and over 60 percent were on bedrest for a month or longer. To make matters worse, they have little access to Western medicine.

When a Shiwiar gets hurt in this way, his or her kin group takes care of the person until they're better. In one case, a young man who suffered nerve damage from a snakebite was shuttled from safehouse to safehouse by allies during wartime. Without this kind of help, many Shiwiar would have died from their injuries.

The example of the Shiwiar shows why we humans, reflexively, like to take care of our own. In our ancestral past, we couldn't accumulate wealth or stockpile resources. We were hunter-gatherers, and once we had hunted and gathered all there was to hunt or gather in a given area, we had to move on. Social relationships were the only bank deposit you had. To keep your group from going extinct, you had to provide your group members with resources when they were struggling.

"Since networks of alliances are the only health insurance policy available in small-scale societies, it follows that, when the likelihood of illness increases, individuals should be motivated to ensure both that their premiums are paid and that their coverage is extensive," wrote Carlos Navarrete and Daniel Fessler in a 2006 study. Your premiums are ties to other people. Your coverage is how they help you when times get tough.

Most researchers agree that the successful groups of our ancestral past were like the Shiwiar. They were basically like little hippie communes, with more, or perhaps less, nudity, depending on which particular communes and cavemen you're picturing. They lived in close-knit communities and looked out for one another. There's some debate, however, about how willing our ancestors were to help people *beyond* the Shiwiar down the block. Some anthropologists and psychologists argue that less porous groups were, in past millennia, more likely to survive and thrive than groups that would accept just about anyone. In other words, according to this theory, we humans have always favored our own little band of hunter-gatherers and remained wary of anyone else. Today, some people say illegal immigrants are taking "our jobs." For thousands of years, according to this theory, we were worried they'd steal our freshly killed meat.

Others, though, paint a rosier picture of our Pleistocene fore-bears, suggesting that some of them were actually less fearful of outsiders than humans are today. Nomadic foragers, as these early people were called, lived in groups of about twenty or thirty, but they switched groups often and would frequently trade and inter-act with groups that lived even hundreds of miles away. A family might live with the parents of the wife for a while, then travel around with the parents of the husband for a bit.

These hunter-gatherer groups lived free from leaders or borders. Population density was low, so if you encountered someone, your first impulse was not to hate them. There's little evidence that we waged war until about ten thousand years ago, says Douglas Fry, an anthropologist at the University of Alabama. "We'd rather party than fight," is how he put it to me.

We saw this party preference among foraging groups even in re-cent centuries. Nineteenth-century accounts describe a group of Aborigines in Australia who lit a huge signal fire whenever they found a beached whale. The signal was meant to draw people from all over. It meant, Fry says, "Hey! Here's a dead whale, plenty of food for all of us. We'll get to renew acquaintances, we'll get to have sex with other people, we can exchange art objects." (Like I said, commune.)

So if this was our past, when did we become so hateful toward outsiders? How did we get from whale party to fascism? Apparently, it was when we started farming, about ten thousand years ago. Farming involved settling on patches of land and interacting less with outside groups. When we did encounter outsiders, the differ-ences between us and them seemed more significant. Plus, unlike a forest full of berries, a carefully tended field was something we felt was rightfully ours. The earth's climate changed. Social hierarchies developed in which some had more, and some had less, and you could fight your way from one rank to another.

Then came organized religion, money, and rulers—all of which diced people up into subgroups and, in some cases, pitted them against one another. Warfare, according to some scholars, has actually *increased* since "civilization" took hold. Even as society grew supposedly more sophisticated, humans were becoming more ethnocentric and parochial.

Our blissed-out ancestors would have been *so* disappointed.

More recent history, of course, has supported Tajfel's theory: We tend to sort people into groups based on their differences, even when those differences are laughably minor. Then, we rank the groups in relation to our own.

In New York in the late nineteenth century, doctors and charity workers focused their anxieties on the influx of Eastern European immigrants, and particularly, on one of these newcomers' troubling habits: eating pickles. According to the food writer Jane Ziegelman, pickles were seen as too pungent and, for the families who ate them, oddly addictive. This supposed "addiction" was apparently evidenced by the, uh, relish with which poor immigrant kids snapped them up. More likely, penny pickles were about the only luxuries they could afford.

As one doctor wrote at the time, "the spices in it are bad, the vinegar is a seething mass of rottenness." She called the pickled cucumber "depraved." Once they were school-aged, as Ziegelman wrote in the *New York Times,* immigrant children were indoctrinated by the city's board of education into a blander, more "normal" American diet of creamed fish and applesauce. Today, of course, few people can tell the difference between the descendant of an Eastern European New Yorker and one whose ancestors came on a slightly earlier boat. And even fewer would look twice at a New Yorker eating a pickle.

Irish Catholics and Irish Protestants might also look alike, and—at least to a foreign ear—sound alike. But the Troubles of the late twentieth century, in which the mostly Protestant unionists fought the mostly Catholic nationalists, is further proof, like so many other sectarian clashes, that even small dissimilarities can spark hatred. With tensions running high, the two groups found surprising ways to tell one another apart. One such shibboleth was the letter "h": Protestants pronounced it "aitch"; Catholics, "haitch." Paramilitary gunmen were known to force people to say the letter aloud to determine whose side they were on.

In 1998, the Irish writer Nuala O'Faolain described in an *Irish Times* article how high-stakes this verbal twist could be. "You spell out a word to someone who's filling in a form and she looks up and smiles: 'You said haitch instead of aitch,' she says. 'You must be Catholic.' With that, you realize that she must be a Catholic or she wouldn't have risked the remark."

The idea that a diverse array of people is okay—or even good—to have around is a rather new concept. In the early 1900s, American state legislatures took it upon themselves to deport "criminals, lunatics, and other social misfits" beyond their borders, writes Peter Schrag in his book *Not Fit for Our Society.* In 1901, Missouri went so far as to forbid the "importation of afflicted, indigent, or vicious children."

Henry Cabot Lodge, the turn-of-the-twentieth-century senator from Massachusetts, called for reduced immigration on the basis of State Department reports that southern Italians are "generally rustic and of the lowest type of the Italian as to character and intelligence," and that European countries were sending their worst people—"criminals, vicious characters, and paupers"—to the U.S. in order to pare down their own charity rolls. "The immigration of people removed from us in race and blood is rapidly increasing," Lodge wrote, and "these people are almost wholly illiterate." Of course, some Southwestern states want more people, he acknowledged, but they can't come at the expense of "lowering the standard of American citizenship."

Henry Goddard, a psychologist, was dispatched in 1912 to Ellis Island to sort out which incoming immigrants were afflicted with "feeblemindedness." Goddard's method of diagnosis was simple, Schrag writes: he would look at the immigrants and instantly be able to tell. By this measure, fully 82 percent of Russians and 76 percent of Jews turned out to be "morons." Perhaps unsurprisingly, they were two of the most loathed ethnic groups at the time.

This attitude culminated in the 1916 book *Passing of the Great Race,* by the eugenicist Madison Grant. He denounced the flood of Polish Jewish immigrants—with their "dwarf stature, peculiar mentality, and ruthless concentration on self-interest." The "swarms" of Jews were driving "native" (meaning white, in Grant's view) Americans to retreat from public life and lowering their birth rates. He recommended state-mandated sterilization for "social failures," "weaklings and defectives," and "worthless race types."

*The Passing of the Great Race* was published in Germany in 1925, and at one point Grant was said to have received a letter from a fan who called his book "my Bible."

The fan letter's author? Adolf Hitler.

The entire twentieth century practically frothed with hatred toward immigrants, as the political scientist Joel S. Fetzer describes in his book on public attitudes toward immigration. (This was, of course, on top of Americans' well-documented exploitation and dislike of both native-born and enslaved people of color.) One news article described the lynching of Mexicans in the early 1920s to be "so common as to pass almost unnoticed." On the now ultraliberal West Coast, there was a campaign to "Keep California White."

In the 1930s, the Hitler-admiring Catholic priest Father Charles Coughlin promoted anti-Semitism through his radio show and oddly named newsletter, *Social Justice.* Bands of his followers vandalized Jewish stores and advocated "liquidating" the Jews from America. Japanese Americans returning home from internment after World War II were met with signs that said "No Japs Welcome."

As late as the late 1970s and early '80s, when my family and many other Russian Jews immigrated, many white Americans remained staunchly opposed to anyone who looked or sounded different. A campaign was launched to make English the official language of the U.S. In Detroit in 1982, two white auto workers beat a Chinese American man, twenty-seven-year-old Vincent Chin, to death with a baseball bat, erroneously believing him to be Japanese, and therefore, a competitor in the car industry.

Fetzer notes that for much of this time, the amount of hostility directed at a given immigrant group depended on "how much the newcomers' culture diverged from the dominant WASP norm." This was especially the case when there was a big influx of a very different group. The "exotic" Chinese and Japanese had it rough, while fair-complexioned Brits and Scandinavians were mostly accepted. Though economic factors played a role in any given year's levels of xenophobia, immigrants weren't, for the most part, hated for taking our jobs. They were resented for usurping our culture. Americans were worried that newcomers would commit the worst sin of all: never being quite like "us."

In love and romance, too, nothing has, historically, been hotter than conformity. The idea that people should embrace you "just the way you are" is nearly as new as the sext. After a brief dip into bohemianism in the 1920s, and before the tuning in and dropping out of the late 1960s, Americans of the late 1940s and '50s craved convention. The rise of bureaucracies within corporations made standardized practices and dress codes more important. "You see a filling out of middle management," explained Micki McGee, a sociologist who has studied the history of self-help literature. "You see women employed as assistants, secretaries, and you see conformity around what's supposed to happen."

Add to that the virulent anti-Communism of the era, as well as television programs and magazines that had vast penetration, and you get a cultural monolith. People were falling into "helpless conformity," as Betty Friedan called it. Those who aroused any suspicion of disloyalty to the U.S. risked being fired from their jobs. Even liberals were considered, in the words of one U.S. intelligence officer, "a hop, skip, and a jump" from sympathizing with the Reds. Various societal ills, including mentally ill children, were blamed on "wives who are not feminine enough and husbands [who are] not truly male," as one 1950s writer put it. Standing out simply wasn't worth the risk.

The historian Stephanie Coontz, who read dozens of 1950s- and '60s-era advice books and women's magazines for her book *A Strange Stirring: The Feminine Mystique and American Women at the Dawn of the 1960s*, says that everyone was on the lookout for Mr. or Mrs. Right—but there was only one way to be right. "With only a few exceptions," she told me, "they all emphasized the importance of a woman adjusting to her husband's work, friends, interests, and hobbies, and especially of putting her own interests and aspirations second, if not entirely aside."

"I quote one writer," Coontz added, "who says that if a wife must take a job, she should be sure that it's not interesting enough to compete with her dedication to him."

Women, in particular, were expected to mold themselves to fit their husbands' expectations, and those who had marriage trouble were asked by therapists if they were keeping themselves attractive enough. (Freud's theory of "penis envy" was twisted to imply that women who chased after male privileges would soon wear themselves out.) Men, meanwhile, were expected to display their manliness and wealth. Many unwed mothers gave up their children for adoption or risked being ostracized. Women who didn't want this life, Coontz writes, were pitied.

As Coontz explained it to me:

Countless short stories of the day told the tale of a girl who was just too serious about school to get a man's attention, with the trick ending that she had only enrolled in the class because she thought he would like it if she shared his interests. The happy ending was when she admitted she didn't like or understand chemistry but had wrongly believed that pretending to be interested in it would make her interesting to him.

People were getting married young. In the postwar economy, men tended to be breadwinners, and women stayed home. It was easier for society to funnel young women toward demure Stepford-wifery than to help them figure out if they're a Carrie or a Samantha.

"Remember your most important job is to build up and maintain his ego," Edward Podolsky advises wives in his 1943 book, *Sex Today in Wedded Life*. "Don't bother your husband with petty troubles and complaints when he comes home from work...Be a good listener. Let him tell you his troubles; yours will seem trivial in comparison."

By being the perfect companion, a good wife or girlfriend could help the couple achieve that midcentury nirvana, conventionality. *Fascinating Womanhood*, a 1965 bestseller, told married women they should aim to be "the perfect follower." Betty Cornell's *Teen-Age Popularity Guide*, published in 1951, advises that "you have only to fit yourself to the mood of your partner" when at a dance. "You'll always find that you get along better and are better liked if you abide by the standard procedure." *How to Pick a Mate*, published in 1946, advised that women let men do most of the talking and try to "fall in with whatever mood he is in." If a man has an idea about a place to go on a date, you should "enthusiastically accept" it. Clifford Rose Adams, the book's coauthor, urged young people to ask themselves things like, "Will this mate bring you social approval?," noting that "you want a mate that other people will like, that other people will admire and respect." Another important question, according to Adams:

Will this mate embarrass you by nonconformity? The man wants a wife who will not act unbecomingly in public, who knows how to say and do the right thing when other people are present, who will conform to the customs that will cause their neighbors to think well of her. The girl wants a man who is not discourteous or sloppy, who will get to work at the time he is supposed to report, who will not embarrass her in public by doing things that will make them criticized by others.

Happy wives, Adams wrote, quoting one psychologist of the day, "tend to be conventional," while unhappy wives "seek spectacular activities" and "want to be on the move."

Micki McGee, the sociologist, explained that even as nonconformity became a social trend, beginning with the Beats of the 1950s and into the antiwar movement of the mid-1960s, it wasn't as liberating as it seemed. True, books like *Sex and the Single Girl* encouraged women to have sex before marriage—a radical notion at the time. But it also admonished women to "light up when a guy calls" and always shave their armpits. "Encouraging women to embrace gender norms and pander to male bosses to advance their own social and financial position can hardly be read as a nonconformist position," McGee said.

Indeed, we seem to always find a way to hammer every nonconformist impulse into just another norm. Goths in high school reject the polo shirts of the preppie world, but they all dye their hair an identical black. Young hipsters in cities eschew cookie-cutter suburbs in order to live in cookie-cutter apartments. (I think I've seen the same "unique" IKEA lamp in about ten different "unique" Asian-fusion restaurants in Washington.) In its famous "1984" ad, Apple promised to literally break you free from a monotonous dystopia, but, as McGee pointed out, "when every single person has an iPhone, how is that being different? The paradox of the ethos of finding your own way is that if everyone's doing that, it's not actually being different."

In the latter half of the twentieth century, workplaces evolved from begrudgingly tolerating diversity to awkwardly cheerleading it. After the Civil Rights Act of 1964 forbade employment discrimination on the basis of race and sex, companies began sitting their employees down for antidiscrimination trainings, which were initially only aimed at ensuring compliance with the law and preventing lawsuits, as Rohini Anand and Mary-Frances Winters describe in their study of the trainings' history.

But then, the Reagan administration loosened regulations around employers' antidiscrimination practices. With less federal oversight, companies scaled back their diversity trainings. Trainings in this era focused on making women and minorities fit into the existing corporate culture, rather than the other way around. Women and people of color were urged to be more confident in the face of adversity—but relatively little was said about stopping the adversity itself.

The 1990s saw a pivot toward trainings that were targeted toward everyone, not just minorities. But the result was not necessarily better. "Many interpreted the key learning point as having to walk on egg shells around women and minorities," Anand and Winters write. "Some surmised that it meant White men were villains, still others assumed that they would lose their jobs to minorities and women, while others concluded that women and minorities were simply too sensitive." As a result, by the turn of the millennium underrepresented groups were still not seamlessly embraced by their coworkers.

Then again, perhaps we shouldn't blame past generations for being so wary of outsiders. After all, their brains made them do it.

When we see people who belong to other races, ethnicities, or groups, our brains snap into action, scanning the intruder and branding them in red warning letters: DIFFERENT.

The amygdala, the threat center of the brain, becomes activated when we see a face belonging to someone from another tribe. Several studies reveal that the amygdala responds more strongly to pictures of people of other races, but this can also happen with any group our brain perceives as different or threatening. The amygdala's activity causes us to stare at or distance ourselves from the person. Our heart rates rise and blood flow surges in preparation for a fight. (On a more adorable note, in a paper called "The Cooties Effect," researchers showed that the amygdalae of kids tend to react less strongly—and thus less negatively—toward the opposite sex as they get older.)

The brain also exhibits less empathy-like activity when it comes to people who are from groups outside our own, be they supporters of rival sports teams or people from other races. In experiments, people who watched others get poked with needles reacted as though they were feeling the pain themselves, but only when the people being prodded were of their same race. When outsiders are in pain, there's activation in the brain that looks more like schadenfreude.

David Amodio, a professor of psychology and neural science at New York University, has found that white people even process black people's faces in a way that dehumanizes them. Rather than seeing them as having human faces, white people process black faces more like they would an upside-down human face or the face of an animal. Then, because they don't see the black faces as very face-like, the white participants are less willing to allocate money to the black faces. Meanwhile, viewing pictures of social outcasts—people like the homeless and drug addicts—elicits in many people brain patterns consistent with disgust, similar to looking at a picture of an overflowing toilet.

As the brain is doing all this processing and threat-preparing, it is also zapping an area on its side, the anterior temporal lobe, and telling it to serve up all the stereotypes you might have associated with that person's group. That means if you see a transgender person, your brain might play you *Tootsie,* Caitlyn Jenner, and size 13 stilettos, in a kind of very primitive, insidious Netflix queue. We tend to remember people by whatever it is that makes them unusual—a dwarf doctor is memorable because he is a dwarf, not a doctor—and we assume that people will be just like other people who have their same unique trait.

In a 2002 article, the Princeton psychologist Susan Fiske described most people's feelings toward outside groups, like the disabled or elderly, as one of "cool neglect." Most people rarely express open hostility toward outsiders; they just don't like or respect them as much as their own group. In fact, most people who are biased against other groups tend to perform worse on cognitive tests after being exposed to members of other races: they're focusing all their energy on tamping down their prejudice so they can seem fair-minded. Even if our brains are swirling with bias, to the outside world, we try to look impartial.

Amodio thinks these hypersensitive neural responses might have served a purpose at some point in humans' ancestral past. Today, though, this instinct sets us up to avoid or alienate people who don't look or act like us.

Our distrust of outsiders might even explain the surprising rise of Donald Trump, who frequently targets minorities and the "other" on Twitter and in his policies. Michele Gelfand, the psychologist who studies tightness and looseness, has suggested that Trump's campaign-trail reminders of "threats" such as Mexican immigrants and Syrian refugees sparked voters' desire for cultural tightness.

Recall that tightness is how much we stick to norms. It means a return to law and order, another Trump standby. In Gelfand's research, concern about various threats predicted both people's psychological tightness and their support for Trump. Normative tightness, Gelfand found, predicted voting for Trump beyond .001 percent of a statistical doubt. "Perceptions of threat tighten societies, leading to social coordination at best, and intolerance at worst," she and her colleagues wrote in 2016.

Multiple studies and surveys have now shown that it was a fear of losing status to other groups—like immigrants and people of color—that motivated many white Americans' support for Trump. As I wrote for *The Atlantic* in 2018, Trump supporters were more likely than Clinton voters to feel that the "American way of life is threatened," which is about as clear a signal as seizing a sociologist by the lapels and screaming, "I'm feeling status threat!"

Perhaps it is no surprise, then, that many traditionally white counties that experienced rapid increases in Latino newcomers flocked to Trump in 2016. The immigrant influx was gauged by something called the diversity index, a measure of the chance that any two people in an area will belong to a different race or ethnicity. Trump won two-thirds of voters in counties where the diversity index rose by 150 percent or more, according to a *Wall Street Journal* analysis.

When I asked Chris Crandall why this might be, why a handful of immigrants are fine, but a sudden inpouring is scary, he explained it this way: One person speaking Spanish in Wisconsin is a deviant. Some people might see her as inferior, but it's ultimately about her, not the group.

A lot of Spanish speakers suddenly appearing in Wisconsin, meanwhile, is a threat to the way things have always been. And threats have the potential to unnerve us.

Trempealeau County, in western Wisconsin, voted for Barack Obama in 2008. It voted for Obama in 2012. But between 2012 and 2016, something happened that changed the county's politics.

Like many other places in the Midwest, throughout the 2000s the overwhelmingly white county began attracting large numbers of Latino immigrants. Most of the new arrivals to the county found work in agriculture or at Ashley Furniture in the town of Arcadia. By 2016, the city was one-third Latino.

Latinos I spoke with who live there described somewhat of an integration Catch-22. At first, when there were relatively few of them, they were mostly accepted, but sometimes discriminated against because they were so new and different. But later, when more and more immigrants began trickling in, some people lumped them all together, writing them off as criminals who take advantage of the system. There always seemed to be either too few or too many Latino immigrants to make all the white people perfectly comfortable.

A woman I'll call Gloria moved to Arcadia with her young daughter and husband in 2010, when the city was only about 6 percent Latino. Originally from Mexico, Gloria and her husband were living in Arizona when they were driven out by the recession, which had gutted the state's job market. Gloria was pleased that her husband found a job within weeks of moving to Arcadia.

Despite having lots of experience working at a bank, Gloria had trouble finding similar work in Wisconsin. She got the sense that she would have to know someone in order to find a position.

Gloria speaks highly of the town, where she was eventually able to find good work and make a home. Since the move, she's had another child. Over time, more Hispanic grocery stores and restaurants opened up, providing the town's immigrants with familiar cuisine.

But she also says some of the white people were rude to her. "It's a small community where everybody knows everybody," she explained. "They kind of feel like they kind of own part of Arcadia. It seems like you were just…coming to their place."

When she finally did get hired at a bank, some customers implied that she didn't know what she was doing. One woman screamed at her and called her stupid for not performing a simple transaction the exact way she specified—a more convoluted way than necessary.

"You feel kind of awkward," Gloria said. "Sometimes you don't know if you should say something or just stay quiet. After a while…you kind of learn their way. You kind of learn when to step up or when just to move out of the way."

Gloria told me she would only speak up for herself when she felt like some good would come of it. Everything else, she let go.

For most of our interview, Gloria sounded upbeat, but when she talked about situations like these, in which she was talked down to and insulted, her energy drained. "You know you have to go to work because you need the money," she said at one point. "You come to the house, and sometimes you are in a bad mood."

"Physically," she added, "it destroys you."

At the time, anti-immigrant sentiment in the region was just beginning to percolate. In 2006, Arcadia's then-mayor John Kimmel proposed making English the town's official language and penalizing businesses that employed undocumented workers. This prompted such an outcry that most of his proposals were scrapped. However, when an immigration raid in 2010 led to several arrests, one local news station wrote, "Several people in Arcadia who did not want to appear on camera told us they're glad illegal immigrants are being arrested and deported."

In news reports, some locals called the newcomers "a blessing," but others worried they would bring crime. On social media, whenever a Hispanic committed a crime, one resident told me, it seemed like the comments would turn into a fury about how "all" Hispanics are criminals.

It's commonly thought that the main reason behind opposition to immigration is a fear that immigrants will take Americans' jobs, but research on anti-immigrant sentiment suggests that's not quite true. Instead, what seems most important is how culturally different the immigrants are from the native population. Specifically, what matters is if the immigrants speak English. To wit: more than 90 percent of Americans believe a person "must speak English" to be an American.

Several studies show that Americans view immigrants who speak English more favorably than those who speak other languages. Worries about English being dethroned are a key motivator of anti-immigrant sentiment. (It's not just in the U.S., either. Cultural similarity is so important to the acceptance of immigrants that Swiss authorities once ran an ad campaign featuring an African migrant arriving to work on time each day, as if to emphasize that Africans can be just like the timely Swiss.) "If assimilation into the host society is a central norm that immigrants are commonly perceived to violate, language is perhaps the most visible signal of that norm," write Jens Hainmueller and Daniel J. Hopkins in their study on this topic. It turns out we don't want to safeguard our jobs so much as our norms.

What happened in Trempealeau County seems closest to what Hopkins described in a 2010 paper: hostility toward immigrants rises when communities undergo an influx of immigrants *and* when national leaders are at the same time talking about how dangerous immigrants are. What's more, few of those immigrants to Trempealeau County spoke English as a first language. Intensifying matters, when people have *negative* experiences with other ethnic or religious groups, they are more likely to connect those experiences to the person's ethnicity and generalize those negative attributes to the rest of the group.

In 2016, not long after Trump called Mexicans rapists, and after Latinos had moved in at a rapid pace, Trempealeau County had the perfect storm for hostility toward outsiders. In 2016, Trempealeau County went for Trump.

"If you'd seen the way things have changed in this town," one fifty-one-year-old Arcadian told the *Wall Street Journal* that year, "you'd say, 'Something needs to be done about it.'" One resident of Arcadia derided "border jumpers" to the *Milwaukee Journal Sentinel* in 2016 and said he wanted Trump to "just make it where it was, where a working white guy has a chance." Another woman told the paper, "There are too many Hispanics here that are trying to overpower all of us."

It wasn't just Trempealeau County, of course. As Peter Schrag put it, as Latino immigrants moved from traditional immigrant destinations like California and Arizona to the Midwest, "the backlash spread with them."

After the 2016 election, Gloria noticed that some Latinos were leaving Trempealeau County for Canada.

Victoria, a twenty-five-year-old Mexican woman, has lived in Arcadia since she was nine years old. (I'm using a pseudonym for her because the future of Deferred Action for Childhood Arrivals, or DACA, the program she relies upon to stay in the country, has been in jeopardy in recent years.) Back in grade school, she estimates, there were only about five other Hispanic students in her school. She remembers other kids being surprised that there were kids in existence who didn't know English. When her brother started kindergarten in Wisconsin, he was embarrassed to bring Mexican food for lunch.

In the early years, Victoria's family mostly kept to themselves. As soon as she did learn English, Victoria was helping her parents, translating school forms for them and calling to make appointments. "Since there weren't a lot of us, [white Arcadians] were more accepting," she told me. "Things aren't all the same really anymore."

To be clear, she and everyone else emphasized, most people in Arcadia are welcoming. But Victoria, too, now hears the occasional crack that there are now too many Hispanics, or that people don't want their kids growing up speaking Spanish. Once, someone at her job claimed that immigrants don't pay taxes, so Victoria defiantly showed them her pay stub. When Victoria and her brother, who is also undocumented, went off to college, they were ineligible for in-state tuition.

One particularly strange moment for the family came in September of 2017, when a police officer who seemed new to the area pulled over Victoria's father, who does not speak English and doesn't have a driver's license. (He was unable to get one, as an unauthorized immigrant.) It was two-thirty in the morning, and Victoria's terrified father called her to come help him. When she arrived at the scene, she says the officer brusquely interrogated her about why her father doesn't have a license. The officer let her father go with a ticket, but the incident seemed to rattle the family.

Victoria speaks perfect English with a Midwestern accent, yet she says she feels more Hispanic than American. Her younger brother does too, even though he barely remembers life in Mexico. Victoria watches Spanish-language TV, listens to Spanish music, and cooks Mexican food.

I came away from our conversation wondering if the actions of some of their fellow Americans might have helped push Victoria and her brother into the arms of Mexican culture. Some of their neighbors only disliked immigrants more as there came to be more of them, and they voted for a man who vowed to kick them out. They became wary of the immigrants because their behaviors, their food, their appearance, their *language,* to them, were weird.

Victoria tells me she wishes she could return to Mexico and visit her extended family, but her immigration status prevents her from traveling internationally. Her own parents haven't seen their parents in years.

Her brother, too, dreams of returning to Mexico and becoming a politician. After seeing the toll that immigration took on his parents, he wants to make his home country better—so that families don't have to emigrate anymore.

EMMA, PART I

When I was seven, we became U.S. citizens, and a coworker of my dad's bought me a subscription to *American Girl* magazine, whose arrival I awaited each month like a little junkie expecting her dealer. When it came, I tore into the features about typical girls in places like Boring, Oregon—not as boring as it sounds! I felt trapped by Midland, and I looked to the magazine to open my horizons, one Iowa corn parade at a time, or whatever.

One month, there was an article about the life of an Amish girl. The girl's face was not photographed out of respect for her religion, so we readers had to settle for wisps of light-brown hair sticking out of the back of her bonnet. She described a life of reading by kerosene lamplight and obeying her parents *no matter what*. It was reality television for melodramatic second-grade girls: at last, someone whose life was incontrovertibly worse than mine.

After I gobbled up the Amish story, I raced over to a neighbor's house. I had to let her know, without delay, that the Amish exist and that they don't have *Mario Kart*. I didn't know how to pronounce it—I had only ever seen it written—so I called it "Ame-ish," like a religion made up of people named Amy.

"Maybe you're Amish," she said.

"Maybe *you're* Amish," I retorted.

We were both relieved that I was simply Russian, not Amish. After all, my parents forbade artificial food dyes, on account of a cancer article they heard about once, but they took no issue with Super Nintendo.

It was around then that the same coworker of my father's asked me to write an essay about what being "an American" meant to me. I had never given it much thought, and I had no idea what to write. The Amish were Americans, but who the hell wanted to be like them?

I asked my dad what it meant to be American, and he said it meant I could vote. I was a kid, though. Of course I couldn't vote. My dad occasionally expressed pride in being an American, but he usually meant it sarcastically, and usually only after he found he was obligated to spend money on some bureaucratic necessity. *"Ohhho!"* he would bellow from the kitchen, having ripped open his car-registration renewal letter. *"I'm proud to be an American! Register car! Bullshit!"*

For my essay, I ended up spewing some patriotic hyperbole and calling it a day. It was good practice for my liberal arts degree, perhaps, but it didn't get me any closer to the answer. What made an American girl? What did it mean to have an American life?

The Swartzentruber Amish, one of the most conservative orders, call leaving the Amish "going high." Perhaps it's because their lives are so modest, so basic, they could be considered earthy, low. The women in Emma Gingerich's Missouri order could only wear dresses made of dark red, black, blue, green, or gray. After childhood, their clothes are fastened with straight pins, not buttons. Her house had no phone, and her family spoke a German dialect at home.

A tourist photo taken of Emma and her siblings as small children, in the early 1990s, shows the girls in black bonnets, black dresses, and white aprons, running barefoot to church past bales of hay. She was forbidden from cutting her hair or leaving home without a cap and bonnet covering every strand. The Amish have essentially made a deal with modernity. Unlike many Americans, they rarely feel lonely or lost; their communities give them constant purpose. All they must do in return is conform.

Emma's order did not practice *rumspringa,* a period in which Amish teenagers try on worldly lifestyles, mythologized in tequila-soaked TV shows like *Breaking Amish.* Instead, Emma was so shielded from the facts of life that she usually only realized that a new sibling was joining the family when she heard the cries of a newborn in the next room. When she got her period, her mother told her she was like a hen sitting on her eggs. To Emma, her life often seemed lower than low: sunken.

She was the kind of kid who begged to go to the local schoolhouse before she was old enough. Her mother would begrudgingly pack her a lunch and send her off. Unlike the other kids, Emma loved school. She tried to hide her interest in it, since she knew others would mock her if they found out. Eighth grade, when she was expected to end her education, loomed.

She had thirteen siblings, but her father often singled her out for criticism. If something wasn't on the table in time for dinner, it always seemed to be Emma's fault, even though there were eight other girls who could have fetched it. (Girls are the default attendants of the domestic realm in Amish culture.) Taking care of her brood of siblings made a lifetime of womanly drudgery appeal even less to Emma.

Emma bucked against the many norms of her community. She never understood why they couldn't have a toilet or electricity. She acquired a small radio and hid it in her room, tuning it to music stations late at night.

She also felt somehow different from other Amish girls—vaguely inadequate, or like everyone else was in on a joke she didn't understand. By sixteen, Amish girls are long done with schooling and are considered old enough to be schoolteachers themselves. Each year, the local Amish school board would choose a sixteen-year-old girl to be a teacher the following year. Emma had expressed an interest in teaching, but she was never asked to be one, even though younger girls were.

Sixteen was also the age at which Amish girls started dating, and by seventeen it was considered unusual not to have a boyfriend. Yet, girls were also not supposed to reveal if they had crushes on certain boys. They were instead expected to wait until someone set them up.

One day, some male friends of Emma's brought a guy over to her house. Just a few minutes into the date, this new boy walked out the door. Emma thought he was just going to the bathroom, but then she heard his buggy pulling away.

"That really hurt my feelings," Emma told me. "I was like, 'Oh, my goodness. I am definitely an outcast or something.'" When all the other teens found out about this misfire, they blamed Emma.

It took forever for anyone to set Emma up again, and when someone finally did, it was not with the boy she'd hoped for.

Still, she continued seeing him, since it was expected. Every two weeks—as expected—he would come to her room. Without speaking a word, they would climb into bed together. Sex was forbidden, but this strange co-sleeping stage was required. She and a boy whose name she scarcely knew were to lie side by side in a narrow bed together all night and determine whether they wanted to spend the rest of their lives together. Though this is the community's sanctioned form of "bed courtship," a patina of propriety had to be maintained. The following morning, the boy would wake up before dawn and leave under the cover of night, to avoid being seen. After about a month of this, Emma told him she didn't want to see him anymore.

That's when the headaches and nausea started. According to her memoir, *Runaway Amish Girl,* published in 2014, Emma's parents took her to a quack doctor who "treated" her by shoving balloons up her nose and inflating them. The painful treatment made Emma even more miserable than before. She couldn't figure out what was wrong with her: everyone else seemed to accept their Amish fates. It felt like God had put something in her that made her doubt.

Emma and several others I spoke with seemed to have a period where they're excluded from the larger group, even if in a minor way. After people "communicate" to a norm violator that they broke the rules, Chris Crandall explained to me, the group might spurn the norm violator. Established group members might feel like they have to do so in order to make the group "mean" what it always did.

In fact, some of Emma's Amish friends might have been making her feel like a loner on purpose. One thing peripheral group members can do is to marginalize someone else—Emma, in this case— in order to curry favor with the rest of the group, says Michael Hogg. In pushing to the side someone even weirder, the weird can feel normal again.

When Emma was seventeen, she revealed to a non-Amish friend of the family that she yearned to leave, and he gave her the phone number of a family that agreed to help her.

One January afternoon in 2006, when her parents were out of town, Emma took off her cap and tied a scarf around her hair— she was afraid to leave home bare-headed. She walked out of her family's farmhouse. Using a cell phone smuggled to her by another rebellious teenager, she dialed the acquaintance's number. It was the first time she had ever spoken on the phone.

The note she left for her parents read: "The time has come for me to leave, I am not happy here anymore. I am sorry to do this to you but I need to try a different life."

Being American, it turns out, sometimes means having the freedom to decide how much freedom you want.

## ASMA, PART I

The first time ten-year-old Asma saw the small, Southern town to which her father was proposing to move her family, she cried. The place was littered with run-down buildings, some of which looked as though they were left over from the days of sharecropping. Unlike her previous elementary school, which was brightly painted and had student art projects on the walls, her new school seemed cheerless and gray. The fifth-grade students were covering material Asma had learned years ago.

(Asma asked that I not use her real name or identifying details so that she could speak freely about a place she has mixed feelings about, but in which her parents still live.)

Asma was born to a devout Muslim, African-immigrant family and spent her early childhood in a northern part of the U.S. But midway through her childhood, her family had to move to a rural town in the South for her father's job. Asma and her siblings would be the only Muslims in her new school.

When I asked Asma if she ever felt a distinct *I-don't-belong* feeling, she knew exactly what I meant. When they first arrived in the new town, Asma's parents enrolled her in a summer program. Breakfast was served, and she declined to eat the pork sausage.

Other kids stared in awe at this stranger, with her clipped vowels and dietary restrictions.

"I'm Muslim," she explained, and would continue to explain when kids asked why her family didn't celebrate Christmas, or why she wasn't eating during Ramadan, or why her mom wore a hijab.

"What church do you go to?" they'd say, as many good Southerners do upon meeting a stranger. Asma would patiently explain the difference between Christians and Muslims. People would tell her that she needed Jesus, and Asma would politely demur.

After 9/11, her difference seemed to harden, in the eyes of her neighbors, into outright deviance. Research has shown that crises like armed conflicts make groups cohere more firmly. Under threat, groups enforce their norms more strictly and punish those who violate them more severely. After 9/11, being unlike all the white Christians in multiple ways wasn't an easy way for Asma to be.

One kid asked Asma if her father was a terrorist and if she knew when the next attack would be. On the attack's one-year anniversary, her class had to sing "God Bless the U.S.A.," and Asma got the sense that the patriotic zeal wasn't meant to include people like her. In the wake of the tragedy, Asma's realization of her own distinctiveness happened over and over again.

It wasn't just being Muslim that made her stand out. She wasn't like the Christian kids, but she wasn't exactly like the other black kids, either. She felt like many people in her town accepted her, a smart black kid who used stereotypically "white" diction, but not the other black kids, many of whom were growing up in poverty. On some level, Asma sensed that it would behoove her to preserve her newscaster-neutral accent, to be the kind of kid that adults liked.

Asma is still Facebook friends with some of the locals from that town, and she's sometimes puzzled by the town's cognitive dissonance. Some people there wish President Trump would keep all the Muslims out one minute, while wishing her well on her endeavors the next.

In high school, Asma served as a kind of assistant for one of her teachers, helping him with administrative work during her free period. He was a quirky man, and many of the oddball students gravitated toward him. He was kind to Asma, and they had an easy, comfortable relationship.

Later, after she had already graduated, news reports came out exposing the teacher as a member of a neo-Nazi group. For Asma, the revelation led to some uncomfortable questions: *What was it about me that this hateful man was okay with? And am I okay with being the sort of black person that hateful white people like?*

The reason why we often feel unsettled by different beliefs and identities might be rooted in our most basic instincts. Specifically, it appears to be connected to our lizard-brain sense of disgust and cleanliness.

Since the Nobel Prize began in 1901, Denmark has produced more than thirty Nobel laureates per one million citizens. Italy, meanwhile, has generated just one prize-winner per million. South Korea acquires eight hundred international patents per million people per year, but Singapore gets only about eight.

In 2014, the Tulane psychologist Damian Murray set out to determine why this was. What separates countries that churn out lots of luminaries from those that don't?

Predictable factors like wealth, education, and life expectancy made a big difference in a country's level of innovation. But even when Murray took wealth and education into account, he uncovered a surprising circumstance that also affected creativity: how plagued by various infectious diseases—such as leprosy, malaria, and typhus—a given country had been in the early twentieth century. The reason a heavy disease burden dampened the kind of creative thinking required to win a Nobel, Murray found, was because worrying about biological threats made people in those nations more conformist.

A history of infectious diseases didn't make people in those nations dim-witted. But, according to this theory, it helped make them more traditional and avoidant of other people, and thus, less likely to come up with new and interesting ideas. Often, what leads to innovation are, precisely, norm-violating, nonconformist ideas. (In lab settings, for example, people who are more outraged by norm violations tend to register as less creative. People who notice and react very strongly to social norm violations tend not to think outside of the box, Michele Gelfand told me.)

Murray found that the more pathogens burdened a given society, the more its citizens became increasingly authoritarian, less individualistic, and less creative. They came to distrust anything, or anyone, that seemed weird. As a result, they were safer, perhaps, but also less inventive than their historically healthier neighbors.

According to a newish theory in psychology, this happens because in addition to our regular immune systems, which vanquish germs and keep us healthy, we are equipped with so-called *behavioral* immune systems. Our behavioral immune systems predispose us to avoid people who break our social norms because we, subconsciously, fear they might harbor illnesses we are not equipped to fight off. There are three ways this instinct might work. First, people who don't follow local customs are likely to be from faraway lands, and they could bring in unfamiliar pathogens that could wipe out your tribe. Second, people who break certain norms, like the one against having lots of sexual partners, might be more likely to spread diseases even if they *are* from your tribe. Finally, an unusual appearance or strange behavior might signal an infectious disease—think leprosy, which disfigures the face. All three kinds of people, our gut reaction tells us, should be avoided. Thus, we may shun people who break our local norms, even if there's nothing actually wrong with them.

As I described in a 2016 *Atlantic* article, our fear of getting sick appears to make us less open to outsiders in several ways. Several studies have now shown that when people are more worried about disease, they react more negatively toward foreigners and norm violators. (Is it any wonder that immigrants are often referred to as "animals" or "parasites" or other terms for disease vectors?) People in more disease-ridden countries are less likely to be extroverted or open to new experiences, suggesting that they want to stay away from the unfamiliar and avoid exposing themselves to even more sicknesses. Pregnant women in their first trimester are more prone to infections, and as it happens, during that trimester women exhibit more ethnocentric and xenophobic attitudes than when they're further along in their pregnancies. One study found that states and countries that are more plagued by infectious diseases tend to have stronger family ties and greater levels of religiosity; the authors interpreted these measures as indicating a preference for sticking with your own kind of people.

Though not all studies have supported this connection, a substantial body of research has found that people who are more easily disgusted are more likely to be tough on crime, anti-gay, and even politically conservative. People who are more sensitive to the smell of sweat and urine are more likely to support authoritarian political leaders—perhaps because these leaders would be more likely to keep disease-bearing outside groups out. People who searched for more news about the 2014 Ebola outbreak were more likely to vote Republican, which suggests, to some researchers, that they were worried about the virus and wanted someone in office whose immigration policy might keep supposedly Ebola-infected outsiders away. (Sometimes pundits make this connection explicit: in one 2005 broadcast, Lou Dobbs's show claimed illegal immigrants were spreading leprosy in the United States. Later, his correspondent was found to have confused a thirty-year figure with a three-year one.) The behavioral immune system operates like a strong gag reflex. It instinctively keeps away anyone who might bring something weird to the table, all with the goal of keeping us healthy.

Gelfand, the researcher who examined tight and loose cultures, also found that a high level of threats leads to cultural tightness—the cultures with stricter norms. In her 2011 study, she found that tight nations had fewer natural resources, including less farmland and food reserves. They were more densely populated. They had worse air and water quality, experienced more natural disasters, like floods and droughts, and had a greater risk of invasions. Tight countries had more deaths from communicable diseases and had higher child mortality rates. "When you have a collective threat, you can't solve it on your own," Gelfand told me. You need to stick—firm, close, tight—with your fellow man. Perhaps because of how many threats they've faced, people in tight societies are less willing to live near people unlike themselves, one study found.

Some researchers think the behavioral immune system is not a psychological impulse so much as a cultural one. It's not necessarily any healthier to avoid outsiders, this line of thinking goes, but groups have historically grown and prospered when they were closed off to outside influences. (For example, the Mormons, who proselytize aggressively and mandate everything down to the style of underwear adherents must wear, are fast-growing, while membership in the Unitarian Universalists, whose beliefs are much more flexible, is basically stagnant.) Group leaders, then, might be manipulating our natural sense of disgust toward unfamiliar diseases in order to stoke xenophobic feelings whenever it's convenient. If a politician wants people to start turning against immigrants, he might just start talking about Ebola-ridden immigrants sneaking across the border.

This theory fits with how the Hindu caste system in India developed. As Yuval Noah Harari writes in his book *Sapiens,* about three thousand years ago Indo-Aryan invaders stratified the Indian population into castes in hopes of permanently subjugating them. The Indo-Aryans placed themselves at the top of the heap. Mixing with the lowest castes, which were kept from having access to good sanitation, was considered "polluting" oneself. The very lowest caste became known as the "Untouchables," and other people, accordingly, avoided even touching them. It behooved the Indo-Aryans to stoke the behavioral immune systems of their subjects, so they did.

This being psychology, some researchers think the entire behavioral immune system concept is, basically, bunk. Some scholars I reached out to told me the effect sizes of these studies tend to be small, which in science-speak means they don't really explain all that much. Favoring your own kind, some argue, has more to do with government effectiveness than with diseases. In places where governments don't take care of the roads, schools, and clinics properly, people seem to invest more in their immediate families and groups as a form of social security—not because they're disgusted, but because they have no other choice.

Douglas Fry, the anthropologist, told me the idea of the behavioral immune system "sounds crazy." Germ theory, after all, is only a few hundred years old. People in our ancestral past would have had no idea they were avoiding invisible particles that caused sickness. And, he points out, in modern hunter-gatherer societies, people still have all sorts of supernatural explanations for illnesses that don't correlate with outsiders coming in or out. Returning to the Nobel study, another anthropologist, Agustín Fuentes, told me you can't compare modern-day countries as different as Denmark and Singapore, since they have very different histories.

One of the major studies in this field, the one about family ties and religiosity, was met with a slew of critical commentaries. The critics claimed there are other things, like a country's wealth, that might explain why countries that have more parasites are more religious. One person offered up a study of fifty-six Mayans to show that religious people tend to get sick *more*, not less, because they're always out proselytizing and helping the poor. So if religious people want to avoid germs, they have a funny way of showing it. Other critics said it's not always the case that foreign pathogens are any worse for you than local ones, so it wouldn't necessarily benefit our ancestors to avoid foreigners for health reasons. The study authors had responses to all of these critiques, but I'm going to spare us all and just say this field of research is, well, controversial.

Mark Schaller, a University of British Columbia psychology professor who has studied the behavioral immune system, explained that yes, the effect sizes are often small, but that in psychology, "even small effects can have big consequences." The behavioral immune system is one reason why xenophobic attitudes exist, he argues, but that doesn't mean it's the only one. The Nazis compared the Jews to rats, which are associated with infectious diseases, but they also claimed Jews were hurting the economy, which has nothing to do with disease or disgust. And while it's true that people have not always approached avoiding disease logically or rationally, that's just the point, Schaller says. The behavioral immune system isn't rational. It's reflexive, and it's willing to endure a thousand false alarms for every real threat.

Some researchers I spoke with are beginning to make connections between the behavioral immune system and our actual, biological immune system. People who carry a particular variation of the ACP1 gene are more susceptible to parasitic and infectious diseases, and, Murray and his colleagues found, they also happen to be less extroverted. In other words, they avoid going out and meeting new and different people, who might be carriers of unfamiliar pathogens. If you are the kind of person who gets sick easily, your body might just nudge you to get out less and expose yourself to fewer new people.

The emerging picture from these studies suggests the two immune systems work in concert, alternately kicking in and backing down as they're needed. People who are more careful about germs—who, say, open the bathroom door with a paper towel—have less inflammation, which is the way our body typically protects us from pathogens. When you're taking pains to avoid germs—when your behavioral immune system is revved up—your body realizes there's less of a need for it to fight infections below the skin, so it turns down the inflammatory activity.

For some of the nonconformists I interviewed, there was a noticeable pattern of being avoided—almost literally—like the plague. Their ideas seemed to, frankly, gross out their neighbors. These days, "catching the gay" is an outdated joke about bigots, but for some outcasts, it still feels as though their peers fear being infected with their ideas. They spend their lives being kept at a distance by others' behavioral immune systems. Next, we'll learn just how damaging this kind of alienation can be.

# CHAPTER 4

# The Sting

One week in 1995, the psychologist Kipling Williams and his colleagues at the University of Toledo, in Ohio, decided to experiment on themselves. He and four of the other researchers in his department would ostracize a different person among them every day for a week. Each day, a randomly selected colleague would have a scarlet letter "O," for "ostracized," taped above his or her office door. That day, the others would ignore and otherwise subtly reject that colleague. They would avoid eye contact and conversation with that person. The ostracized colleague would not get so much as a hello or goodbye.

Some of the scientists thought the project would surely be a bust, since they all knew about it to start with. One of the researchers even worried she would start giggling while attempting to faux-ostracize her coworkers. Others thought the treatment wouldn't be so different from what they already experienced in their everyday lives. One researcher, a young immigrant, wrote that she thought it would be easier for her to tolerate the ostracism; since "this is not my country, people don't acknowledge my existence all the time."

Even though the researchers knew the experiment was fake, the diaries they kept during the week revealed a surprising amount of angst. "I feel like I am a ghost on the floor that everyone hears, but no one can talk to," one of the participants wrote on his "O" ostracism day. They felt stupid when people didn't laugh at their jokes. Even a few seconds of accidental eye contact felt "wonderful." One of the ostracized researchers, on his O day, would annoy his colleagues just to get any kind of attention. Some of them grew a little paranoid. "No matter how much I know why they're [ostracizing me], there's a part of me that wonders if it isn't something else," one of the participants wrote in his journal.

"Despite knowing the reasons behind the ostracism, and knowing that a predetermined end was in sight," the ostracism felt unpleasant, they wrote in a journal article about the experience after the fact. "We questioned each other's motives, had difficulties carrying out our day-to-day duties, and felt disengaged from our friends and colleagues. As targets we felt disconnected to the group, frustrated by our lack of control, uncertain of the value of our contributions, and unrecognized." Even though the ostracism was temporary and experimental, it nevertheless made its painful mark on the ostracized.

The "Scarlet O" study and others like it underscore just how distressing social isolation can be. There are, of course, some people who feel untroubled by their societal exclusion. In my reporting, I've found, for instance, that polyamorous people tend to recognize that their lifestyle is considered strange by society, but they will nevertheless defend it vociferously. They seem certain that monogamous normals are the ones who are really missing out.

But for most people, realizing you are on the periphery of your group can, in itself, lead to significant unhappiness. Misfortunes, the superstition goes, come in threes, and for whatever reason, so do the sad statistics on bullying. In studies, it only takes three minutes of ostracism by total strangers for people to start feeling bad emotionally. About a third of kids are bullied, and about a third of *them* grow up to have what one researcher calls "adult post-bullying syndrome," a condition marked by struggles with trust and relationships, mental illness, people-pleasing, and addiction. And about a third of all depression among eighteen-year-olds can be explained by childhood bullying.

Most of the people I interviewed were happy to be pursuing

their solitary path. But some nevertheless found it at times painful to be on their own.

## EMMA, PART II

When Emma Gingerich left the Amish, she did not know who the president was. During her first few weeks with the family that helped her escape her order, she learned to take a shower in running water, to shave her legs, to apply deodorant, and what contact lenses were. At her first-ever haircut, a hairdresser lopped off twelve inches. The family that had helped her escape the Amish handed Emma off to some acquaintances in San Benito, near the Texas-Mexico border. There, she quickly felt the pain of being ripped from the only social group she'd ever known.

Emma was, at that point, a natural-born American citizen with no Social Security number or birth certificate. She had to learn to drive, got a job at Dollar General, and then someone stole her truck out of the parking lot. No one had ever told her to lock her doors.

After long days of work, she struggled to keep her eyes open to study for her GED. She started college, but it took her about two years to learn English. All day, her brain rang with the unfamiliar sounds emitted by her professors.

She had not known what sex was, yet within the first seven months of her new life, she was raped twice by a laborer who worked at the subdivision where she cleaned houses. She would cry and ask God why he was putting her through all this. In 2010, four years after her escape, as she was sobbing herself to sleep one night, God seemed to listen. She heard a voice say, "I'm here." She opened her eyes and saw Jesus standing in her doorway. She fell asleep and awoke the next morning with a renewed sense of strength.

To pursue her bachelor's degree, Emma moved to Stephenville, Texas, a small town between Fort Worth and Abilene. There, Emma struggled socially nearly as much as she did among the Amish. She had trouble trusting people. When she finally made a friend, she turned out to be an insecure girl who sought constant reassurance of her status as a "best friend." It wasn't terminology Emma was familiar with. *What's the difference between a friend and a "best friend"?* Emma felt like she was constantly trying to please her, a feeling she remembers alternately as "cowering down" and "treading water."

At times, she felt like people could see through her business-casual separates and envision her wearing a long dress and bonnet. She speaks with a subtle, but noticeable, Germanic lilt. People ask her all the time where she's from, and sometimes she's too exhausted to explain it all. Even finding a new church was difficult. Emma is still a strong Christian, but she found the Baptist church she encountered in Texas too insistent that she attend every Sunday, or even twice a week.

I first met Emma in person a few years ago, when I interviewed her for an *Atlantic* article about her use of technology. At the time, I noticed that she seemed to have dueling impulses about whether she needed more personal space, or less. For a while, whenever someone knocked on her front door, she would scream.

The negative consequences of social exclusion were a subtle but inescapable part of what my family and I experienced in Texas. Texans' friendliness is the best thing about the state, but like too much Sweet 'N Low, in overlarge quantities it carries an acrid note. Polite concern about which church you go to and "how y'all doin' tonight" can slip into outright nosiness—or even a vague insinuation of superiority. Cashiers at grocery stores often ask my parents, who both have heavy accents, "Where y'all from?" They then proceed to guess countries—*Germany! France!*—that are inevitably wrong. This is not rude, per se, but it is yet another reminder to my parents of how glaring their outsiderdom is.

At one point, in high school, I got a job selling clothes at a men's clothing store. I liked the job. Many of my fellow cashiers were boys from other schools in the area, and it was a chance to interact with them on neutral territory. Decked in my mandatory khaki pants, I hoped to recast the shopgirl version of me as slightly cooler and slightly less good at math. Slightly less Russian, even.

I also liked it because men do not ever try on clothes. They simply pick up a polo shirt, measure it roughly against their torsos, and throw it over their shoulders like they just chopped down a tree. I had zero tasks most days, yet I received the same $6.50 an hour as the poor saps endlessly folding silky camisoles at Banana Republic.

But, of course, I also had a mandatory name tag, so customers would often ask me where I was from.

"Do you like it better here?" one older customer asked, after I told him I was from Russia.

"Uh, sure," I said. "I mean, I was really young when I left."

"Well, it must be nice," he said, "having all this freedom."

"All this freedom" is something we heard a lot. *Aren't you enjoying all this freedom?* Texans felt they had given us something that was so dear to them—freedom—and seemed hurt it was not more transformational for us, that we were not like snow-people whose icy exteriors melted away at the first bite of hot, nourishing freedom. But more often than not, people who are expected to feel persistently grateful instead wind up feeling subtly inferior.

There was another element to it. Though my Scandinavian mother could always pass for an average white American, my father looks like Saddam Hussein, and perhaps as a result I, too, don't blend in perfectly with most of the people I grew up around. A friend of mine says this is because a certain stratum of upper-class, white Texans look "like pilgrims," and she's not entirely wrong. The popular girls at my high school looked like they had been born to a hardy germ line of Bavarian pioneers, then lightly sandblasted by scorching winds to a rugged perfection. I'm blond, but that's about where the similarities end. My classmates said I looked like a mouse, or, on my better days, a turtle. As a Brooklynite makeup artist once informed me before an early-morning TV appearance, "You have vary exahtic featchas." Whatever physical differences actually existed between me and my classmates only magnified the fact that I was already considered too nerdy and too foreign to date.

At the clothing store where I had my summer job, the workload at one point became so minimal that anarchy took hold. One time, all the boys emptied an entire canister of air freshener in the bathroom, clouding the place with a synthetic lavender scent that stung our eyes.

Despite their antics, I began to notice one of the boys in particular. "Brad" had gone to a different high school than mine. He had acne, which—it feels good to say now—I was willing to overlook. He was the "funny guy," though the only funny thing I can remember him doing is the dancing monkey scene from *Zoolander.*

It was the summer before college, I had never been on a date before, and I decided to try out a new, more forward approach. I spent weeks flirting with Brad, which largely consisted of my laughing hard at his monkey impression and his hopping around more vigorously in gratitude. When I strategically mentioned that I do yoga, he asked if I'm "super flexible," and I said, "Hrrm, no. I would say I have standard levels of flexibility," which even my mother, who had no interest in getting me laid, thought was a missed opportunity.

Still, there were days at the store when I suspected he was talking to me more than was absolutely necessary, or looking in my direction more than was required for the job. I began to think that perhaps my "flirting" was working.

One day, I brought a stack of jeans back to the stockroom, where I found Brad perched on a ladder, chatting with a few of our other coworkers.

"Hey, Olga," he said. "Would you go out with me?"

All of my blood rushed to the very center of my mouth. No one I liked had ever asked me out before, and now it was happening, just like *Seventeen* magazine promised. Granted, I didn't think it would take this long, but better late than college.

In fact, I thought, maybe this was finally happening because it *was* that liminal summer before college, when kids were trying on cosmopolitan identities. He was willing to date an immigrant. He was willing to meet my dad and hear all about his Siberian fur rug. He was willing to do that, for me.

I had heard Brad talk about art once. Maybe he would take me to an art museum. I had visions of us riding public transportation and wearing tweed, like city people.

It was important not to seem too excited.

"*Sure!*" I said, not quite as coolly as I'd hoped.

My life was finally beginning.

I remember a longer-than-normal pause. I remember thinking it was odd that he had chosen to do this in front of so many other people. Then I remember him saying the thing that made my heart plummet through the floor

"I'm just kidding," he said.

He and everyone else in the stockroom broke into giggles.

I felt like inside me a vacuum seal had broken and the air was rushing in too fast. My skin was expanding, and soon it would burst.

"Okay," I said. I walked back out to the main floor completely coated in an icy sweat. I took my place behind the register.

Not long after, a female coworker was either sent out to see me by the others or was driven out by her own guilt.

"We were just messing around," she said.

I had to pretend not to be humiliated.

"Of course," I answered.

"I hope you don't take that serious," she said.

"No," I said. "Why would I?"

In college in D.C., my Russianness no longer made me a curiosity. But it was actually after college that I hit the low point of my social well-being, when I was preparing to move to Los Angeles for graduate school.

It was 2009, the depths of the Great Recession, and I had suffered a string of unrelated misfortunes. Within a few-month span, I was laid off from my job, forced to move from my apartment, and dumped by my boyfriend of nearly two years.

Immediately after, I had a fling with a guy whom I wooed with lines such as, "What's the point of anything if everything in life gets ruined anyway?" He, in turn, dumped me for "being an Eeyore." Then, two of my best friends left Washington to further their careers—one headed to Massachusetts and the other to Baghdad. I, meanwhile, packed up my Nissan Versa and drove across the country by myself to go to school in a city where I knew no one.

L.A. is a very expensive place to be both friendless and penniless. I was staying at a second cousin's house, and though I am grateful for her generosity, I have no idea where she disappeared to while I was there. Shortly after I arrived, she stopped coming home after work and stopped answering my calls and texts. She also stopped paying her gas bill.

After several "PAST DUE" notices, the stove and hot water were shut off. I switched to taking cold showers and eating nothing but yogurt. I finally found a cheap group house on Craigslist, through a process that can feel a bit like an ancient mating ritual, in which a woman meets a man for the first time and then immediately moves into his house and begins cleaning it. I had settled on this house because it was in a good area, it had free parking, and the people there didn't seem as insane as everyone else I had met so far. On moving day, I was dragging my belongings into my room when I accidentally let out the house's golden retriever.

Dogs are among the many things I'm highly allergic to. I've never had to handle a dog or call one or even touch one. There was no one else home. I pleaded with the dog to go back inside for what seemed like hours. In the middle of the struggle, I realized my new housemates had not cared enough to try to be home on the day I was moving in, or to answer their phones or check in to see how it was going. I also had no one—not one single person— to call for help.

I finally got the dog inside. Then I sat down on the curb between my two boxes of wool sweater dresses, buried my face in my hands, and sobbed.

Researchers believe this kind of social isolation is not only making us physically ill, it's changing the ways in which we seek companionship. Loneliness is not simply introversion. It isn't the same as preferring to be alone. Rather, it's a gap between the amount of social interaction a person would *like* to have and the amount they experience.

We can even see this loneliness gap in other species, like rhesus monkeys. Normally, scientists determine loneliness by giving people questionnaires about how they feel. That doesn't work so well on monkeys, which are otherwise a fitting animal model for human loneliness, so John Capitanio, a research psychologist at the University of California, Davis, had to devise a new method. He observes the monkeys and divides their socializing into "attempts" and "successes." For example, the monkey might walk by another monkey in the hopes that it will give it a signal that it wants to interact. "Lip-smack me, or touch me!" the monkey seems to say. If the "attempt" is successful, the monkeys might move on to actual socializing, by, say, grooming one another.

The lonely monkeys make a lot of these attempts at socializing, but they have trouble converting them into true social experiences. Not unlike lonely humans, they are forever asking other monkeys to the prom and getting shot down.

Capitanio sees loneliness as being an instinct almost like hunger. Evolutionarily, it could be our body's way of telling us that we must urgently go out and seek connection. But that's easier said than done: lonely humans have an overactive sense of social threat—a fear that they'll be rejected if they try to reach out and socialize. Lonely people *want* to be around others, but they are afraid that if they try, they will be rejected.

The monkeys' brains closely resemble our own, and Capitanio has found that loneliness affects humans and monkeys in similar ways. The lonely monkeys' urine contains more norepinephrine, which suggests their "fight or flight" instinct is more highly and frequently activated. What's more, the bodies of lonely monkeys (and lonely humans) tend to have more of a certain kind of white blood cell called monocytes, suggesting that they are in an inflammatory state. And, in an especially strange twist, the lonely monkeys also have higher levels of cortisol, an anti-inflammatory molecule.

"Those should not be happening together," Capitanio says, of the monocyte and cortisol combination.

Here's what that combination would look like, using an above-the-skin example. Let's say you brush up against poison ivy and develop a rash—that's inflammation. It's your body's way of trying to contain the offending substance. You would go to the drugstore and buy hydrocortisone anti-itch cream. Hydrocortisone is a type of glucocorticoid, similar to cortisol.

Normally, cortisol is supposed to tamp down the inflammatory response, but the cells of lonely people—and monkeys—aren't as responsive to the cortisol. It's like they have internal poison ivy, but not even buckets of anti-itch cream can soothe it.

People who are chronically lonely tend to withdraw socially because they start to feel like other people aren't trustworthy. Socially isolated people view their interactions with others more negatively, so they keep their distance, perpetuating a cycle of loneliness. People who are already lonely, paradoxically, are more likely to lose friends over time. As one paper on this subject notes, "These reinforcing effects mean that our social fabric can fray at the edges, like a yarn that comes loose at the end of a crocheted sweater."

That's why it's important to acknowledge that though being the sole Russian in West Texas certainly played a role, I brought a lot of my social isolation on myself. After a few of the popular kids made fun of me, I tended to assume they spoke for the masses and avoided all of my classmates—even the ones who probably would have happily befriended a girl with a strange name. I've carried this feeling forward into adulthood, at times distancing myself from people out of fear they'll discover the "truth" about me—I'm an immigrant, surprise!—long after this strategy stopped being rational or useful.

Ultimately, loneliness can spark a number of health problems. Below the skin, the body can't tell the difference between loneliness and any other type of threat. It perceives loneliness just like it would the possibility of being lanced with your enemy's spear: something, it thinks, may need to be mended right away. Your body begins to treat loneliness much like it would any other kind of bodily damage, springing into action to try to fend off the millions of bacteria that might be pouring in every second.

Typically, the immune system spends most days fighting a long, slow battle against viruses, the minor colds and sexually transmitted diseases that hop from human to human. When it senses a threat like loneliness, though, the immune system pivots to preparing to fight bacteria instead.

The way the body fights bacteria, somewhat unfortunately for the body, is also through inflammation, explained Steve Cole, a professor of medicine and psychiatry at the UCLA School of Medicine. He described this inflammatory process as one in which immune cells "destroy everything in sight around them," causing lots of collateral damage. During inflammation, cells called macrophages release dozens of different molecules—proteins called cytokines—to float around and communicate to other cells. White blood cells are summoned to help destroy bacteria. T cells do what Cole calls a "Pac-Man-style chomp" on anything that might have a pathogen inside, even if it's just healthy tissue.

The problem is that loneliness is not an actual, physical wound, so this inflammatory response is pointless. You could be lonely for days, weeks, months. The entire time, the immune system is gearing up to fight off bacteria that aren't really there, pumping you full of inflammatory chemicals in the process. The inflammation shreds the blood-vessel walls, leading to plaque buildup, which is why lonely people have more heart attacks. Inflammation destroys cells, and as the cells are replaced, there's a chance some of the new DNA might come with mutations, which can lead to cancer. This is one reason why lonely people have worse cancer outcomes. Scientists are still trying to figure out how, exactly, inflammation leads to neurodegenerative diseases, but it's known that lonely people are more likely to develop dementia. Meanwhile, the immune system is so distracted by bracing for the supposed bacteria that it takes its eye off the virus ball—and indeed, lonely people are more prone to viral infections.

## JOI

As Toni Morrison put it, "In this country, American means white. Everybody else has to hyphenate." Perhaps for no one is that truer than for African American women, who are weighted with modifiers and bombarded by both racism and sexism. As a result, they suffer some of the most intense effects of social exclusion.

In so many situations, black women are historically underrepresented, and they continue to face acute prejudice because of that underrepresentation. Researchers think the strain of being discriminated against might be one reason why African Americans tend to experience more of certain types of health problems than white Americans do.

When I first met Joi, a thin, pretty black woman with a degree in electrical engineering, she was not someone I expected to have a harrowing health story. She's friendly, financially comfortable, and in a loving relationship. She shops at Whole Foods.

She hadn't been trying to get pregnant when she did at age thirty-eight. A few months in, she developed a searing pain in her gut. The culprit was fibroids—tumors of the uterus, which black women are more likely to develop than white women are. Joi spent much of her pregnancy lying in bed in agony.

Her son, Alexander, was born three months early, bright red and weighing less than two pounds. In a photo taken on his first day, his arms were pinned into a t-shape by tubes. The next day, Joi was allowed to hold him for an hour.

There is a difference between being a racial or ethnic minority in this country and simply being unique. For Americans of color, the othering experience is far starker, and often more dangerous, than it is for even the quirkiest white people. As I described in a 2018 *Atlantic* article, several studies have now shown that racism might help explain why black women like Joi are about 50 percent more likely than white women to give birth prematurely. There might be several possible mechanisms at play, including racism-induced stress sending the body into labor too soon.

What's more, income doesn't appear to inoculate minorities from the stress of discrimination. Even when compared to the same class of white medical-school graduates, African American *doctors* were more likely to suffer from cardiovascular disease and diabetes twenty-five years later. Perhaps what ate away at them was what W.E.B. Du Bois called "double consciousness," or the fact that even successful African Americans are forced to constantly be "measuring one's soul by the tape of a world that looks on in amused contempt and pity."

Joi's son, Alexander, stopped breathing at least four times a day, and it became harder and harder to revive him each time. He also had pneumonia and a problem with his heart, and he had to be intubated. He was too small for the tube, so the doctors had to push it down his throat, scarring it on the inside. In all, Alexander was in the hospital for six months before being released to a regimen of oxygen tanks and specialists. During his first winter, Joi had to keep Alexander quarantined inside the house.

Joi, who now does web development and works in academia, tries not to dwell on racial grievances. But there were incidents that made her wonder. There was a time in a bar when she felt her hair moving, and turned to find a man groping it. There was another time in a restaurant in a gentrified hipster neighborhood when a waitress threatened to call the police because Joi's boyfriend had knocked over a bowl. Thinking of the woman's eagerness to call the cops on a black man, Joi worries about her son.

Joi loved engineering school, but work was another story. The place where she worked—she asked me not to say where—was dominated by white men. They would "mansplain" to her, take credit for her ideas, and express surprise when she finished projects quickly, she said.

You "push your feelings down," she told me, "so you won't be the angry black woman." But your feelings can affect you, even from deep down.

People often feel injured when they're lonely or socially excluded, and inside their bodies, it's almost as though they are. But some of the worst consequences of social exclusion might be the ones that occur in the mind.

In 2017, three psychologists led by Zachary Hohman of Texas Tech University recruited 152 people to take a fake personality test. The participants hailed from all political parties, races, and education levels, but they were all Americans. The test arbitrarily told each participant their personality type was more similar to the typical American or more similar to the typical French person.

The Americans who were told they resembled the French felt much more uncertainty about themselves, their futures, and their place in the world. They were then more likely to answer that they "agree" with statements like "I feel that I am not really the person that I appear to be" and "Even if I wanted to, I don't think I would tell someone what I'm really like."

To a typical, red-blooded American, something about being told they resemble a Frenchman must be very unsettling indeed. "When people are made to feel that they lack fit within their group, they question who they are," Hohman and his coauthors wrote.

Other studies have shown that when people—say, honors students or sorority members—are told that they're very different from the other members of their group, based on personality tests, they will more heartily embrace the stereotypes associated with that group, such as "hardworking" or even "superficial." Told that they do not fit in, people will do anything to try to prove that yes, they really do.

Feeling excluded can be so painful, in fact, that people will turn to terrible alternatives to avoid it. Researchers are increasingly finding that the roots of various kinds of terrorism and radicalization lie in the rather banal sensation of feeling cut off from your social circle.

In the wake of the 2015 Paris terror attacks, the economist Thomas Piketty wrote an op-ed in *Le Monde* in which he argued that "only an equitable model for social development will overcome hatred"—suggesting, in essence, that economic equality is the key to extinguishing the global terrorist threat. Efraim

Benmelech, an economist at Northwestern University, read the article and decided to investigate whether economic inequality really does drive terrorism. Benmelech looked at the number of fighters flowing in to join ISIS from countries other than Syria and Iraq. What he and his coauthor, Esteban Klor, found was very peculiar: rather than coming from economic backwaters, ISIS fighters were pouring in from supposed democratic-socialist utopias. The countries that yielded the most ISIS fighters, relative to their total Muslim populations, were Finland, Ireland, Belgium, and Sweden.

So if economic inequality didn't nudge certain Muslims to join ISIS, what did? Benmelech suspects that in addition to the fighters' personal religious ideology, it might be a country's level of overall cultural homogeneity that makes Muslims feel like they aren't welcome. Places like Finland might provide generous welfare benefits for much of the population, but some refugees and immigrants there feel so unwanted that thousands have canceled their asylum applications. The majority of Finns, after all, say they feel "Islam is fundamentally incompatible with Finnish values and culture." After Finland saw an increase in the number of refugees from Iraq, roving bands of men calling themselves "Soldiers of Odin" began patrolling the streets looking for men who appear Middle Eastern, under the guise of "keeping our women safe." Feeling alienated in this way, some disaffected, radical Muslims in Finland might have warmed to ISIS's message of a global Islamic caliphate, one in which Muslims are glorified.

This connection between cultural marginalization and an attraction to terror groups has held up repeatedly in research. ISIS recruits are more likely to be second- or third-generation immigrants, for example, which suggests that they gravitate to the group because they feel uncomfortable in either culture. In a 2015 study of first- and second-generation Muslim immigrants in the United States, those who felt alienated from American culture and discriminated against also felt more insignificant. In fact, the more "culturally homeless" they felt, the more the discrimination made them feel insignificant. That insignificance, in turn, was associated with greater attraction to a hypothetical fundamentalist group that "promised belonging" and justified extremism to support its cause.

And it isn't just ISIS, of course. Research on other types of political radicals, and even school shooters, suggests many of them are motivated by a desire to punish the groups that excluded them. White supremacists often target insecure and lonely-looking teens as potential recruits. Angela King, a former neo-Nazi who now runs a group that helps people disengage from hate groups, has described falling in with some young skinheads after being bullied as a child. And bullied kids seem primed to be taken up by such groups: lab experiments on social exclusion—which typically involve college students getting "rejected" by a fake group—have found that exclusion reduces cognitive skills and self-awareness.

Feeling uncertain about your identity for any reason—either because of job loss, disconnection from your culture, or even rapid technological change—"can leave you with a thirst to identify with other people," as Michael Hogg put it to me. People in situations like these often want a leader who will tell them exactly what their group's purpose and identity are. Across several studies, researchers have found that when people feel like they're bobbing in a sea of uncertainty, they will float toward the buoy that seems steadiest. They will crave a leader who is ethnocentric and autocratic. They flock to cults, gangs, and other groups that will assign you a new identity and leave no room to question its nature.

Exclusion is one of the things that can trigger what the psychologist Arie Kruglanski calls a "significance quest"—a plot to restore your place in society by becoming "somebody" again. You can restore your significance constructively—by, say, volunteering at your mosque, or destructively, by volunteering for ISIS. It all depends on what paths you see available to you, and who your friends are. Kruglanski says that many women who become suicide bombers have been made to feel insignificant in the eyes of their culture. They might be infertile or stand accused of extramarital affairs. Having lost their place in their society, they seek to restore it. Meanwhile, much of ISIS's propaganda involves highlighting the various ways Muslims have been humiliated by Westerners. Your quest for significance gets triggered, Kruglanski explains, by real or perceived discrimination against you or your group.

This is how social exclusion can become so perverse: it can insert ideas into your head that you don't even possess. You might not be unusually hateful, but you're lonely, and that can be enough. Many white supremacists, in fact, don't even start out with extreme views on race. "People think you develop really racist attitudes, then you go out and find a group that expresses those, but that's not exactly how this works," the sociologist Kathleen Blee told PBS in 2015. "It often works in reverse, that people start hanging around with people who are racist and they learn really racist attitudes by participating with those people in racist ways."

The process of *de*radicalization, meanwhile, often means helping extremists find new groups of people who are not violent or hateful, yet can still provide them with an identity. This new group can help them achieve significance through positive contributions to society, like humanitarian work or a trade. Some programs, for example, teach former fundamentalists new vocational skills, so that they can begin to craft a new "self" outside their hate.

I asked Arie Kruglanski if he worries this kind of research could be construed as excusing extremists. Some of these studies imply that hate-group members aren't that bad... they just need a hug!

He said that it is a moral dilemma whether to forgive people who have committed heinous crimes, and thus, "each person must offer or deny forgiveness based on their own moral convictions."

"I can understand a serial killer, but that doesn't excuse the deed," he added.

Indeed, because so many people are drawn to terror groups precisely because they feel misunderstood, one way to stop them might be to finally try to understand them.

Overt social exclusion also leaves a terrible mark on people who break gender norms. Supporters of the bathroom bills often portrayed the measures as a way to protect innocents from trans people, who, they seemed to believe, preyed on unsuspecting girls and women in their most private moments. But the people who need protection when it comes to bathrooms might be trans people themselves. Transgender people who have been denied access to gender-appropriate bathrooms or other facilities have a higher risk of suicide than those who haven't, a 2016 study found. And that's on top of the already astonishingly high rate of suicide attempts among young trans people—around 35 percent, in some studies. What's more, in 2013, 54 percent of transgender respondents in a survey reported experiencing health issues from avoiding using public restrooms, including dehydration, kidney infections, and urinary tract infections.

Here's how one transgender woman described the act of using the bathroom to a group of researchers writing in the journal *Transgender Health* in 2016:

> Then of course there are always restrooms, which are, let's call them, "nightmarish," for lack of a nicer term. I do everything possible to avoid using the restroom in public. Going into the bathroom, you're always worried that someone's gonna harass you or call you out about something, or say something mean or attack you, or do some other horrible thing.

The increased suicide risk among transgender people occurs, the researcher Kristie Seelman wrote, because of "minority stress," or the strain that marginalized groups face because of society's constant, low-level poor treatment.

In addition to racial minorities, there's especially strong scientific evidence that minority stress affects LGBT people, whose very identities are at the center of so many culture wars.

Here is how minority stress plays out: compared to straight people, gay, lesbian, and bisexual individuals are more likely to need treatment for anxiety or to take antidepressants. Another paper published in 2016 found that gay men who had been insulted, felt ashamed, or felt rejected because of their homosexuality were more likely to develop mental-health problems. In that study, the men were not, necessarily, being called slurs or kept from dating people of their preferred gender. One measure simply asked whether they'd ever been avoided in locker rooms or mistreated by doctors. The implication is that even small incidents have the potential to send people into an anguished vortex: *Is it because I'm gay?*

The consequences don't end at mental health. Gay, lesbian, and bisexual people who experienced homophobic language get more headaches and chronic diseases, and they are in worse overall health. (HIV, which weakens the immune system, may explain some, but not all of these disparities. Gay women, who have a lower risk for HIV than gay men do, are also less healthy than straight women, and among gay men, some of the disparities persist after controlling for HIV status.)

It's not clear whether these mental and physical health issues arise because LGBT people have to hide their true identities or because they face prejudice after coming out. A study that followed HIV-positive gay men for nine years found that the infection progressed more rapidly among those who were in the closet. But another study that sampled the saliva of gay and bisexual men throughout the day found those who were out to their workplaces had higher levels of cortisol, a stress hormone. The study authors weren't sure why this happened, but they suggested it might have been because the out men were experiencing more discrimination at work—or perhaps because they were just anticipating it.

This is what this heightened anticipation looks like, from another of the transgender women interviewed by researchers for *Transgender Health* in 2016:

> Any time I'm in the presence of someone who knew me before—so, past family members, past friends, anybody like that—it's almost like every muscle in my body is in a heightened state of alert and my blood pressure, I can almost feel it pumping…I'm ready for them to say the wrong pronouns or use the wrong name, or speak to me in some negative way even if they haven't done it or aren't going to. Usually, by the time that situation is over, whether or not anything bad happened, I'll just burst into tears or just decompress emotionally after it's done because I'm so ready to be hurt, expecting to be hurt.

The distress, for trans people, may come from realizing that some people will continue to treat you as though you never transitioned. In some cases, the authors of one 2005 study wrote, "the consequences of disclosure can be more harmful than those of inhibition."

Throughout my reporting, I met several trans people for whom transitioning resolved the stress of gender dysphoria. The stress of standing out, meanwhile, persisted.

## VIVIENNE, PART I

Before Vivienne Ming became Vivienne Ming, a mother, scientist, and entrepreneur, she wasn't sure she wanted to be, period.

Vivienne, who was assigned male at birth, was then living in Monterey, California, a bucolic valley that served as the setting for John Steinbeck's *The Pastures of Heaven*. Growing up there in the 1980s, her life might have seemed similarly ideal: she was a high school football player and strong student from a well-off family. But as adolescence wore on, Vivienne began to realize that the person inside her refused to line up with the person she was expected to turn into. She preferred long evenings spent cooking dinner with the women in her family to fishing trips with the men. At football games, she longed to run off the field and shed her bulky pads. When someone remarked how broad her shoulders were getting, she nearly burst into tears. *Who asked for this?* she thought. At night, she imagined herself dying in horrific ways, being beat up or held underwater by anonymous strangers.

After high school, Vivienne reluctantly enrolled in college, where she was crushed by the weight of expectations she felt unable to live up to. She felt her father expected her to somehow become both a Nobel Prize winner and an NFL kicker. Just a few weeks into her freshman year, she became too depressed to attend classes. She made a nest of pillows and blankets in her closet and virtually moved in, spending all her time reading in the dark hideaway. She felt bad, but she also felt bad about feeling bad: she was supposed to be a great athlete and student, but she was letting all that potential wither away. And she wasn't quite sure why.

When her college expelled her for not attending classes, Vivienne moved into her Chevy Suburban, which she parked in the lot behind an old industrial center in Mountain View. For a year, she lived out of the back of the car, friendless and adrift.

One night, Vivienne got hold of a gun, and in the throes of self-loathing, determined it was pointless to continue living. She would shoot herself, she decided.

## ALEX, PART I

A few years ago, another young Californian I spoke with, Alex Grady, was starting to seriously question his religion. This was, in part, because his church leaders were sending him to a place where almost no one else shared it.

By the time Alex was in college, he had been preparing to go on his Mormon mission for over a decade. Most devout Mormon men go on one. During their mission, young Mormons take a break from college in order to live in foreign countries, do good works, and attempt to convert other people to the Church of Jesus Christ of Latter-day Saints.

After Alex submitted his paperwork, he was told he would be sent to the Mormon mission in Sofia, Bulgaria. Though he didn't get a say in his destination, he was thrilled at the prospect of a foreign adventure.

To prepare, he was dispatched to a missionary training center in Provo, Utah. He was told to bring suits and ties and to have his sideburns shaved no lower than the middle of the ear. (Female missionaries, meanwhile, wear skirts that cover the entire knee when standing or sitting.) In Provo, for nine weeks, he spent fourteen-hour days learning Bulgarian and studying scripture.

Alex bid goodbye to his girlfriend, whom he would only be allowed to call once, on Christmas. The other phone call he was allowed each year of the mission was to his mother, on Mother's

Day. (These days, missionaries are allowed to contact their families more frequently.) He was assigned a companion who would be constantly at his side. Two days into missionary training, he became so depressed he cried.

Alex decided to make the best of the situation, but on the ground in Bulgaria, missionary life was similarly regimented. He and other missionaries would wake each day at 6:30 a.m. and exercise for thirty minutes. They'd study in solitude for an hour, then eat breakfast, then study with a companion for another hour. Then they would take to the streets, knocking on doors or stopping pedestrians on the sidewalk to tell them about the church. All day long, Alex repeated variations on *I'd like to share a short message about the Church of Jesus Christ of Latter-day Saints,* over and over again, dawn till dusk. At night he had an hour of journaling before lights out. The next day would be exactly the same. There was no slacking off, since every night he reported to a leader. There were also no movies, arcades, or bowling allies. His only days off were for laundry.

Alex found that the Bulgarians were not especially eager to become Mormons. Most Bulgarians belong to the Orthodox Church, though only a small percentage attend services regularly. To Alex, the country seemed unusually hostile to Mormons, specifically. A 2015 State Department report described fourteen instances of physical assault and harassment on Mormon missionaries in the country, including one in which three missionaries in the town of Shumen were beaten and their property defaced with antireligious graffiti. Ultimately, the Shumen missionaries had to close their church. According to Alex, some local Bulgarian papers printed articles urging kids to throw rocks at missionaries, or alleging that Mormons eat babies. He was heartened when one day he saw a more positive article. It read something like, "Mormons: Not as bad as you think."

So it's perhaps unsurprising that all day long, every time he knocked on a door, Alex mostly heard the same answer: *Ne, ne, ne.* No. I'm not interested. Because of Bulgarians' antagonism toward the faith, the goal for each missionary in Bulgaria was just two baptisms into the church, compared with the two or three hundred new acolytes that Alex said missionaries in some South American countries were expected to recruit.

Alex was lucky: he wasn't attacked on the street like a few of his friends were. But people would frequently slam the door in his face or even personally escort him out of the building. Sometimes, the snubbing came as a relief. He hated door-knocking, and several rejections in a row were a good excuse to go try a different building or part of town.

One day, a local invited Alex and his missionary companion to a school play. As soon as they entered the auditorium, the local leader of a far-right political party walked over and glowered at the two missionaries' Bulgarian friend. "We don't want them here," he said in Bulgarian.

More than a decade later, Alex still remembers the tense moment. "That was my first experience of feeling like," he said, "*this place is out to get me.*"

Emma, Joi, Vivienne, and Alex all saw the downside of feeling like outsiders in their environment—as have so many others. But as we'll see next, there are also some hidden advantages to being unique. Sometimes it just takes a while to stumble upon them.

PART TWO

# THE WEIRD
# ADVANTAGE

# CHAPTER 5

# Creativity

For much of my life, all I wanted to be was normal. I wanted to be as American as my classmates; later, I wanted the privileged background of my peers in journalism. I wanted a past that when I explained it to people, no one asked "why?" about any part of it.

Or maybe—in exploring Christianity, or Judaism, or even Russian language classes later—what I was seeking was a rudder. I wanted a group, a home, an identity. People wouldn't be able to blow me over, I thought, if I had something firmly tethering me to the ground. It could be a boisterous bunch of aunties with unpronounceable soups, or a long lineage of stoic "Jr."s and "the III"s. Any kind of posse would have been fine. Without one, everyone was always able to say what I was supposed to be like, and I had no standing to argue.

There are a million little signals we get that suggest difference is inherently bad. "Living in interesting times" is supposed to be a curse. Interestingness, according to this bit of apocrypha, is inferior to normalcy. Boringness is tranquility, and divergence will inevitably hurt. For people who are considered interesting, that is often the case.

But probe a little deeper, and you find that being weird isn't always difficult. Even when it is, there are moments of glory amid the turmoil. Almost all of my interviewees could pinpoint certain skills they honed, strengths they cultivated, or lessons they learned from the interesting times they lived in.

In fact, science suggests people actually *prefer* to belong to a group that is neither too inclusive nor too exclusive. It can feel good to not fit in quite perfectly, or to be a little weird. This "inverted U" of belonging is known as the "optimal distinctiveness theory," with the optimal level of fitting in being at the apex of the upside-down "U." Just like the indie band stops being cool after everyone you know is listening to it, it sometimes feels better to be in an elite group than in a large, amorphous crowd.

Of course, not everyone feels their weirdness has an upside. I spoke with several people suffering from major mental illnesses, for example, who would love to calm the storms inside their heads, even if it made them less creative or special or journalism-profile-worthy.

But believing that your weirdness is your superpower can also be hugely beneficial. There is evidence that thinking about your circumstances in a different way—a process called cognitive reappraisal—can help you cope with challenges. Perceiving what makes you weird as being what gives you strength can, ultimately, make you happier. If you already possess the lemons of social rejection, you might as well make a really odd lemonade. In this section, we'll see examples of how weirdness can be a strength.

After my entire life vomited me up in 2009, I was invited by the University of Southern California to come to L.A. to interview for a scholarship slot in its master's program in journalism. When the email hit my inbox, I saw it as a minor miracle. I had no job prospects in D.C. It was the start of the recession, and everyone I knew was getting laid off. As if to mirror my inner gloom, a freezing winter rain lashed my face as I scurried around town to my fifty-dollar freelance photography assignments.

When he broke up with me, my boyfriend told me it was because I'm too risk-averse. He was looking for someone more adventurous, and I wasn't that. If I got the USC scholarship, I thought, I would surely prove him wrong. How much more adventurous could you get than a cross-country move to get trained in a dying profession?

I convinced myself that if I went to grad school, I could solve all my problems at once. Say what you will about L.A., but it did not contain my ex or any of the haunts that reminded me of him. I'd be in a new city, which would make it less painful, I hoped, to be separated from my D.C. friends, who were all decamping Washington for their own career moves. Most importantly, I had always wanted to be a journalist, and this was a chance to chase my dream.

The scholarship opportunity was explained to me thus: a group of applicants would, via a long day of interviews, compete to win a limited number of scholarships. If I didn't win one, I wouldn't be able to afford to go, and my journalist dream would essentially die.

My friend Kelly agreed to fly to L.A. with me for my interview. She said she wanted a little vacation, but I suspect she was also afraid that if not under constant supervision, in my despondent fugue I would try to hop my rental car over the guardrail of the Santa Monica freeway.

L.A. was not, perhaps, the most natural environment for a clinically depressed Texan and a tough Irish-Catholic girl from Philly. One night, Kelly and I went out to a bar in Venice. Two guys came over and, rather than hitting on us, chided us for drinking vodka tonics—didn't we know vodka sodas had fewer calories? ("Men know about calories?" we asked one another later.)

One night, we went to a small get-together at the house of my second cousin, a rocket scientist who gives driving directions like a person who understands trigonometry. On the way back I got us lost in the tangle of highway numbers. Kelly and I ended up far from where we needed to be, and we had no way of knowing how to get back.

I started crying, and the crying morphed into a sort of hollow wailing, which turned into banging on the steering wheel and screaming, *"Oh...my...God!"* For me, getting lost was yet another sign that I couldn't survive in the world now that I had been abandoned by my boyfriend, job, and friends—except of course for Kelly, who sat in the passenger's seat, staring blankly at me in abject terror. We found our hotel after hours of driving around L.A.'s side-street maze. I lay down, exhausted, and cried myself to sleep, a process that repeated itself nearly every night during our time in L.A.

The night before the USC interview, I woke up in a panic. It occurred to me that the rest of my life hinged on performing well the following day. I didn't have time to be depressed. If I failed to convince the university higher-ups that I was worthy of a full scholarship, I thought, I would be stuck in this hole forever, moping around D.C. jobless, friendless, and alone.

I got out of bed and went over to the little executive table that's in all hotel rooms, even the ones that are definitely not for executives. I flicked on the table light and opened my computer. The interview would require selling the administrators on my vision for online journalism, at a time when advertising dollars were evaporating and newspapers were shutting down. I had no experience thinking about the Internet or business plans, since I had frittered away my time in college on a political-science degree I never really used.

I opened up a Word document and began googling new-media-thinker blogs, websites about coding, and excerpts from books by popular "journalism 2.0" luminaries. I started to notice patterns in the buzzwords and arguments the journalism futurists used. None of them seemed to know what they were talking about, but they all talked in the same way, and that seemed good enough to get them branded "thinkfluencers." And it would have to be good enough for me.

By the time our alarm clock sounded that morning, I was still maniacally googling and muttering things like "platisher" every few minutes. Kelly glanced over at me and shook her head in dismay.

We got dressed and went to USC's campus, which looks like it was designed to play the role of "college" in a teen movie. (In fact, it has, many times.) The grounds were perfectly maintained. Students sped between the dusk-colored buildings on beach bicycles. I half expected a kid to lead the marching band in a rendition of "Can't Take My Eyes Off of You."

Also, there were fountains. Everywhere.

"Jesus Christ, what's with all the fountains?" Kelly said, narrowly avoiding stepping in one.

"Yeah, this seems...expensive," I said hesitantly.

"Olga, out of curiosity," Kelly said, "let's say you don't get this money, how much is this going to cost you?"

"Mm, like fifty grand a year."

Kelly bit her fist.

"Holy shit, Olga," she said. "Holy shit. That's a lot. You better get that scholarship, is all I'm saying. You don't have that kinda money."

Somehow, that fact had not escaped me.

The interviews were structured like a video game, where you do easy rounds with lower-level professors before meeting the Big Boss, the director of the journalism school. In the morning, all of us scholarship contestants were brought into a softly lit conference room for a brief USC propaganda talk. I surveyed the competition. One guy was a laid-off investment banker. One girl was fresh out of college.

"Which college?" I asked.

"Harvard," she said.

I wondered how much practice it must have taken to say that word in a way that sounded neither embarrassed nor haughty.

The USC professors told us to help ourselves to coffee from the Keurig machine. "A Keurig machine!" I said to one of my rivals. "This school really *is* expensive."

"Yeah, well, I don't intend to pay for it," he said, somewhat menacingly.

My first interview of the day was with a writer who taught magazine journalism. I was so tired and borderline deranged with anxiety that when he asked me to lay out a plan for an independent news site, I just started yelling smart-sounding phrases louder and louder while waving my finger in the air. "I'm going to make a health site!" I intoned, like Blogger Mussolini. "Where readers can connect with people who have similar *health conditions*! And it will have *audio slideshows*."

Toward the end of my rant, he was leaning forward in his seat and shouting a bit himself. "You've got me excited!" he said. "I wanna come work for you!"

*Level one down,* I thought.

My very last interview of the day was with the journalism school director, whose facial expression could have best been described as "not amused." She asked me how I planned to get people to pay for news online, given that digital ads were basically worthless, news is depressing, online content has become a race to the bottom, oh, and we're in the midst of an economic calamity.

At that point, my lack of sleep tugged on me like a whiny toddler. I let out a jumble of words about multimedia. "Uh-huh," the director said, distractedly.

I desperately spewed a few more sentences about Twitter.

"Riiiight," she said. She looked like she was gathering her things to leave.

At that point, something clicked in me. It didn't feel like "you got this," or any other pseudo-empowering aphorism. Instead, the voice inside me said, "Nothing in the world cares about you. Your career is nonexistent. Your parents hate this journalism plan. Your boyfriend broke up with you because you're boring. These professors have seen twelve people like you today. Kelly maybe cares a little bit, but she can't help you now. If *you* care about you, it's time to think of a way to save yourself."

I dug hard in the back of my brain for a string of jargon I hadn't said already. One that made slightly more sense, or was slightly closer to what these people wanted to hear.

"The thing is," I ventured, "we have to scale users up the engagement ladder."

The director paused. She wrote that down. "Hmmm," she said.

Then she grasped my hand weakly and said she'd be in touch. I was free to go.

The next day, Kelly and I went to the Santa Monica Pier, an old-fashioned boardwalk perched out over the ocean. As we wandered past the arcades toward the water, Kelly asked me how my interview went.

"Eh, it went okay," I said. "I was honestly so tired I had no idea what I was saying half the time. Plus the other people are like real geniuses. I highly doubt I beat the Harvard girl at this."

We had walked to the tip of the pier, where a multicolored Ferris wheel loomed over the crashing waves below. I suggested we ride it, thinking it might be my only chance to do so.

As we waited in line, my little silver flip-phone rang.

"Olga," said the voice on the other end, "congratulations, we'd like to offer you a full scholarship to USC."

Kelly and I leapt up and down, screaming, this time, with joy.

I'll never know if the digital gobbledygook I spewed in those meetings is really what got me the scholarship. But I would later come to understand how my brain snapped itself out of its funk and powered me through my interviews.

In a study a few years ago, researchers found that being rejected or feeling uncertain, much like I had been in the lead-up to the L.A. trip, can actually motivate people to conjure creative solutions. Sharon Kim, a business professor at Johns Hopkins, told me she had always noticed that some people credit their creative successes to being loners or rebels. She was skeptical that those two qualities actually correlated, so she decided to test the theory by inviting some volunteers to her lab to solve word problems. Before they began working, Kim and her colleagues "rejected" some of the study subjects by telling them they weren't picked to work as part of "the group." (There was no group, of course—Kim and her team just wanted to make them feel left out.) Another, control, group of participants weren't snubbed in the same way. Kim then had all the participants perform a pair of exercises on paper. First, they were asked to determine what unites a group of unrelated words ("fish, mine, and rush"—the answer is gold). Then, they were told to draw an alien from a planet very unlike our own.

The rejects, it turned out, were better at solving both types of problems. The non-rejected participants drew standard, cartoonish-looking Martians. But the aliens drawn by the rejected participants looked radically different from humans—they had, for example, all of their appendages sticking out of one side of their bodies.

So there *was* a relationship between rejection and creativity. But this advantage was only seen among the participants who considered themselves unique—who had an "independent self-concept." Those who felt like they already weren't part of any particular group were more creative when they were rejected by an arbitrary collective. There appears to be something about being a weirdo that uncorks your mind and allows new ideas to flow.

This is similar to what the Brown University psychiatrist Arnold Ludwig found when he examined the lives of more than one thousand eminent people—including creatives such as Frida Kahlo, Jean-Paul Sartre, and Howard Hughes—for his book *The Price of Greatness*. The creative individuals, such as writers and actors, in his sample were more likely than, say, businesspeople or soldiers to be "odd or peculiar" as children and to be considered "different" in adulthood.

In his 1962 study of architects, the psychologist Donald Mac-Kinnon also found that the families of the more creative architects moved around a lot when they were kids, which "appears also to have resulted frequently in some estrangement of the family from its immediate neighborhood," he wrote. In almost every case, he writes, their family "differed in its behavior and values from those in the neighborhood." Perhaps expectedly, the creative architects often said they felt alone and isolated as children.

Even though acing the scholarship interview was leagues below painting a masterpiece or designing an iconic building, it still required a fair amount of creativity. Unlike the media visionary I made myself out to be in those interviews, at that point I was actually a bit of a Luddite. I had only ever really worked for a human-rights nonprofit and a tiny newspaper. The most complicated technology I had ever navigated was Microsoft Word. That USC interview was the first time I had used the Internet to help me prepare for a job interview. It was also the first time I tried mimicking the language of a subculture—online journalism, in this case—to seem as though I already belong to it.

I do not know why I reacted to my rejection with a burst of creative insight, rather than by crawling further into my hole. Perhaps, at that time, I had simply run out of a hole to crawl in. In those months, I felt like I had washed up on the edge of the world. I was stranded, so I had to chart my own course.

Creativity is defined scientifically as a process that results in a "new and useful" product. It doesn't have to be art—a new assembly-line procedure can be as creative as a painting. And its usefulness doesn't have to be physical—joy can be as useful as productivity. Throughout my interviews with the individuals in this book, creativity seemed to be one of the more common advantages uniqueness conferred, whether by pivoting the person to a new perspective, or by forcing her to invent life-hacks. Next, we'll delve into some of the other ways difference can promote creativity.

In the late 1980s, Chay Yew, an aspiring playwright living in California, returned to his native Singapore to complete his compulsory military service. While there, he joined a small theater company called TheatreWorks, for which he wrote a play about a straight, HIV-positive Chinese man and his relationship with a gay social worker. The script was swiftly banned by the Singaporean government for its homosexual themes, which were considered out of step with the country's traditional values. (Gay sex is still officially illegal in Singapore.)

Rather than scrap the idea, Chay rewrote the play entirely, keeping the identity of the gay character intact but striking the overt homosexual references. He swapped specifics for euphemisms, and he wrote stage directions that conveyed the hidden message—the male characters "glided" onto the stage, for example.

"Government censorship taught me how to write between the lines with subtext," Chay told the *Los Angeles Times* later.

Chay's bicultural identity as an immigrant living far from home, then returning, might have been the very thing that helped him think creatively under the tight constraints of censorship.

Several studies have found that being "weird" in one's culture—as Chay, a gay Singaporean immigrant, was throughout his young adulthood—can enhance what's known as "integrative complexity," the ability to recognize and tie together several competing points of view at once. People who are better at integrative complexity tend to handle uncertainty well and are better at reconciling conflicting information. They can see a problem simultaneously from multiple perspectives. Like *Fiddler on the Roof*'s Tevye the Dairyman—also technically bicultural, given that he's a fictional Jewish peasant living in Russia—they are able to consider things on "one hand" and many "other hands." Chay knew that his play was good by Western standards, but he also knew it wouldn't fly by Singaporean standards. So he found a way around both.

In fact, people who don't fit neatly within any specific identity have been found, over and over again, to perform better at innovative thinking. Children who are exposed to multiple languages are better able to understand an adult's perspective, which suggests to researchers that they go on to become better communicators overall. In one experiment, people who had spent time living abroad were better able to find hidden solutions to word and conceptual problems, perhaps explaining why the Russian Nabokov wrote *Lolita* while in the United States, as well as why Picasso, a Spaniard, began experimenting with Cubism while living among eccentric writers in Paris. A study that looked at the openness of Japanese society to foreign influence between the years 580 and 1939 found that periods of greater immigration and foreign travel corresponded with more national creative achievements two generations later.

Bicultural people who view their cultural identities as blended, rather than in conflict with one another, are the ones who tend to exhibit greater originality in their thinking—at least when they're in situations that draw on both their cultures, like a fusion restaurant or a cosmopolitan city. "Internalizing distinct cultural perspectives and finding the thread that connects them can enhance creativity," the authors of one such study write. They suggest multicultural education and even international cuisine can help people get into the culturally blended headspace.

Chris Crandall, the professor we met a few chapters ago,

explained that people who are on the periphery of all sorts of groups are often freer to innovate and change social norms. For example, he says, "Fashion norms come from the bottom up." African Americans launched the trend of baggy pants; lesbians pioneered the hipster look. "American urban youth culture has more freedom because they're on the outs with status quo forces," he told me. Later, high-status people monetize those outsider innovations. Outsiders are already not concerned with what the in-crowd thinks of them, so they have more leeway to experiment and come up with the next iThing or bestseller. We see this outsider's innovation phenomenon among immigrants in the U.S. today: statistically, they are more likely than native-born Americans to start businesses, to hold high-quality patents, and to have children who become highly educated.

Freud believed that creative people have a "looseness of repression." Artists' minds, he posited, work like those of children engaged in make-believe or an adult in the midst of a dream. Similarly, being in a strange land seems to liberate you from normal thought patterns. For one thing, living abroad might simply expand the number of ideas you're exposed to—as long as you try to absorb the local culture, rather than cloister yourself. What's more, people who are outsiders to a culture tend to seek out "unconventional knowledge," as one study put it. That made me think of a Citibank ad from a few years ago, in which an American woman in Iceland takes a dip in the Blue Lagoon and realizes the silica mud at its bottom would make for a great face mask. (The upshot: she needs a Citibank line of credit for her new business!) Leaving aside the probable illegality of exporting chunks of a major tourist attraction, the ad encapsulates the basic idea behind the creativity surge of foreignness. You go somewhere, you see something new with fresh eyes, and you apply it back home.

Happily for those of us who have never traveled abroad, this creativity boost can even happen to people who live in unusual frames of mind, rather than in exotic locales. Rodica Damian, a psychology professor at the University of Houston, and her colleagues had college students engage in a virtual reality exercise in which the laws of physics didn't apply. In this virtual world, things fell upward, instead of down. When compared to another group who performed an exercise in which the laws of physics functioned normally, those who had the physics-warping experience were able to come up with more creative answers to the question "What makes sound?" Damian found the unusual experience helped boost cognitive flexibility, or the ability to come up with lots of different kinds of solutions to problems.

Damian has a theory she is currently researching that suggests all kinds of unusual experiences—be they trippy virtual-reality adventures, Chay Yew's biculturalism, or even the adversity I experienced in the lead-up to my USC interview—can enhance creativity. Even people who have had unpredictable, difficult childhood experiences, such as illnesses or parental deaths, seem to attain higher levels of creative achievement. These experiences might trigger the need for new perspectives on one's problems, as well as the capacity to come up with unconventional solutions to those problems.

Importantly, having a medium level of these weird experiences—but not a very high or low level—is what appears to be associated with increased out-of-the-box thinking. "The idea behind this is that once you've experienced things that violate norms and rules and expectations, you're more open to more things like that," Damian told me. "You experienced that the world doesn't have to work by your rules, so you can break the rules."

Damian gave me an example from her childhood in Romania, where traditional dishes don't typically mix sweet and savory flavors together. "It never occurred to me while I lived in Romania that you could put sugar in a savory food, or you can add mandarins in your salad," she said. But after she moved to the U.S., the land of honey-glazed hams, she developed a love of combining different flavors and making spice mixes from scratch. "Maybe next time I'll think, what about spicy and sugary?" she said. One weird thing can lead to another.

However, more weirdness is not necessarily always better. If something *too* jarring or traumatizing happens to you, just coping with it might use up all your mental capacity. Someone whose house was destroyed by a tornado is not, understandably, going to be basking in their newfound creativity. They're going to be calling their insurance company.

To further qualify these findings, the creativity gains seem to only be evident among people who have what Damian calls "adaptive resources." These are the things that can help you overcome trauma, be they personality traits (such as how self-sufficient or self-assured you are), how much money you have, or how much social support surrounds you. Intelligent people seem to have an easier time spinning their weird straw into creative gold, as do people who are more open to experiences. People who have lots of these resources are able to view their unusual experiences as "challenges," rather than "threats," and as performance-reviewey as that sounds, that seems to make a big difference in whether your difficult experiences result in personal growth.

If you don't already have a lot of adaptive resources, the good news is that people are able to change their personalities—more on this in later chapters—through therapy and other tactics. After making these changes, people might be able to generate different explanations for their weird experiences and view them in a more positive light.

The problem is, that process of finding new explanations for your experiences sounds, even to Damian, a lot like creativity. This field of study can get a little circular. Damian is currently trying to untangle whether creative people are just more likely to find themselves in unusual situations, or whether, as it currently appears to her and others, creativity actually does spring from weirdness.

If that is true, it leads us to a philosophically difficult place. If people who are kicked around by life end up more creative, that might imply that a little kicking-around—in the form of discrimination, trauma, loneliness—is fine, even healthy.

But that would be too much of a leap. Creativity, after all, can only happen if you have the kind of life that allows you to be creative. Working three jobs to make ends meet because you've been discriminated against will leave little time for creativity. Immigrant kids who are locked out of scholarships may never reach their creative potential, because they won't be able to afford college. Your creative potential doesn't mean much if it's never given a chance to flourish.

But, Damian says, if you're already unique in your environment, it can only help you to think about your situation in a more positive way: "I'm different, but that means I have something special to bring to the table." Your weirdness is attached to you. But rather than a millstone around your neck, it can be a jet pack.

Being unusual doesn't just make you, yourself, more creative. Dissenting voices can also boost the creativity and decision-making power of the broader group you're a part of.

Across several studies, groups with a nonconformist member came up with more—and more creative—ideas than groups in which everyone agreed. Exposure to dissenting views appears to encourage the group to consider lots of alternatives, reexamine their premises, or even just to think harder.

In a 2001 study, for example, researchers examined a parcel delivery service in the Netherlands that was divided up into teams of five or six members. Each member submitted a survey about his or her perceptions of the team, and then the researchers interviewed the workers' supervisors a few months later.

The workers were asked how often a few of their team members disagreed with the majority of the team, as well as how much all the individual team members took part in the overall decision-making process.

Research assistants then asked the teams' supervisors about any innovative procedures or methods their teams implemented to improve their work, like making a computer program to keep track of sick leave or building a box in which to keep the address cards.

Among the more democratic teams, in which all the workers took part in the decisions, the teams that had dissenting opinions in their midst came up with more innovative solutions than the teams in which everyone agreed.

Earlier, we learned that people rarely seek friendship with

people they disagree with. So why did the teams with dissenters come up with better ideas? It could be that while friendship is about encouragement, innovation requires pushback. The friction of dissent is often what ignites the creative spark, and it takes weirdos to make dissent possible.

The presence of a person who voices a competing perspective to the predominant one of the group has also been found to reduce our tendency to throw good money after bad. In a phenomenon called the sunk-cost fallacy, people are tempted to see a terrible idea through to the end once they've committed to doing it, even if it seems less and less brilliant as the problems pile up. (Those who have stuck with a terrible TV show or relationship because of the time they've already invested know this phenomenon well.) But when there's a lone dissenter, she pumps the brakes, prompting everyone to question why they're doing whatever it is they're doing. In this way, nonconformists can also keep groups from making actively *bad* decisions.

Solomon Asch's famous 1951 experiment revealed the occasional ludicrousness of conformity. When told to compare a line with three other lines—one obviously the same size, one obviously shorter, another obviously longer—about one-third of the participants selected the clearly wrong option, all because others in the group, confederates working with the researcher, gave the wrong answer also. The experiment has become a classic example of how willingly people follow the crowd, even when the crowd is leading them off a cliff's edge. When asked why they conformed in this way, participants said they were worried about being seen as "peculiar." That is, they didn't want to be considered weird.

But less well-known is a variation of the experiment in which Asch introduced yet another confederate—this time one who gave the right answer alongside the crowd trying to mislead the main participant. Having just one person who broke with the majority reduced conformity among the participants by up to 80 percent. The participant in those trials must have felt like he and the other dissenter could at least be weird together. Shockingly, participants were less likely to conform even if the dissenter disagreed with the crowd, but was *still* wrong. It didn't even matter what the dissenter thought, only that they appeared to give the participants permission to disagree. "Defiance per se, the explicit flaunting of a majority's claim for truth, significantly reduces the grip of conformity on observers," write Benoit Monin and Kieran O'Connor, regarding some of these follow-up Asch studies.

This liberating element of alternate viewpoints has been replicated in other studies, and it underscores the value of having a diverse array of people around to poke holes in the prevailing idea.

The reason why minority views are so potent, according to research on persuasion, is that in certain circumstances, people tend to scrutinize a minority viewpoint more carefully. When we hear a dissenting view, we think more critically about what we're hearing. Listening to a minority viewpoint prompts, in the listener, a consideration of information about different sides of an issue. Majorities, meanwhile, spur us to think only about data that supports the majority perspective. As the researchers Charlan Nemeth and Jack Goncalo put it, "Minorities stimulate more originality, while majorities stimulate more conventionality of thought."

Finally, studies show people in the minority tend to support diversity more than people in the majority do. People who are in the minority see differences of opinion as a benefit, rather than a drawback. Not only do people with weird opinions help open up the group to new perspectives, in other words, they also help it embrace other weirdos.

Unfortunately, though, when people stop being weird, these benefits go away. When people who were once in the minority become the majority, research shows they become more closed-minded. This, perhaps, explains groups like the Puritans, who went from being radical dissidents to literal witch-hunters within just a few decades. Weirdness has its perks, but nothing is weird forever.

# CHAPTER 6

# Truth

In Russian, interesting facial features are sometimes referred to as *izuminka*, or "little raisin." The English translations for this term include "highlight," "zest," and my favorite, "bewitching little detail." (Of course, it also means "dried grape.") I'm not sure of the etymology, but there is, indeed, something about a raisin that conjures a small beauty mark. The word has always reminded me of the hidden value of uniqueness. In dark moments, like when I'm staring at a Google-image-search page of nose-job photos, it's nice to remember that maybe there is a silver lining—a highlight—to be found in unusualness.

Unique traits are our calling cards. They *are* the bewitching little details that captivate and charm. In psychology, the "bizarreness effect" holds that odd things are more memorable. When study participants read lists of sentences that were either normal—"The maid spilled ammonia on the table"—or bizarre—"The maid licked ammonia off the table," they were able to recall the strange items more easily later on. Strange and funny things stand out from the other detritus in our memory banks, and they are therefore top-of-mind when it comes time to recall them. We see evidence of this concept in the romantic realm, too: in a study that was structured a little like a dating site, both men and women preferred nonconformist partners who "stand out from the crowd." Meanwhile, across three continents, nonconformists reported more success and satisfaction in dating.

Being different, in other words, can help you stand out in a positive way. And as the people we'll meet in this chapter found, *doing* something different can help you find your true calling, your true self—and even true love.

One November day in 1997, Terri Muir, a twenty-nine-year-old schoolteacher on Vancouver Island, was using her dad's computer to research a family vacation when she saw a banner ad for a site called Match.com. Vancouver Island is a visually striking but somewhat secluded strip of land off the west coast of Canada, and it was hard for Terri to find dates there. Intrigued by the possibility of meeting people from other parts of the world, she signed up for Match that night.

The very same evening, a twenty-eight-year-old steel broker in Portland, Oregon, named Tom Buckley had just gotten back from a Thanksgiving dinner that was made somewhat awkward by the fact that he was the only single adult in attendance. He saw the same Match.com ad, and he clicked on it.

The Internet was so young back then that they said they were not even able to upload their pictures to the site. (The earliest Match screenshot I could find, from 2000, shows a web portal adorned with cheesy, yet era-appropriate, clip-art hearts and lots of exclamation points.) Both Terri and Tom typed in a few facts about themselves, only taking the Match questionnaire half-seriously. Terri said she liked tennis and reading. Tom said he was Catholic, but not a Bible-thumper, and that he liked rugby. Tom's profile was the first one Terri clicked on. The questionnaire asked them how far they were willing to travel to visit someone they met through the site. They both entered "500 miles." From Tom's door to Terri's was 499.

The first people to try out a new trend often face stigma, but some are nevertheless willing to defy social norms in order to live their best, truest lives. The revolutionary nature of what Tom and Terri were doing is evidenced by the fact that two years after they signed up, in 1999, Match.com still had only two million subscribers. Today, Match and its associated brands have more than fifty-nine million members. Online dating, when Tom and Terri were doing it, was so new that it was considered dangerous. "If romance blossoms on line [*sic*] and you arrange a face-to-face encounter, take precautions," wrote a *New York Times* story about the trend. "Experts advise that first dates be held in public, preferably in daytime." Today, it's probably rare that two people who found each other on Tinder would *ever* see each other in the daytime.

In the early days of Internet dating, if you managed not to get axe murdered, there was always the chance your social reputation would get killed instead. In 2006, the summer before my junior year of college—libertine, everything-goes college—I connected with a fellow student at my university through MySpace. We quickly migrated to more time-honored forms of courtship, like awkward phone calls and even awkwarder sex. But we had to keep the fact that we had exchanged our initial messages through the Internet a closely guarded secret. Even then, online dating was considered desperate, a nerdy last resort for those who weren't lovable under normal circumstances. Ugh, you met him through the *Internet*? Why couldn't you just spill your Red Bull–vodka on him in a bar like a normal person?

In 2002, a *Wall Street Journal* story described online dating as "at least one rung lower than meeting in a singles bar." "Even happily matched online couples remain uneasy about telling friends and family how their love affairs started, despite a surging use of dating services," wrote the *Journal* reporter. "They don't tell the truth until things get serious—and sometimes not even then."

Before the rise of swiping left or right, there was an impression, milked by rom-coms, that soul mates "just found each other," ideally by physically colliding in an art gallery. To admit that you were so lonely you were willing to put your information on the Internet—at a time when virtually nothing was on the Internet—was bold. And to some, it was weird.

————————

Tom and Terri began emailing through their Netscape and AOL accounts, then moved on to phone calls. Because the calls were between the U.S. and Canada, they racked up $1,000 phone bills. When Terri wanted to email Tom, she had to be sure to tell her mom not to pick up the phone, because doing so would kill the dial-up connection.

After a few weeks, they agreed to exchange pictures. Neither had an Internet connection strong enough to upload a photo, so they had to send them through the postal service. After two weeks, both were relieved to open their envelopes and find the other person wasn't secretly a senior citizen.

A few months later, they decided to meet in person, in Vancouver. Terri's mom begged her not to go. "What if you get kidnapped?!" she asked. Terri's coworkers wondered why she would do such a thing.

Terri told Tom to meet her at Starbucks in the airport—only to get there and realize there were several Starbucks in the airport. Three hours later, she finally found a man who looked like Tom's photo wandering among the coffee shops in the slowly emptying terminal.

Terri and Tom didn't know anyone else who had met online, so they told anyone who asked that they had met at a rugby match. A year and a half later, they were married in one of the first few Match.com weddings. They didn't tell people how they met until their wedding day.

I heard a similar story from a woman named Dawn, who in 1994 was a twenty-four-year-old living in Annapolis. Unlike most people she knew, she had a computer, and one day she logged on to her Apple PowerBook, a gray beast of a thing, and went into a chat room, where she struck up a conversation with a military wife. The wife told Dawn she had a single friend who would love to have someone to talk to: Why doesn't Dawn email him?

Dawn is the maternal type, and she liked the idea of having someone to emotionally tend to. The man Dawn ended up corresponding with was James Wright. James was a Marine going through naval flight school in Florida and had only gotten a computer so he could play *Doom*. But he, like Dawn, was curious. Before long, they were sending each other song lyrics and poetry. After a few months of emailing and phone calls, he mailed her a plane ticket. "I'll be the half-Asian guy with a vest," he wrote.

Dawn's parents were terrified for her, and her coworkers joked that she was going to meet Ted Bundy.

"You just don't understand!" Dawn said. "We get each other! It's just meant to be."

To round out the almost unbearably 1990s nature of their romance, for their first date, James took her to a Cranberries concert. They were married within a year.

Talking to these couples, I didn't sense a shred of embarrassment from them about how they met. Granted, neither couple generally *admits* how they met, other than to close friends. The Buckleys still say "rugby" and the Wrights say "through a friend." But both couples leapt at the chance to be interviewed, and they seemed to remember unusually rich details about their interactions. More importantly, they are happy they met online, even though doing so was considered strange at the time.

Terri did not want to settle for whoever was in her small town. Plus, she liked the freedom of her email courtship. She felt like she could say anything to Tom, and like she and Tom had actually communicated more than the average couple before they began dating in person. Between their phone calls and dates, she had the emails to reread and reflect on. "When we met in person," she told me, "I felt like I had known him for a long time."

Dawn said something similar, that she felt she and James were more authentic over email than they could be in typical dates. Dawn thought James seemed bolder and more romantic than most men. James found "the whole computer thing" intriguing. No one was writing personal emails at the time, and it added some excitement to the dating grind. James liked women who tried new things, and email, at the time, was definitely one of them.

For pioneers like Dawn and James, breaking the norm helped set them apart. It also brought them together.

In an experiment in the early 1960s, the psychologist Stanley Milgram found that 65 percent of his subjects would be willing to administer a shock of 450 volts—equivalent to being stung by a bee with a six-inch stinger—despite the protestations of their supposed victim (the victim was actually an actor, and the shocks weren't real).

To Milgram, it was another sign that ordinary people could behave in extraordinarily evil ways. "Gas chambers were built, death camps were guarded; daily quotas of corpses were produced with the same efficiency as the manufacture of appliances," he wrote. "These inhumane policies may have originated in the mind of a single person, but they could only be carried out on a massive scale if a very large number of persons obeyed orders."

However, fourteen of Milgram's forty subjects defied orders and refused to deliver the strongest shocks. They were nonconformists. They said things like, "I can't go on with this; no, this isn't right." And "I'm sorry, I can't do that to a man. I'll hurt his heart. You take your check...No, really, I couldn't do it." They felt morally unable to continue hurting a fellow human being.

What's more, in versions of Milgram's experiment where there were two confederates who refused to deliver the most intense shocks, only 10 percent, rather than 65 percent, of participants revved the shocks to the highest level. It's a finding that has surfaced again and again in studies: "Principled deviants," as psychologists call them, tend to rein in the cruelty of their compatriots and prod them toward their better angels. These upstanding outsiders help show the group how to do the right thing.

People with strong virtues are often able to resist following social norms, as the psychologists Jolanda Jetten and Matthew Hornsey describe in a review paper, especially when they can see those norms leading to a dark place. These individuals will seem weird to their contemporaries, but later on, they may appear sage by comparison. In a 2003 study, Hornsey and some coauthors found that among students who felt that gay couples should be recognized under the law, those who felt their view was the morally correct one were willing to stick by their beliefs even when they were told their view wasn't popular. For some people, it's simply more important to stand up for their beliefs than it is to fit in.

But these moral rebels aren't always rewarded by the rest of the group for being so virtuous. Sometimes, extremely principled people serve as an admonition that the rest of us could *also* have stood up for what's right, but we chose not to. "By reminding us of our freedom to act," Jetten and Hornsey write, "the rebel makes us confront our own past actions, leading to an existential crisis."

## LESLIE

Having a strong moral basis for her dissent was what helped Leslie Wagner-Wilson when she needed it most: escaping the infamous cult in Jonestown, Guyana.

For Leslie, life as a peripheral member of the cult was painful. But ultimately, her outsider status is what helped her break free from the groupthink and take a huge risk in order to defend her principles—and, as it would turn out, her life.

To use the popular phrase the cult gave rise to, Leslie did not "drink the Kool-Aid." But on the day she fled, 918 people, including U.S. Representative Leo Ryan, died in what was at that point the single largest deliberate loss of American life in history.

When I first reached out to Leslie, she seemed reluctant to do yet another interview. People call her from all over the world—a Swedish talk show was the latest supplicant—to ask her to recount one of the most traumatic times of her life. But when we met at a bar near her home in Phoenix, Arizona, she spoke candidly and with occasional humor about life as one of the few people to ever exit this notorious sect.

Some victims of trauma have concerns about people getting too physically close, so when we sat down I asked if I could scoot toward her for the benefit of my voice recorder. "Come on!" she said, beckoning me to slide across the booth. After Jonestown, where adults shared large, communal outhouses, she said she doesn't have many personal-space boundaries.

Leslie is in her early sixties, is African American, and has high-arching brows that make her look like she's just made a really good point. When she was thirteen, her mother joined the Peoples Temple, as Jim Jones's group was called, because she thought it would be good for Leslie's sister, Michelle, who had gotten involved with drugs. Throughout her teens, Leslie was proud to be part of an organization that was supposedly helping the world by spreading socialism and fighting racism. She wanted to be a revolutionary. The church provided a strong community, which was enveloping and comfortable and made you feel worthwhile. Whenever doubts crossed her mind, Leslie thought she was the only one questioning it. And, it's worth remembering, Leslie was twenty when she lived in Jonestown—the age at which many people join sororities and fraternities in a quest for identity. She compares the lure of a cult to the toxic embrace of an abusive relationship. "Maybe if I do better, I'll feel better about it. If I'm not doubting, not thinking about myself, maybe this will pass," she explained.

"Of course," she added, "it never did."

Leslie calls Jones "a brilliant monster." After sprouting branches in Los Angeles, the Redwood Valley, and San Francisco, Jones and the Peoples Temple came under scrutiny in the media. It became obvious that the "healings" Jones staged were fakes, performed with the aid of chicken gizzards, which he told Temple members were cancerous lumps. Jones announced a plan to start a settlement in Guyana, a country on the north coast of South America. He told his followers that in the jungle, they would finally live a utopian existence free of racism and capitalism. Fictitious promotional videos filled with picturesque scenes helped seal the deal.

By that point, Leslie was already beginning to see through him. Jones, who insisted that Temple members avoid nice clothing and jewelry, at one point informed his flock that he needed a Mercedes for protection. It struck Leslie as far-fetched that a man who cast himself as an all-powerful "Father" would need a luxury car to guard him.

Even before Jones departed for Jonestown, Leslie had started to pull away from the church, finding a series of jobs that conveniently interfered with the Temple gatherings.

But the Peoples Temple was very efficient at breaking its members' egos. At so-called "catharsis" sessions, family members would be called to inform on family members, accusing them of capitalist decadence and stripping them of their self-worth. Gradually, Leslie's self-esteem disintegrated. She married a fellow Temple member named Joe Wilson. But after she and Joe had a son, Jakari, the couple drifted apart, and Leslie allowed Joe and a friend to take Jakari to Jonestown. "I thought he was better off without me," she explained. "I felt like I was not a good socialist."

She had no intention of ever following them to Jonestown. But in 1977, she received a phone call from a Temple member who informed her it was her time to go. Leslie feared that if she didn't move to Jonestown right away, she would never see her son again. That prospect terrified her enough to board a bus to Miami, then a plane to Guyana. From Georgetown, Guyana's capital, she took the twenty-four-hour boat trip to the settlement. Upon arrival, her passport, like those of the other Jonestown members, was seized.

When Leslie first arrived in Jonestown, she was happy to be forgiven and welcomed back into the fold. She was impressed with the settlement in those early days, before an influx of nearly a thousand newcomers would strain its capacity. Jakari laughed and played with the other children like they were brothers and sisters. The church members had cleared the jungle and built cottages and cabins. She was surprised to see armed guards, but she believed what she was told, which is that they were there to protect the settlers from dangerous local villagers.

Very soon, the image of a tropical socialist paradise began to fade. Rations grew more meager as more and more Temple members arrived by the boatload. Residents' legs were ravaged by ulcers from the heat. Leslie was told she would be sent to Cuba to train to be a doctor—a career path that excited her. But then she was randomly reassigned to cover a white woman's fieldwork job. The explanation, from the supposedly antiracist Temple, was that the white woman would burn in the sun. To Leslie, it was a galling sign of a racial disparity at Jonestown.

Jones had a habit of rounding up his acolytes in the middle of the night and forcing them to prepare for an attack he said could come at any moment. If that occurred, he told them, it would be time for "revolutionary suicide."

No one spoke of the children's future. Would they attend college? Would they spread the socialist word? Jones, at various points, weighed moving Jonestown to the Soviet Union, which Leslie thought was a strange choice for a predominantly African American congregation that was already beset by hunger and harsh weather. Or as she put it to me at the bar: "A bunch of black folks in Russia? Really?"

Anyone who complained about Jonestown, however, was swiftly and severely punished by Jones. After "the overwhelming realization that you have made one of the biggest mistakes of your life," Leslie explained, "you then have to hide that and whisper about it [to] someone you thought you could trust. That kind of stress is almost unbearable."

When Leslie wrote a letter to a close friend confessing her desire to leave, Jones discovered it. Leslie was reprimanded and sentenced to a "learning crew," which performed the most difficult manual labor and were kept isolated from their families and children.

Around this time, she learned that a friend, Shanda James, had been raped by Jones, then medicated to the point of oblivion. Leslie began to grow seriously worried about what lay ahead for her and her son. During our interview, recalling this time, she sounded not so different from the moral nonconformists in the Milgram studies. "What I was experiencing was not right," she said. "It wasn't true, it wasn't honorable."

She prayed that it would be her final year in Jonestown.

Leslie is the kind of person—perhaps surprisingly so, for a former cult member—who follows her gut, analyzes situations carefully, and sticks firmly to her decisions. Those traits are what brought her to Jonestown. They would also be what got her out.

She began dropping hints to a friend, Diane Louie, that she was ready to leave. Diane invited her to join a group that was planning an escape on the day of Congressman Ryan's visit, when it was thought that everyone would be too distracted to notice a few missing people.

Leslie could not risk bringing her family members, who by then had also moved to Jonestown. Not knowing what was about to happen, Leslie thought she could return and rescue her family once she, herself, was free. The morning of the escape, she was only narrowly able to wrest three-year-old Jakari away from his father, who was by then one of Jones's closest aides.

Sixteen months after she arrived in Jonestown, Leslie and nine others slipped past the guard shack and set out for Matthews Ridge, a hetown nearly thirty miles away from Jonestown. As Leslie walked through the jungle with Jakari strapped to her back, her only fear was getting caught. When the group arrived at a police station in Matthews Ridge, the police captain told Leslie there were hundreds dead in Jonestown. Later, Leslie would find out the casualties included her sister, brother, mother, and Jakari's father, Joe.

Jonestown, in the end, was more mass murder than mass suicide. The children were poisoned first, sapping the parents of their will to live. Guards trained guns and crossbows on those who resisted drinking the poison. Ultimately, 907 people drank the cyanide-laced Flavor Aid. (It was more economical than Kool-Aid, and Jonestown at that point was cash-strapped.) Sixteen attempted to defect with Congressman Ryan, whose entourage was fired on by Temple gunmen, killing Ryan and four others. Three men at Jonestown consciously did not drink the poison, and one woman hid. Just thirty-six people who woke up in Jonestown on November 18, 1978, lived to see the next day.

From Leslie's vantage, there are a number of reasons why so many people came to Jonestown, and why they didn't leave as soon as its horrible reality became clear. The Jonestown settlers may have been brainwashed, but they were also functionally imprisoned. Many of the Temple members had signed blank pieces of paper that could be filled out with fake crimes and used for blackmail. Subsisting on rice and gravy, they were too malnourished to run fast or overpower guards. Those who complained were drugged with sedatives or physically beaten. Some were senior citizens who had sold their possessions before leaving America—they had nothing to return to. A few might have been true believers, but many were, Leslie said, "holding on to this little thread of hope that things would change."

Leslie's example does not, therefore, imply that others in Jonestown were too weak-willed or timid to escape. For instance, moments before the massacre, Christine Miller, a sixty-year-old woman, opposed Jones's plan of mass suicide, telling him, "We all have a right to our own destiny as individuals." Hyacinth Thrash, a seventy-six-year-old woman who survived by hiding under her bed during the poisoning, later wrote that she had "double feelings" about Jones and had devised an escape plan. Leslie's salvation likely only came because she had long ago started to disbelieve Jones's teachings, had committed herself morally to breaking from the group, and, crucially, had chanced upon the escape party. Countless others were not so lucky.

For years afterward, Leslie was wracked by survivor's guilt and posttraumatic stress disorder. She hopped from boyfriend to boyfriend in an attempt to replace the family and friends she lost overnight. When we spoke, the son for whose sake she escaped, Jakari, was in prison for attempted murder. This is, she acknowledges, in part the result of a childhood spent in an unimaginably violent place. The children of Jonestown were physically and mentally tortured. They were trained to say that they would do anything—put their mother's hand in a garbage disposal, cut off her breast—for the cause. They were groomed to be child soldiers, a second generation of miserable devotees.

Toward the end of our conversation, I asked Leslie how we could keep another Jonestown from happening. The short answer? We can't. Though precise numbers are hard to come by, there appear to be hundreds of cultlike groups operating in North America today. It's a need to belong, Leslie said, that explains their power.

The human desire for love and kinship is so strong that charismatic monsters like Jones can turn it against us. The only antidote is trusting that inner, moral sense that *something* is not quite right.

## ALEX, PART II

Alex, the Mormon missionary in Bulgaria, soon grew tired of the "I'd like to share a short message" opener, so he instead began offering the people he met free English lessons, or just to be friends. (The English lessons, he told me, didn't have to mention the Church.) He told himself that at least he was making connections—ones that might lead to a religious conversion later on.

But as his mission progressed, Alex's enjoyment of it did not. He realized that this was an experience he would never get to share with anyone else. He would not be speaking Bulgarian back in California. He would not remain friends with the Bulgarians he met when he was out proselytizing.

He threw himself into practicing dancing, his lifelong hobby, and he learned to play "Clair de Lune" on the piano. He began to study French on top of Bulgarian, just for fun. Perhaps, he thought, he'd at least come back a better person. When he allowed himself to, he made mental lists of things he missed: ice, vending machines, customer service...not to mention his girlfriend, his family, his life.

It's worth noting that Alex's experience is not necessarily typical of Mormon missionaries. I also spoke with a man named Taylor, a missionary who served in the Czech Republic, which bills itself as being one of the most atheistic places on earth. Yet, Taylor told me he was never discouraged, not even in the middle of the long, dark winter. Not even when he was shoved into elevators or had knives pulled on him. For Taylor, the experiences only fortified his faith.

Alex, meanwhile, often fantasized about quitting. But doing so would be social suicide: his girlfriend's parents were active in the church, and he felt she was expected to marry a returned missionary. Leaving early might mean their relationship would be over.

In the end, he completed his mission. His girlfriend welcomed him back, and they married not long after his return. The mixed feelings Alex had about his Mormon mission, however, didn't end when he came home. He opposed the church's stance on homosexuality and other social issues. He was associated with an when she organization that, in his view, "caused so many people pain."

He describes it this way: Let's say you remember loving McDonald's as a kid. But then later you're told that the sodas are mostly corn syrup, and that the meat is "pink slime." Would you keep eating there just because it made you happy once?

In 2017, nearly two years after I first connected with Alex, he removed his name from the records of the Mormon church, the final step in a long, soul-wrenching process of quitting.

After college, Alex had made a career as an insurance salesman, where he applied the skills he learned persuading strangers on his mission. Like religion, he told me, insurance "is an emotional purchase that's usually sold with the buyer's best interest at heart."

A few years ago, he considered quitting insurance sales and becoming a law-enforcement officer. Given his Mormon mission experience, he figured he could handle a job that involved walking the streets, approaching people, and, potentially, making himself a target. He felt well equipped for the rigor and strictness of police life. It reminded him of his missionary training.

Alex sailed through the admissions process for the academy. He seemed unusually clean-cut, as someone who had never used drugs and only had his first drink at twenty-seven. After passing the written test, physical, and background check, Alex enrolled in his local sheriff's academy.

That's when he began to get the same ill-at-ease feeling he got on his mission. According to Alex, the academy asked cadets to buy their own uniforms—a $1,500 expense—and their own textbooks—another $300.

There were long homework assignments to be completed at night, extra time the recruits weren't paid for. He didn't like what he considered the patriarchal, fratty culture, in which drill instructors practically hazed the cadets.

When I reached out to the Los Angeles County Sheriff's Department for their perspective, a spokeswoman said recruits do "incur some expenses," including uniforms and study materials, and that the recruits perform homework because they receive college credit. She rejected the characterization of the culture as similar to a fraternity and said hazing is forbidden. However, she added, "The Los Angeles County Sheriff's Department is a paramilitary organization and part of the recruit training involves stress indoctrination and leadership protocol training."

To Alex, though, the academy felt too similar to being on a mission again: the lack of time to oneself, the strict chain of command. To someone who hadn't felt traumatized by a mission trip, the academy might have been tolerable, or even enjoyable. To Alex, it felt too close to a cult. "My missionary experience prepared me to be a deputy," he said, "but also showed me I don't want to be one." He quit and returned to insurance sales.

Leaving his church, he realized, had prepared him to stand up to authority in a respectful way. Being an outcast in his religion taught him the value of questioning why you believe what you believe.

Taylor, the Czech Republic missionary, had a very different metaphor for the church and its missions than the McDonald's analogy Alex came up with: "It's like walking through a rose garden. You can feel the thorns, but when you look back, all you can see is the roses," he told me. But his recollection of what it was like to be the only religious person in a den of unbelievers was strikingly similar to Alex's. "When you're the odd man out," Taylor said, "you have to decide what you believe."

The mission experience made Taylor more dedicated to Mormonism, while it made Alex more dedicated to getting out. Being bombarded with so much antagonism and rejection forced them to look inward and determine what, precisely, animated their spirits. In both cases, being the weird ones helped them uncover what was true about them all along.

## JULIA, PART II

While Julia Landauer, the NASCAR racer, was still a student at Stanford, she appeared on the TV show *Survivor*. Within days of arriving in the Caramoan Islands of the Philippines, she developed a sunburn so severe that a huge blister formed on her cheek. When she lay down, she could feel the liquid inside it sloshing from side to side. She got her period for fifteen days straight and lost twelve pounds.

She worried the other contestants would resent her if she revealed that she was a Stanford student, so she tried not to talk much and, in the process, developed a reputation among the other contestants as cagey and too quiet.

One night while I was visiting her, I watched clips of Julia on the show on YouTube. She was voted off seventh, so she had very little total screen time. It consisted mainly of adult contestants picking apart Julia, a rail-thin twenty-one-year-old in pigtails.

"She's really boring. She genuinely does not contribute anything except a nasally voice," one contestant said. One man sat Julia down and issued her a long series of manipulative-seeming instructions on how to play the game, to which Julia responded simply, "Understood." Another said he would describe Julia as having a "vanilla" personality—"but that would be a great disservice to the flavor vanilla."

The next day, I told her that if someone had said something like that about me on TV when I was that age, I would still be beneath the rock I would have crawled under to die.

"There's only so much you can do about it," she said briskly. "He knew how to play the game."

Not long after *Survivor*, Julia volunteered to be a "case study" in a Stanford consulting class. The other students formed a "U" shape around her and critiqued her "brand."

"My feedback is you're too polished, you're not relatable," she remembers them saying. "We don't get who you are."

To be criticized in that way felt crushing. She kept it together for the rest of the class, then cried all the way home. She gave herself three days to feel bad.

After that, she decided the experience was "the huge kick in the ass that I needed." In those days, early in her racing career, she was less self-assured, and she was getting all sorts of mixed tips from people to "tone down New York, play up New York, tone down Stanford." One person told her not to use words with too many syllables.

After that brutal consulting session, she realized there was just one thing she needed to play up: herself.

A few weeks after Julia sent me her bad-news email in 2018, she emailed me again to say she was able to get into three races, after all, in Canada. It was for the Pinty's series, which is named after a Canadian food company. The series is a little below the Xfinity series, NASCAR's second tier, but it's well regarded and full of seasoned drivers. It's also a less expensive series to run, costing thousands of dollars, rather than millions for the top NASCAR races.

Her ability to race this season was thanks to Joey McColm, a racer himself and the head of a team called Canada's Best Racing Team, or CBRT. It was also thanks partly to Julia's uniqueness within her sport. In a newsone d release, Joey said he liked Julia's "marketability," and his team seemed happy to have the only woman in the race. Julia was open to doing events and speaking engagements for sponsors, Joey told me, which some of the more traditional drivers aren't willing to do. Julia's experience on *Survivor* and in the consulting class had taught her that she needs to open up more, to be less guarded. She shares a lot more about herself with the public now. She's willing to use her experiences to try to connect with fans and potential sponsors' audiences. (She was, after all, allowing me to follow her around for the weekend.)

The thing is, "Canada's Best" wasn't technically the best in the series—at least not as far as winning was concerned. When I was following Julia, the team was ranked ninth. Several of the men with CBRT only worked part-time in the garage, and Julia knew the team was underfunded going into it. Joey, the owner, told me that while all teams, including his, are on a fairly tight budget, it doesn't affect the components of the car, only how many races they can enter. One expert I talked to said the reality is probably somewhere in the middle: that is, if they had more money, teams like CBRT would be able to afford more workers, which could affect how well the cars run.

Because of all of this, Julia told me as she drove me to the CBRT shop, she'd be happy to finish in the top five in her upcoming race.

By race day, she had adjusted that expectation to the top ten.

One day, Julia drove me to the team's shop, which is situated in an industrial part of a small town outside Toronto. Joey's father, a middle-aged mustachioed man named Kevin, showed me the car Julia drove in Halifax the previous weekend. "She brought back half of Nova Scotia with her," he said, pointing to its tires, which had heated up so much that they were now covered in a layer of gravel.

Drivers reuse the car's metal bodies until they get too smashed-up to drive. The vehicle is called a "stock" car, but it's actually built solely for racing. There's nothing inside but a driver's seat and a bunch of equipment, bolted down and unadorned. Even the headlights are just taped-on stickers.

When you're Julia's size, pretty much everything has to be custom-made. She wears the smallest possible Hans device, a neck brace meant to prevent whiplash. She has the smallest possible seat, the better to cushion her lithe body in case the car crumples into a wall, as occurred once in 2008.

She climbed into the car and asked Joey to tighten the seatbelt. Being tightly strapped in gives her more leverage when she steers and keeps her safer if she crashes.

As a final flourish, she and Joey cut out the decals for the nonprofit she works with—called One Love—and stuck them to the black metal sides of her car, along with her racing number: 25.

Julia went back to her hotel room to watch more racing videos and eat the remains of her pad thai lunch. Eating leftovers saves her money she can put toward racing.

Her uncommon attributes and hard work helped Julia get into the race. But they were no match for Canada's weather.

"I hope you brought your rain gear," Julia said when I arrived in Ontario to watch her prepare for the race. "Because it's gonna rain all weekend."

This was important because if it rained, there would not be a qualifying session to determine the order in which the cars lined up to race that weekend. If there is no qualifying session, the cars start in order of how many points they've accrued in past races.

But at the Nova Scotia race, her first in months, Julia's rear axle snapped in two, forcing her to withdraw before the end of the race. Since Julia's car performed so poorly, without a qualifying round she would probably start near the back—a huge disadvantage. Plus, when it rains, there's a higher chance of a really bad crash. The grass around the track gets slippery, so if the car slides onto it, it goes "Shoof! Into a wall," Julia said, swinging her arm wildly to represent the trajectory of a rain-slicked tire.

The day before the race, we headed to the track for a practice run. It was dry that morning, and Julia hoped it would stay that way. She suited up for practice, taking off her pearl earrings and tugging on a fireproof shirt and white, fireproof racing suit, which she topped with a fireproof hood and fireproof helmet. In 1964, Edward Glenn "Fireball" Roberts—so named because of the fastball he threw as a young baseball player—actually did burst into flames during a NASCAR race in North Carolina. Roberts was heard screaming "Help me!" as he burned. Today, there are layers of precautions: Julia even drives with a fire extinguisher strapped by her side.

Zipped into her racing suit, Julia had the air of a conquering hero. Her chest thrust forward, she paced around the car lot, ensuring all was well in her kingdom.

Men came up to take her picture and shake her hand. A group of little girls in yellow earmuffs encircled her for autographs. An old man in a cowboy hat walked up to me and said, "Gotta have a few women in, or the field's no good."

She fist-bumped her family and her old go-kart coach, Glenn, who had come to watch her race. She jumped in through the driver's-side window and revved up her engine.

Things seemed, to my non-expert eye, to go fine during practice. It was overcast but not rainy, which I was told is the perfect weather for racing. But when Julia emerged from her car a little over an hour later, she was red and panting. "That was so fucking scary," she said.

Mechanics crawled under the car, and Glenn and Julia's father peered under the hood. She hadn't been able to hear the radio for parts of the practice session. The car was vibrating because the tires were old. The shifter broke, and the brakes were so mushy that she could never be sure they'd bring her to a full stop. She had no reverse, and her power-steering fluid leaked. It would all need to be fixed before the following day.

Julia headed into a big tent to sign autographs alongside the other drivers. The sky blackened. Julia greeted her fans warmly, but she seemed tense. She turned and quietly asked me if it was raining.

It was. So heavily that rainwater was leaking under the tent.

Outside, the air chilled and a dismal scene unfolded. Pit crews in ponchos pulled tarps over their cars and rolled them into the haulers. Julia's family ducked for cover and silently looked on.

The qualifying session was canceled. Julia would be starting the race twenty-first out of twenty-six cars. Her task would be to fight her way to the very front from the very back.

There is one scene in the movie *Dumplin'* that is a terrific representation of the conundrums facing people who are unique in their environments.

*Dumplin'* is, in many respects, not very good. It's the story of a looks-obsessed Texas mom and her plus-sized daughter, Willowdean, who rebels by signing up for the teen beauty pageant over which her mother rules with an iron fist. Jennifer Aniston, weepy and coiffed, plays the mom with too much twang and not enough Prozac. Every other scene is a schmaltzy opportunity to hammer home the value of being yourself. It was kind of hard to watch, as a writer of a book about the value of being yourself.

Still, what it lacks in artistry, it makes up for in psychological case studies about what it's like to be weird. Willowdean joined the pageant to make a statement, but her friend Ellen, who is thin and conventionally pretty, mostly did it to support Willowdean. Willowdean acknowledges this state of affairs, referring to herself and the other outcasts in the pageant—another overweight girl and a goth feminist—as "the weirdos." In one scene, the pageant contestants are assigned to learn a dance, which they would then rehearse as a group. Rehearsal begins—and lo, the weirdos don't know the steps. They never bothered learning them. As the other girls dance, Willowdean stands in the back sulkily while the goth feminist flings her arms around, as though to mock the whole thing. Ellen, meanwhile, gracefully executes the steps with a smile.

*Dumplin's* world, like all of ours, is ruled by norms. With Dolly Parton songs and floral dresses, the girls live under a sugary code of Southern femininity that they are trying desperately to subvert. The girls, each in her own way, are determining how to navigate their weirdness. Should they openly flaunt the mainstream, like the goth feminist; ignore it, like Willowdean; or embrace it, like Ellen?

The Hollywood depiction is cheesy, to be sure, but it is also strikingly similar to the decision process my interviewees underwent. Should they correct everyone who makes an unenlightened comment, or ignore them? Should they behave like what's typical for their gender, or like what's typical for their profession? In the end, each of them has found a specific approach to life that has allowed them to remain unique while, for the most part, being blessedly free of the kind of impostor syndrome and social anxiety that often plague even the normiest of normals.

Next, we'll learn their secrets. We will follow these real-life Willowdeans, and we'll examine the many ways they negotiate the codes of their world.

# PART THREE

# HOW TO BE
# DIFFERENT

# CHAPTER 7

# Getting Support

## JULIA, PART III

On the day of Julia's race, light finally came to these immortal gods and mortal men. That is, the weather in Bowmanville, Ontario, was actually good—cloudy and dry, just what Julia had been hoping for. This did not deter Kevin, Joey's father, from issuing a dark prognostication.

"It's gonna get hot," he said, glaring at the heavens. "Ohhh, it's gonna be like a sauna."

Julia's hauler was set up next to that of Kevin Lacroix, the superstar Canadian driver from the race we watched in her hotel. She headed to the drivers' meeting, where row upon row of white men and their teams heard a list of instructions and rules for this course. Unlike the oval courses typically associated with NASCAR, this was a road course, which includes both right and left turns. "You guys and uh, ladies...," the official said at one point, seemingly catching himself. (This, too, doesn't faze Julia, who considers herself a "guy" in the chummy, summer-camp way it's usually said.)

The drivers bowed their heads in prayer. *Father God, thank you for every person's path that you have ordained to be here today....* Julia cracked her knuckles lightly.

When I asked her what it's like to sit in a room full of men every time she deals with anything NASCAR-related, she shrugged. "I've been doing it for sixteen years, so it's all I know," she said.

Julia's goal in the race was to work her way out of the back of the pack as quickly as possible, since the trailing cars tend to be sloppier and less predictable, and possibly more dangerous.

The drivers prepared to roll out of the staging area and onto the track. One woman kissed her racer husband tenderly before he climbed into his car. Glenn, Julia's former coach, swept a strand of hair out of Julia's fateen coulce. Julia tugged on her helmet. The inside of the car reaches 140 degrees, a swelter mitigated only by a cold-air hose she plugs into the top of her helmet. In the summer, Julia trains for this by rolling up her car windows and driving around North Carolina, where she lives, without the air-conditioning on.

"Alright kiddo," her dad said, "have fun, enjoy, be smart."

The cars started, popping off like miniature explosions and sending us civilians scattering away with our ears covered.

I walked with Julia's family to an area by a snack stand, where a large contingent of francophone NASCAR fans were cheek-kissing in anticipation. From this perch, Glenn would watch Julia make some key turns and give her a heads-up, via radio, if someone was about to pass her.

Over the loudspeakers, the radio announcer said Julia "doesn't take anything from anybody. A top-fifteen or -ten finish might be in the offing for Julia Landauer." That would mean she'd have to climb at least six spots up. Julia's family looked calm, like they were about to watch an opera instead of their child hurtling around in a sheet-metal box. Maybe they were just used to it.

The first few laps were promising. Julia advanced two cars almost right away, and by lap four she was in sixteenth place. A few laps later, she was fourteenth. Periodically a car would let out smoke or flames, and I would look worriedly at Glenn, who would reassure me that Julia was just fine and not on fire.

Suddenly, a car belonging to a driver named Ryan Klutt spun out into the barrier, to "oooh!"s from the audience. Klutt's pit crew patched up his car and sent him back out onto the road. But the incident was enough to raise a yellow "caution" flag, meaning all the cars had to slow down while driving in the same order they were already in. This was good for Julia, since she would now be able to close up the gap between her car and that of the driver ahead of her, but not so much for Kevin Lacroix, who was in second and had a huge lead.

When they picked back up to normal speed, Julia tried, once again, to pass. But this time, she missed her mark and ended up far outside the other cars. Julia thought the problem might be her shock absorbers, so she took a pit stop so her crew could check out her car. But even after that, each time she rounded the corner, her wheel yawned away from the wheel well, as though threatening to detach. The car looked lopsided, drunk. Over the radio, Julia told Glenn she felt like she was on a roller coaster.

She gradually lost places, finishing sixteenth—just outside the range the announcers had pegged as a possibility for her. Kevin Lacroix finished second. The winner was a guy whose car was sponsored by EpiPen.

Julia drove her car back to her hauler. She came out clutching her sides, saying her obliques were sore. She felt like she had been holding the car together with all her might. The sway bar, a large metal rod across the front end, had come undone, leaving the car's right side practically dragging along the ground.

Could the technical difficulty have happened because CBRT, Julia's team, isn't as flush as some of their competitors? When I asked Jeff Pappone, the motorsports journalist, if a sponsorship might have made the difference in something like a sway bar or axle breaking, he told me that a very well-funded team could afford to simply replace a sway bar that looked the tiniest bit unstable. Better-funded teams also have more people checking all the parts to be sure they're working. "The teams at the front don't have as many failures," he said. Stuff like this still happens to well-funded teams, but not as much.

After the race, two men walked over to Julia to tell her she'd have been in the top ten if her car hadn't failed. Another driver grabbed her by the shoulders for a fan picture, and she smiled gamely.

Kevin McColm took her to the side for a rare serious moment. "I'm so proud of you," he said.

Given the long stretches between wins, the lack of consistent sponsorship, and the dearth of other women to commiserate with, I was at times baffled by why Julia was able to handle her outsider status so well. What made her so resilient in the face of so many setbacks?

She's clearly in love with racing, for one. No matter how many times journalists ask her, she's easily able to come up with new ways to describe the high of making an incredible pass or falling into a fluid rhythm on the track.

"I'm probably a little crazy and very optimistic," she told me, by way of explanation. "You can't just get frustrated and give up. If you did that and you were a parent, your kids would be neglected. If you were running a company, your company would go under."

It probably helps that she isn't easily "triggered," to use modern parlance, by low-level sexism, or even by the kinds of outright insults hurled her way on *Survivor*.

Lastly—and this is the frustrating one, the one where people don't have as much control, where they can't just cultivate themselves and try harder—it helps that Julia's family is so involved and supportive.

Julia and her two siblings are still so close that they Skype once a week for an hour. Once, her little sister, Emma, accidentally broke her brother Aidan's wrist while playing basketball, and Aidan kept it a secret for weeks so that Emma wouldn't get in trouble. Aidan, who is now in his early twenties, has also advanced far in racing, and he peppers Julia with feedback after he watches her practice. Both siblings attend as many of their sister's races as they can.

Julia's father loves racing and still pitches in as a spotter for her during some races. All throughout the weekend of the Bowmanville race, Julia's parents and Glenn, her former coach, surrounded her, like the Secret Service jogging with the president.

That description might strike some as reminiscent of helicopter parents, the ones who just can't bear to eject themselves from college dorm rooms. But some research suggests that not only is the "helicopter parent" threat overstated—one study found having an overly involved parent only explains 9 percent of the variation in student well-being—parental involvement in young adult children's lives can actually be a benefit. Grown children who receive "intense" support from their parents—whether financial or emotional—several times a week were, according to one paper, better adjusted and more satisfied with their lives than grown children who did not receive this kind of support.

Of course, shielding your children from the impacts of their actions can be a major parenting mistake. But Julia's parents don't do that. They both have high-paying jobs, and they could probably afford to simply pay for some of her racing, rather than leave her to hustle for sponsorships. After Julia's sway bar broke, her father said only, "That's part of racing," rather than trying to fight the judges or the team owner. Her family seems to have struck the ideal balance: supporting and encouraging her, but leaving the actual racing to Julia.

I suspect having a cheerleading squad of a family works to Julia's advantage. At the very least, when the treachery of racing gets to her, Julia can remember that while there may be no one quite like her in racing, there are four people just like her on the sidelines.

## AILEEN AND SARAH

How free you feel in making unique decisions depends in part on whether your environment empowers you to make those decisions. The people I met who had strong support systems—whether through friends, family, or even faith—seemed to have an easier time making pathbreaking choices and sticking with them. Everyone else might have thought they were weird for doing what they were doing, but those opinions didn't seem to shake them. Like trained sculptors, they seemed tranquil and steady, molding something only they fully understood from the outset.

Most things become more accepted as they grow more common, but single parenthood is the rare phenomenon that remains stigmatized even as it becomes more widespread. In 2010, Pew Research Center reported that seven in ten Americans think the trend toward more single moms is "bad for society," and the majority of Americans thought children need a mother and father to grow up happily.

An especially unique subset of single mothers is "choice moms," or single women who have a child on their own, often by using anonymous donor sperm. Perhaps because they get pregnant so intentionally—through a long, deliberate, often expensive process—choice mothers are seen, by some, as rejecting all the trappings of family. They combine two of our biggest societal taboos: single motherhood and determined women. A fringe minority of people think choice moms are selfish or rash. More often, people volley choice moms with endless questions about their decision, making them make the choice, over and over, wherever they go.

I spoke with several choice moms who were able to withstand these societal pressures. The difference in how easy it was for them appeared to be how supportive their social circles were.

Aileen Budow was always independent, and she always wanted to be a mother. But she was forty-two, and she felt that perhaps her subconscious "ticktock" was becoming a bit of a turnoff on dates.

When she told her best friends she was considering becoming a mother on her own, they said, "We've been waiting for you to say this." Her parents said, "What can we do? How can we do it?" Once she made the decision, it was easy, she said, to discard the notion of the stereotypically picture-perfect family and go it alone.

She describes the process of her pregnancy as one of being enveloped by positive energy from her family and friends. She did a "picking party" for the donor with her girlfriends. When they all picked the same three top contenders, she considered it *beshert*— Yiddish for "destiny."

Her girlfriends cheered her on as she lay back with her legs in the air at IVF doctors' appointments. Her office had a maternity leave party for her, and her coworkers chipped in to buy her a baby stroller.

Aileen sounded like one of the most empowered women I had ever met. Other women call her an inspiration and a mentor. (She nearly convinced me to have a child on my own, and I can barely keep plants alive.) When men on dates raise eyebrows at her being a choice mom, she simply deems them assholes, orders the most expensive tequila on the menu, and calls it an early night. She and her son live in New York, a city filled with diverse families in which plenty of kids have gay parents, biracial parents—the full gamut. People rarely ask her questions about where "the dad" is.

She's happy to be the only one making parenting decisions for her son. When father-and-son things do come up—like a recent parents' day at camp she couldn't attend—her friends come to the rescue again, sending their husbands to be with her son for the day.

Today, she has no misgivings about being a norm-breaker. "You should not look at everything with these glasses of what the norm is," she told me. "You look at what's right for you."

The psychologist and philosopher Cristina Bicchieri studies trend-setters, people who violate society's norms and set a path for others to follow. Trendsetters, she says, tend to be more autonomous and less sensitive to risk. They possess a great deal of self-efficacy: a belief that their actions won't be in vain. Trendsetters know that if they start a movement, others will follow.

She has also observed that in order to try new things, different people require different thresholds—a set number of people they need to see behaving unconventionally in order to, say, paint their house purple, or do something else norm-violating. People who have very high thresholds are more cautious: they'll only attend Burning Man once they hear of tech CEOs who are doing it. If someone has an extremely low threshold, meanwhile, they might wear a Beetlejuice costume to an important work meeting on Halloween, even if there's no indication that anyone else will be wearing a costume. (Someone with a threshold of "one," meanwhile, might make a work buddy do it with them.)

Bicchieri, for what it's worth, has a relatively low threshold. When she was growing up in Italy in the 1960s and '70s, women were bound by very strict social rules. They weren't expected to have both a family and a career. But Bicchieri was active in the feminist movement. She moved out when she was nineteen and lived alone, which was unheard of. She went to Cambridge to earn her PhD. One reason she was able to go against the grain at such a young age, she told me, is that a small group of friends did it with her.

Another choice mom I spoke with, Sarah Lenti, had a much more complicated experience than Aileen's.

Sarah is an attractive, successful political strategist who has worked for Condoleezza Rice and Mitt Romney. Still, when she was younger, she had very low self-esteem. She didn't date in high school and she didn't date in college. She didn't date until she was in grad school at Stanford, in fact, and that relationship ended when she had to move to Washington for work.

Then came a three-year slog through limbo with a man who said he didn't want to break up or get married. He would never love her, he told her. At thirty, she wrote a note to herself that if she was still single at thirty-eight, she would think about becoming a mother on her own.

She moved to Colorado and hit the online dating apps, but she met a mix of nice guys she wasn't very attracted to and attractive guys who weren't looking to get serious. Around the time of her thirty-eighth birthday, she was so depressed she was regularly waking up around noon on weekends. A child, she realized, would give her meaning beyond the grind of work. *What the heck is my life about?* she asked herself. Being a mother was the answer to that question.

But unlike Aileen's parents, Sarah's are conservative Christians. They grew up believing that children do best in a home with a mother and father. At the church Sarah attended growing up, there were rows and rows of families fitting a traditional pattern: one man, one woman, and their "natural-born" children.

On the Christmas Eve before her thirty-eighth birthday, Sarah went home to tell her parents she would be trying to get pregnant with a sperm donor. They told her she was being selfish. Sarah was so hurt she left the house, checked into a hotel, and spent Christmas Day alone.

As she was going through the process of injections and embryo implantations, her parents didn't call her. When she called her mom, she says her mother told her, "We're praying about loving them."

In 2015, Sarah gave birth to twin boys. Her parents eventually came around, and today they adore the twins. Sarah became very deft at shutting down any questions from strangers about "their dad": they don't have one, she says firmly.

Along with the twins' births came another major change in Sarah's life: she's no longer religious. Though she acknowledges that faith can be a powerful force for some people, she says science is what gave her children, not God. Her mother prayed and prayed that Sarah would find a partner, but she never did. "If there's a God who listens to the desires of your heart," she told me, "he wasn't listening to mine."

I do not know if Sarah would feel the same way if her choice motherhood had gone as smoothly, socially, as Aileen's did. But it's clear that norm-breaking isn't always costless for everyone. And having people in your life who encourage you can reduce the price of difference.

# CHAPTER 8

# Comfort with Discomfort

## BEVERLY, PART II

At one point during my visit to Wichita Falls to see Beverly Stiles, the sociology professor, I stopped by a Taco Bell for lunch. When I spelled my name for the cashier, he said, in a deep drawl, "Oh, I know how to spell your name, because my wife and I are really into the last Russian czar. And his daughters' names are Olga, Tatiana, Maria, and Anastasia. If my wife and I ever have a girl, her nickname will be Atom, which is a contraction of all of their names."

I stared blankly back at him, this being the most interaction I'd had in a restaurant in probably decades. Also because, even when I pry my mind open as far as it will go, an encyclopedic knowledge of Russian royalty is just not what I was expecting out of a Wichita Falls Taco Bell cashier. (The stereotypes! Not even I escape their snare.)

I was going around town—in this supposedly most Republican congressional district in America—to interview random people in an attempt to gauge the actual Republican-ness of their attitudes. At first, they seemed to fall in line with my expectations. Several women I approached in a Starbucks told me they didn't consider themselves to be feminists, saying the word implies that men can't do things for women, or that men and women shouldn't be equal. Outside, I asked one late-thirties woman about transgender people, and she said she hadn't met many, but that it's important to look out for the safety of people using bathrooms.

But I was surprised when a twenty-five-year-old young woman with freckles and braids told me she considers herself feminist, knows all about the #MeToo movement, and thinks getting rid of gender-specific bathrooms would be the best way to go. And I was similarly taken aback when, at a mall, a twenty-seven-year-old man with a scraggly beard told me that he was a strong feminist, but also that people should go to the restroom of the gender they're born into, because it "keeps it less confusing."

Wichita Falls has a couple of yoga studios, and I visited one of them, a large, modern space in a strip mall. Carson, the peppy young studio director who has lived here her whole life, told me she thinks Wichita Falls is the perfect-sized city, because it's just big enough to have a yoga community, but small enough so that you don't have to "worry about traffic." Still, it's the Bible Belt, so some people are concerned that yoga will clash with their existing beliefs. When she hears this, Carson assures them, "Yoga is not a religion, it's a way to connect you to a higher power."

In other words, yes, a lot of people here hew to traditional, conservative values. But not everyone. And as Beverly would find, they are also open-minded.

Ultimately, Beverly decided not to pursue a job in a more liberal state. She felt her students needed her, and that if she moved to, say, San Francisco, she'd be preaching to the wokeness choir.

But she realized she'd need a new approach in order to help her material resonate with her conservative students. Several years ago, she changed the way she conducted her class. She started launching each new semester with an introductory lecture in which she would acknowledge that some students might be alarmed by what she tells them. They might not feel that gender inequality is real, she admitted, and that's okay. She tells the students they are allowed to bring up the Bible, but that she can't personally comment on its teachings.

When her students claim study findings don't fit their personal experiences, she seizes on the opportunity to talk about the difference between anecdotes and aggregate data. Early on, a few men in her class complained that the course devoted too much time to women's issues. Now, Beverly spends the entire first half on men and masculinity, before moving to some of the more female-centric gender-studies topics, like makeup or household chores. Gradually, she introduces the big f-bomb: feminism.

Beverly's strategy reminded me of a nonconformist survival mechanism called "idiosyncrasy credits." If an outsider yearns to be accepted by a group without surrendering their individuality, idiosyncrasy credits are the way to do it. The idea was pioneered by the psychologist Edwin Hollander in the 1950s. By studying the way people interact in groups, Hollander theorized that newcomers to a group are better accepted if they first pay homage to its established values and goals, then start to deviate in small ways. At first, conform; then innovate.

Think of these credits as little tokens you gather for acting like you belong within the group. Go to the meeting and smile along to the useless presentation, that's a credit. Go to the boring baby shower and coo at the onesies, that's another. Later, you can "spend" those credits by deviating from the group norms, say, by telling your boss what you really think of the project, or sitting out the baby's first birthday party. It's a way of gently reassuring people that you can be normal, *in theory*, before you fully unleash your weirdness.

This strategy worked for no less than the Beatles, as the sociologist Ian Inglis described in the journal *Popular Music and Society*. In the late 1950s, most of the top British performers had antiseptic images, and the nascent Beatles were considered too wild. During those infamous nights in Hamburg during which they racked up their ten thousand hours of practice, the Beatles would taunt the crowd and call them Nazis.

Beatles manager Brian Epstein wanted to clean up the band's reputation. In order to help the band accrue some idiosyncrasy credits, Epstein laid some ground rules: They were no longer allowed to drink or swear onstage. They were to wear suits instead of leather jackets, and bow at the end of each song. Ringo had to promise to shave off his beard and to always comb his hair forward. Most egregiously, John Lennon was told to avoid mentioning publicly that he was married to Cynthia Powell and had a child on the way. As Lennon described, somewhat resentfully, years later: "All the rough edges were being knocked off us." Still, the strategy was effective. Bookings picked up, and within months they had a contract and a hit single, "Love Me Do."

At the height of their fame, in 1966, the Beatles began spending all those idiosyncrasy credits. They dispensed with their polished haircuts and embarked on unusual solo projects. Their music changed, too. According to Inglis's analysis, 91 percent of the Beatles' work before 1966 consisted of love songs; starting with "Revolver," just 16 percent did. (To get a sense of how far they had veered from "I Want to Hold Your Hand," listen to the White Album's "Revolution 9," an eight-minute "sound collage" whose only lyrics are the words "number nine." If weird had a soundtrack, this would be it.) Through their seamless conformity, the Beatles had become so popular, they didn't need to be conventional anymore.

Beverly builds these credits by easing her students into the shallow end of sociology, only later encouraging them to plunge further. Many of them come from blue-collar backgrounds, so she shares details of her working-class background with them in order to build a rapport. And she tries to only stick out in the community in ways that matter to her: she doesn't talk politics with people outside her friend group, for example, or put political bumper stickers on her car. And rather than refer to her field of study as "BDSM," she says she researches "sexual minorities." She's even started saying "fixin' to."

She's also come around on living in Wichita Falls. She made some conservative friends, one of which she refers to as her "favorite Republican." A former student regularly tries to convert her to Christianity, but Beverly considers her a close friend and lets her proselytize because "that's who she is."

On weekends, she drives a few hours to Dallas and other cities to perform interviews for her research or get a dose of big-city life. The Royal Theater, in nearby Archer City, brings in local singers, and Beverly and her best friend try to go, even if they haven't heard of the main act. It's not *Hamilton*, sure. But there's more to life than *Hamilton*. When we talked, she had tickets to see Neko Case in Irving, a city a few hours away.

Trump's election hit Beverly especially hard. The day after he won, Beverly showed the movie *Born on the Fourth of July*, in which Tom Cruise depicts a paralyzed man, for a class about disability. Toward the end, she found herself crying uncontrollably in front of the class. It was nothing, she told them—the movie just reminded her of a friend who was a veteran and had recently died. It was months before she could go out to lunch with a friend who had voted for Trump. *It upsets me too much, that you would watch Fox News and believe all that bullshit and vote for that vile man,* she thought.

It has at times been difficult to recruit other professors to Wichita Falls. One professor, a gay man whose partner worked in Washington, D.C., turned down the university after flying out for an interview. She tried to sell him on the possibility of driving to Dallas every weekend for the food and the gay scene, but Beverly admitted to me, "There's gonna be nothing for him here."

Beverly still has students who do things like quote the Book of Ephesians to her: *"Wives, submit to your own husbands, as to the Lord."* But having students who disagree with her, she thinks, has made her the kind of professor who is willing to make her students uncomfortable—a limb not everyone in academia is still willing to go out on.

Over time, society has grown more "woke," for lack of a better word, on gender issues, and it has made Beverly's job easier. The majority of her students, for example, started out a recent semester knowing what the "glass ceiling" referred to. She no longer hears the rumor that she's a lesbian, or that students won't take her class because she's a feminist.

She also sees small signs that she, herself, is making a difference. About twelve years ago, when one of Beverly's students proclaimed that her parents had raised her exactly the same as her brothers, and thus she hadn't experienced gender inequality, another swiveled in her seat and said, "You're wearing makeup. Do your brothers wear makeup?" The girl was so offended she dropped the class—but Beverly believes the exchange itself was a sign of progress. A retired engineer audited Beverly's gender class out of interest and liked it so much he donated scholarship money to the department. At the beginning of each semester, she asks everyone to raise their hands if they consider themselves a feminist. Maybe three people out of forty will. She asks the same question at the end of the semester. One year recently, all but three people raised their hands. "That works for me!" Beverly said.

When Caitlyn Jenner came out as transgender publicly, students emailed Beverly to say her class helped them understand what "transgender" meant. One said she had used Beverly's teachings to explain the concept of gender identity to people in her church, and one preacher's daughter whispered to Beverly that her class had "opened her eyes." Another former student wrote to say the class had fundamentally changed the way she viewed parenting a boy. As she and her young son wandered through a toy store, the boy asked for a doll. "Before I took your class, I would be the first person to say, 'Absolutely not,'" the student said, according to Beverly. "Now I realize how ridiculous that is."

Beverly quoted a phrase from social-science research that sums this up well: "What is becomes what should be." People didn't approve of interracial marriage until there were lots of interracial marriages. Once interracial marriage became "what is," few would discourage an interracial couple from marrying. Norms can change, even in Wichita Falls.

## ASMA, PART II

By using strategies like idiosyncrasy credits, Beverly and others I spoke with were able to stay true to themselves while living in places where few other people shared their beliefs.

Another way my interviewees combated the social anxiety that can arise from standing out was, frankly, by simply not giving a hoot what people thought of them. This was what I noticed when I spoke with Asma, the Muslim woman from a small Southern town.

When I met up with Asma at her apartment in New York, I was instantly disappointed that I couldn't use my journalistic trick of using the person's surroundings to gather clues about their personality. Her place was filled with nearly the exact same IKEA furniture as mine, down to the pillows. They're all Craigslist finds, she noted. She joked that New York is just the same ten pieces of furniture being shuffled from one apartment to another.

Asma found that growing up, she could usually fight off her peers' Islamophobic comments and prejudices, but that occasionally it was easier to conform. One of her high school teachers ran a charity drive for "Christmas giving," and Asma contributed her pocket money, even though she knew her parents wouldn't approve. Along with the rest of the school marching band, she bowed her head to pray before every performance.

Other times, though, she would flout social conventions, even though doing so would attract even more attention to her. She fasted in school on Ramadan, and after college she began wearing a hijab.

The need to explain her differences didn't end at high school. For college, Asma went off to a traditional four-year university in a more diverse area. Before classes began, she thought to herself, *Surely not everyone will drink in college.*

But, of course, it wouldn't be college without keggers. At her first party, every person was drinking except her. Many Muslims, including Asma, don't consume alcohol, but especially in the early weeks, Asma feared that refusing a red Solo cup would mean social exile.

When Asma was growing up, her parents would practically shout "Remember who you are!" out the door at her each morning as she ran for the school bus. Being an outcast might mean alienating yourself from your peer group at times, they taught her, but it also means entwining yourself more closely with the centuries of tradition that got you to where you are. Only later did she realize they were preparing her to feel comfortable even when she's the weird one out.

Asma never gave in to her college's partying pressure. At the beginning, she did carry around a red Solo cup filled with water. But eventually, she adopted an aphorism she learned from a similarly confident friend: "Everywhere I am is a good time."

If Asma was in her dorm room instead of at a frat party, it was a good time. If she was distancing herself from friends who get too rowdy, it was a good choice. That means she sometimes said "no" to a tailgate or happy hour. When she did go out, she no longer needed to hold a virgin drink in her hand to try to fool people. She had grown so accustomed to being different, she told me, that each individual difference—like not drinking or not having sex before marriage—was no longer a very big deal to her.

As much as research tells us that it's painful not to conform, some studies also hint at a way out: you can, like Asma has, change the way you think about your own nonconformity. In one study, a group of students felt threatened when they had to give a speech about health policy to an audience of their political opponents. That is, they felt threatened *unless* researchers told them the goal was to showcase their individuality, rather than to get everyone to agree. In that case, their threat scores went way down, as measured by their cardiovascular readings. Freed from the necessity of fitting in, the participants felt more comfortable disagreeing with the group. Similarly, Asma gets "a lot of satisfaction out of being true to myself," she said.

These days, people sometimes ask Asma what she does at parties—as in, how does she survive them without drinking. "You just hang out!" she casually replies.

I pushed her on this last part. It's one thing to "just hang out" at parties, and it's another to not lay in bed awake at 3 a.m., wondering what everyone thought of the *one* sober girl in the place.

"People's discomfort is theirs and not mine," she said. The way she sees it, if someone judges you for your choices, it implies *they're* the ones who aren't okay.

This attitude has manifested itself in Asma's comfort with other people's discomfort. Social anxiety often surfaces as a fear of authority figures, but Asma has no problem telling her boss that, say, she needs two more weeks to finish a project, or with correcting someone who mispronounces her name. She's unperturbed by the idea that someone might be frustrated with or puzzled by her for a moment—she's been putting up with that her whole life.

I asked her if she'd like to return to a place like her Southern hometown one day. She told me she did find it borderline "irresponsible" to live in a place like New York, where there's a black Muslim on nearly every block. (Literally, Asma knew of another one who lived across the street and even had her same nose piercing.) Asma thinks that because she's proven so capable at making a good life for herself no matter where she lives, "it seems like I should take some of that energy elsewhere."

Someone once told her, "You should try and locate yourself at the most hardcore place where you can still sustain yourself," she said, "and I think that's sort of what I'm looking for."

If you're born and raised to be a nonconformist, she figures, you might as well go to the places that will test your mettle.

# CHAPTER 9

# Better Than the Rest

## MICHELE

When Michele Roberts came home to her family's apartment in a Bronx low-income housing development one day in 1970, her mother, Elsie, had some news for her. When she entered tenth grade the following year, Michele would be attending an elite boarding school for girls located about fifteen miles away.

Michele was angry. She was a strong student, but she had wanted to go to a science magnet school closer to her home. But there was no sense arguing with her mother. Michele had earned a scholarship, so away to the boarding school she went.

Michele remembers being one of five black girls in the school, and that there were no black teachers. She had nothing in common with the other students. For some of them, the only black people they had ever met were those that worked for their families. Some of the girls asked to stroke her hair.

Michele was consumed with the sense that she didn't belong. Even the teachers questioned her abilities: when she did well on a paper, one asked, "Did you really write this?"

The experience was a difficult one, but it flipped something inside Michele. She grew accustomed to being the only African American woman in the room, and the feeling no longer paralyzed her. *I'm not the stupid one,* she thought to herself. *I'm the smart one.* She buried herself even deeper in her studies, determined to outdo anyone who doubted her.

She graduated with a stellar record—she's now grateful for the experience—and went off to college. The racial percentages there were, unfortunately, nearly identical. It was the same story at Berkeley, where Michele earned a law degree in 1980.

After she graduated, Michele became a public defender in Washington, D.C. It's a notoriously difficult, thankless job. Public defenders are overburdened with indigent clients, most of whom manage to secure just a few hours of their busy lawyer's time. Because of that, Michele said, most people expect their public defenders to be distracted or incompetent.

Michele decided she would be amazing. She'd visit her clients in prison on weekends, when other lawyers were relaxing. In court, prosecutors would size her up, thinking a black woman would be easily bested. *Fine,* she thought, *if that means you're going to not work as hard and you're going to sleep a little longer.* When she talked to juries, she would try to put herself in their shoes, appealing to their common sense without condescending to them. Soon, she became so good in oral arguments that other lawyers would come to her trials just to watch her and learn.

Once, early in her career, she was handling a case with a senior attorney, and he asked her for a draft of the opening statement. When he read it, he asked, "Did someone help you write this?"

Michele knew what that meant.

"The problem is, if you didn't write it yourself," he continued, "you're going to have a really tough time memorizing it."

She decided she was going to give the most brilliant opening statement in the history of opening statements. As she entered the courtroom, she glimpsed the senior attorney out of the corner of her eye. *I can't wait to see the expression on this asshole's face when he realizes that I am not only good,* she thought to herself, *but better than he will ever be.*

And then...she nailed it. It was a flawless, powerful statement, delivered expertly. "I didn't find ignorance and prejudice would demotivate me," Michele explained. "I found it would excite me."

Years later, she was made partner at one of the country's top law firms, Skadden, Arps, Slate, Meagher & Flom—thus becoming one of the fewer than 3 percent of law partners who are women of color. In 2014, Michele was named director of the National Basketball Players Association. It made her an outsider yet again: the first woman to head a major North American professional sports union.

In an early appearance before the NBA players, as the *New York Times* described it, Michele told the athletes that the prospect of dealing with male athletes, male agents, male owners, and male reporters didn't daunt her. "My past," she said, "is littered with the bones of men who were foolish enough to think I was someone they could sleep on."

Michele represents another prevalent attitude among the people I interviewed: if you can't join 'em, their thinking seemed to be, beat 'em. Though not all minorities and nonconformists are underestimated, those who are often become driven to demolish stereotypes about themselves and their identities. Success, to them, looks not only like proving they're *as good as* everyone else, but that they're actually better.

This is not always a voluntary choice. A sickening relic of America's structural racism is that many black parents are still forced to advise their children to be "twice as good" as their white peers. Until society starts to see racial minorities, people with disabilities, and other historically marginalized groups as equal to the norm—white men—this cycle of discrimination and striving will likely continue.

This extreme diligence is therefore somewhat bittersweet. Working harder than everyone else is a trick other people can borrow from people like Michele. But for marginalized groups, it's more of a survival strategy. True progress will come when people of color are no longer forced to rely on it. Until then, it allows some people, including Michele, to accomplish remarkable things.

———————

Michele's superhuman effort is commendable, but there can be a point at which this kind of nonstop toil is a sign of a problem. Though this description does not seem to apply to Michele, over-work can also be a symptom of impostor syndrome, or the inter-nalized fear that one has not really earned one's accomplishments, and thus will soon be exposed as a fraud.

Feeling like you don't quite belong is a common trigger of im-postor syndrome. Women—who are underrepresented in board-rooms and corner offices—seem to be especially prone to this phenomenon. As Valerie Young writes in her book on the topic, *The Secret Thoughts of Successful Women,* 90 percent of all PhD dis-sertations on impostor syndrome are by women.

Many people of color, low-income men and women, and others who have historically been locked out of prestigious positions may also feel like impostors once they do break through to the top. Young cites one study that showed that nearly 86 percent of for-eign medical residents in Canada had high levels of impostor feelings—perhaps because they felt different, and therefore inade-quate. As another woman from the Bronx, Supreme Court Justice Sonia Sotomayor, put it, she felt like "a visitor landing in an alien country" when she arrived at Princeton. (This is one argument for women's and historically black colleges—they offer a sense of strength in numbers.)

Impostor syndrome can manifest in a variety of ways, including procrastination or an inability to accept compliments. But one trait several researchers on this topic pinpoint is, paradoxically, a tendency to *overwork.* Because people with impostor syndrome feel that they are not intrinsically smart, and can succeed only by work-ing harder than anyone else, they tend to obsess over even minute details of unimportant projects. These might be minor, internal memos that keep you up all night, or emails that get saved to the "drafts" folder and edited to Pulitzer-worthy perfection later. The nonstop work offers a way to explain, without taking credit, why the ultimate result was a good one: *"Oh, I'm not really qualified, I*

*just pulled an all-nighter."* Thus justified, the next time their skills
are put to the test, impostors are likely to overwork again, thinking, "Well, it worked the last time." Young quotes Joyce Roche,
the former president of Girls Inc. and an African American woman
who grew up working-class, as saying "the threat of failure scares
you into these long hours." Roche regularly worked fourteen-hour
days.

I, too, am no stranger to impostor syndrome. For my first
appearance on cable TV news, I entered the green room thirty
minutes before my time slot. Being on TV for the first time feels
like taking a Zumba class with all your ex-boyfriends watching.
You have to look good, but also like you know what you're doing,
but also like you're having fun, but also don't screw up or it will
remind everyone why they broke up with you. That morning, I
nervously reviewed the flash cards I, an adult woman, had made
so that I could remember what to say during my two-minute seg-
ment. Another woman waiting for her appearance—a journalist
who had been on TV many times before—tried to talk to me, and
I curtly ignored her. *Didn't she see that I needed every precious second
to prepare? Sure, she could relax and have fun—she is smart, but I am
dumb, but we would both be on TV soon, so to my flash cards I turn.*

Many impostors feel like they've pulled one over on the world—
they let me, a total dummy, in here!—but often, the real person
they are fooling is themselves. They have convinced themselves, despite all the evidence, that they're not really qualified. In her book,
*The Impostor Phenomenon,* the psychologist Pauline Rose Clance
recommends that people who overwork to manage their impostor
syndrome try pulling back once or twice, just to see what happens.
Pick a task that is not crucial to your job, she writes, and deliber-
ately spend less time on it than you would otherwise. If you're still
successful, you can later try it with another project. If you aren't
able to bring yourself to work less, though, it's worth asking yourself why not. Is all that work really what's required to get the job
done? Or are you covering up for something?

Indeed, after those first few scary TV appearances, I dispensed
with the flash cards and tried to relax in the green room instead.

It turns out I didn't need to drill myself on the material I had reported just a few days earlier, after all.

Not fitting in can ignite a drive to stand out in a positive way. Norm-breakers are often overachievers: the last ones to leave the office and the first ones to volunteer for every challenging assignment. Through their efforts, they might land at the top of their class or profession.

Sometimes, like in the case of Michele, the breakneck pace stems from a desire to outperform those who doubt us. But we should also recognize when we are working too hard because we're actually doubting *ourselves*. When you're told that you're never going to make it, a version of that message can play in your head on loop, nagging you to put in just a few more hours at your desk. There are times when you're actually trying to beat your competition—and times when your impostor syndrome simply won't let you quit. Recognizing the difference can be as difficult as it is important.

The key to getting over insecurities such as impostor syndrome, meanwhile, might be to try to look at your situation from another person's perspective.

# CHAPTER 10

# The Big Picture

## DANIEL, PART II

Being investigated by Toronto's children's services was the worst period in Daniel's entire career. The weekend after it all began, he had a panic attack in a drugstore. He grew dizzy, struggled to breathe, and had to sit down. *I'm gonna have to leave the field, and this is all I've ever done*, he thought. *My name will probably be attached to "molested children."*

He was especially hurt that the employee had called him racist after he had tried to accommodate her Muslim faith. He says he arranged for someone to cover for her so she could pray five times a day, and he let her keep her prayer rug in his office. "When she said, 'You hate me because I'm Muslim,' I was like, *'Are you serious?'*" he told me. Then he caught himself. "I know it probably wasn't the right reaction to have."

The Children's Aid Society dismissed the accusation, Daniel and his former coworkers said, since the name on the negative review didn't match the name of any parents, and no children had been pulled from the program, despite what the review implied. (Citing confidentiality rules, the agency declined to discuss the investigation with me.)

When I met up with Daniel, his name had already been

cleared. But I wondered, how do you recover from something like that? How do you snap back from the realization that in your chosen field, people will use your gender and sexuality to smear you?

Over the course of many hours of conversation, I noticed something about Daniel that I suspect helps him get through difficult times.

A few years into his preschool career, Daniel went back to school to earn a master's degree in early-childhood education. Even now that he's done with his degree, he buries himself in theory, perusing textbooks on everything from Piaget to feminism. He reads about gender norms, goes to conferences to talk about "queering the early years," and helped organize a workshop for other early-childhood educators on working with LGBTQ populations. He's interested in how society can stop projecting gender norms onto kids. Perhaps, I thought, he's learned from personal experience just how painful such prejudices can be.

The more Daniel learned about the theories behind societal stereotypes, the easier it seemed to be for him to process people's mistrust of him. When a suspicious mom treats him unfairly, he could chalk it up to psychological phenomena, rather than making it about himself.

Daniel has stumbled on a technique psychologists commonly employ to help people maneuver through painful situations: they advise people to view their problems from an outside perspective.

It's a theory called Solomon's Paradox, after the biblical king of Israel. According to the Bible, God appeared to Solomon in a dream and asked him what he wanted. Solomon asked for wisdom, so God granted his wish, giving him "a discerning heart." People traveled great distances to hear Solomon's sage advice. (Most famously, he determined the true mother of a baby by offering to cut the newborn in half—the woman whose child it was would rather give it up than see it die.)

Solomon's own life was a bit of a mess, however. He had hundreds of foreign mistresses, who influenced him to turn away from

God and toward other deities. He then built shrines for the gods his wives and mistresses worshipped. This angered the original God, the God of Israel, who punished Solomon by tearing apart his kingdom. Solomon, in other words, could only solve problems when they belonged to other people.

In 2014, researchers from the University of Waterloo and the University of Michigan performed a series of studies that supported this paradox. People of all ages were better at coming up with good advice if they had been told that a friend's partner, rather than their own partner, had cheated on them. Other studies show it can be beneficial, when thinking about our problems, to refer to ourselves in the third person, rather than using "I."

Similarly, Daniel—along with some of the other people I spoke with—were better able to weather social slights when they viewed their situations with some remove. They intellectualized their stigma, and like doctors delivering a harsh diagnosis, they gained a healthy distance from the problem.

This perspective helped Daniel become more confident and happier in his job. He liked looking at, say, a chaotic nap time as a "big picture" problem to solve rather than a bunch of kids who refused to listen to him, specifically.

After about a year and a half, Daniel left his job at the daycare. Toronto was becoming too expensive for him and his boyfriend, and he wanted to move to Ottawa to be closer to family. When I met up with him at Salad King, he was between jobs.

At that time, he was thinking about zooming even further out, to an even bigger picture, by transitioning to writing and teaching about early-childhood education, or to working in policy. He was even considering getting his PhD. But it's clear that working directly with kids still appealed to him. When he left the daycare, the kids all made a book for him filled with photos of themselves as a goodbye present. In the photos, they all wore big black glasses, just like his.

## DEANA, PART I

In 1997, a stranger stepped into a small house in Gomel, Belarus, where a sixteen-year-old named Deana lived with her mother, brother, and grandmother. The man wore jeans and Justin brand cowboy boots, and he spoke with a twang. He introduced himself as the man who had been sending all those letters to Deana's mother. He was there to take the family to their new home in America.

Gomel, the country's second-largest city and one of its oldest, was beautiful and baroque, but it had frayed under Soviet rule. Belarus was then, as now, ruled by Alexander Lukashenko, a man so authoritarian that he once investigated the producers of a cartoon series for making a character that looked a little bit like him.

Every morning seemed to bring a new struggle for Deana's family. Deana's mother's most recent husband had turned out to be an abusive alcoholic. When Deana's mother asked for a divorce, he wouldn't sign the papers. She used her power as a notary to authorize her own divorce and left the man to raise their kids on her own.

Deana, who was born in the northern Russian city of Norilsk, didn't realize she was Jewish until the day at school when a boy called her *zhidovka,* a Russian slur for "Jew." When she asked her grandmother, Sofia, what it meant, her grandmother told her that for her own good, she should never tell anyone she was Jewish. Deana wished she could afford a cassette player and color TV like the rest of her classmates, but her family barely scraped along on her mother's salary. For a while, her mother talked of moving to Israel, which appealed to Deana, since she knew that was where other Jews like her lived. But a few years later, her mother began hatching another plan.

Deana's mother began sending lots of mail to someone in Texas. In January of 1997, the man, whom I'll call Raymond, came to introduce himself and to stay for a week. He seemed to make no attempt to hide his foreignness, wearing his Ray-Ban sunglasses even though it was wintertime in a former Soviet country. Between his accent and her middle school English, Deana couldn't really make out what he was saying. But she understood when he announced he was there to take Deana, her brother, and her mother back to his home in Texas, where he and Deana's mother would marry.

Deana's stomach churned at the news, but Deana's mother made it clear her daughter's feelings about the situation didn't matter. Besides, mail-order brides were common amid the economic upheaval of the late 1990s. Deana's mother's friends jealously told her that if they weren't married, they would be doing the same thing.

Deana's grandmother had been diagnosed with cancer, and she wouldn't be able to move with the rest of the family. Goodbye now meant goodbye forever. Her grandmother was the person Deana respected most. She was a firecracker of a woman who had worked on construction sites her whole life and swore like a sailor, yet was deeply compassionate. She had survived World War II, and Deana figured she could get through anything in life if she could be like her.

Raymond, smiling and chipper, was clearly on his best behavior during his visit to Gomel. He asked Deana what her hobbies were.

She replied, in broken English, "Listening to Metallica and shit like that."

"In my house, there will be no cussing," he warned. "And no metal music."

She was doomed.

A few months after Raymond's visit, Deana's family headed to Poland and underwent screenings for tuberculosis and HIV. After three days, they were given a visa and put on a thirteen-hour flight to Chicago, and then another flight to Dallas.

On the plane, Deana tried to imagine what life might be like in Texas. The only thing Deana knew about America was that it was home to New York, a city crammed with tall buildings and fancy people. *Maybe it will be like that,* she thought.

She couldn't have been more wrong. The place they moved to was a blink-and-you-miss-it hamlet—one so small, in fact, that I'm not naming it for privacy reasons. She arrived to find that the three-bedroom house Raymond had told them about was still unfinished. Raymond's kids from his previous marriage weren't able to communicate with Deana and her brother, and they kept a chilly distance. Deana's family were issued cards informing them they were "aliens."

While working on this book, I planned a summer trip home during which I was going to meet Deana and several other sources in person. While I was there, I also did reporting for a story on the town where I went to high school, McKinney. The story involved a lot of door-knocking, and almost every person I approached slammed the door in my face or didn't believe me when I said I had lived there.

It was during one such long day, when I was stewing about how much my hometown rejected me, how they distrusted me, how I didn't actually know anyone, that I ripped a hole on the inner corner of my right thumbnail. I've picked at my fingers my whole life, but this time it looked deep enough to see meat. I washed my thumb off with hand soap, then proceeded to, smartly, cook raw meats, use dirty yoga mats, and shake hands with dozens of people I met doing interviews. Midway through the trip to see Deana, my thumb wound started to look brown and cloudy, and the skin around it turned white and puffed up. Pain coursed across my hand and up my wrist. I was beginning to face my first-ever major consequence of skin picking.

I drove to Deana's pint-sized Texas hometown with my thumb looking like a used tampon. I wanted to get a flavor for Deana's little Ellis Island, but I had to deal with my injury first. Across from the central square—a fixture of seemingly every Texas small town—was a pharmacy that billed itself as "old fashioned." Unable to ignore the agony in my hand any longer, I parked my Volkswagen and went inside. A sales clerk immediately greeted me, then emerged from behind the counter to personally show me the "Advil section" and "the Tylenol section," which appeared to be the same section. When I held my oozing thumb out to her, she called over the pharmacist, a middle-aged blond woman. "Bless your heart," the pharmacist said, poking it with a pen.

"I picked my skin," I said.

"I would do the same thing if I didn't have these," she said. She held out her flawless, pink-painted nails. The fact that she was willing to pretend to be a crazy skin picker for my benefit made me feel so good I almost forgot my thumb pain.

"You better take you some Aleve," the pharmacist said. I grabbed some from the Aleve section.

There it was: the charming, extreme involvement in other people's lives that so far I've only encountered in the American South. This was the only time a pharmacist has willingly interacted with me since I moved to Washington for college. I've seen homeless people wailing in agony on the D.C. Metro, and passersby reacting by cranking up the volume on their noise-canceling headphones. When I go home to visit, I now find human connection refreshingly soothing, like a homeopathic elixir. *People giving a shit about each other!* I think to myself. *I'll be darned!*

But, if you're not used to it, having people insert themselves into your day can be overwhelming. (Indeed, the charm wore off slightly when I went to a Chipotle in a nearby town and the cashier interrogated me about my last name.) And extreme neighborliness definitely wasn't the way of the U.S.S.R. Deana was unaccustomed to this kind of probing, and she found it unpleasant. Some of the town's 4,500 inhabitants seemed, to her, to be too nosy and judgmental. People would walk up and ask if she believed in Jesus. Anyone who heard her speak would ask where she was from and how she got there. Admitting that her mother was a mail-order bride only heaped stigma on Deana, who already felt conspicuous. Once, she told someone her origin story, and he simply laughed, shook his head, and said she must be kidding. That was the last time she mentioned it for a while.

Deana felt, far more poignantly than I ever did, the inability to live free from your ethnic identity. When neighbors would come over to the house, she remembers that Raymond would say, "This is my Russian wife and her kids." Deana wasn't Deana anymore; she was the Town Russian.

"Is it cold over there?" people would ask Deana. "Do your people drink a lot of vodka?" In communications research, these are called "accommodative dilemmas," or the struggle to correct people's misconceptions about your identity group without hurting their feelings. (One paper suggests using humor to defuse such situations, which is difficult to do when you don't speak the language.)

The local high school wouldn't enroll Deana, so she found herself stuck in limbo: too old to be a typical American teen, yet with too little English to start college. She spent her days helping Raymond out in his business, and was otherwise stranded at home without a car.

She also had no knowledge of American social norms. Once, her stepbrother invited Deana along to hang out with his friends. As Deana sat on the couch, the group chatted among themselves, making no attempt to include her in the conversation.

Then something happened that sounds minor, but to me sounded so uncomfortable that my skin crawled when I heard Deana describe it. In the middle of the conversation, everyone but Deana got up and walked to the kitchen. Deana wasn't sure what to do. She was not part of their conversation in any way. Did they expect her to come with them? Or just to keep sitting there? Was she in the way? This was before iPhones, the "Oh look, I'm doing something too" escape hatch. Instead, she just sat there, staring off into space as everyone else ignored her.

Given the mail-order mom, the language barrier, the dying grandma back in Belarus, and all the other minor tortures Deana had endured, this couch-or-kitchen conundrum might sound like the least of her problems. But there are times when the world forces you to confront the fact that you fit in so poorly you literally don't know what to do with yourself. And for Deana, this was one of those times.

———————

Deana kept her pain bottled up. She cried a lot and read books, doing her best to learn English. She realized college was her only escape. She began volunteering at the library, got a tutor, and made a plan to apply to local universities. Her tutor handed her the freshman-English canon—*Of Mice and Men, To Kill a Mockingbird,* and so forth. Locked in her own little world, Deana had something to focus on besides her problems. She became absorbed in the books and the insights about human nature they revealed.

Deana was accepted into Midwestern State University, the same college where Beverly teaches, in Wichita Falls. At first, she selected nursing as her major, thinking it would be a fast path to financial independence.

But almost as quickly, she realized that despite her love of metal music, blood and needles weren't for her. She switched to business. One of the first required classes was on psychology, and before long, Deana was in love. The behaviors she found inexplicable about her neighbors—the stereotyping, the prying—all started to make sense. She learned about bias, social exclusion, collectivism, and individualism. She saw how those concepts applied to the very different cultures of the former U.S.S.R. and Texas. She understood how it's often the case that the root of prejudice is fear.whic

Deana, like Daniel, had found a way to intellectualize her experiences. And as occurred for Daniel, her experiences seemed less hurtful when projected through a less personal lens.

That's when things started to change for Deana. She understood Texans better, so she stopped expecting Texans to behave differently. Gradually, Texan culture, though no less distinctive, was no longer as freakish to her.

My own social anxiety was far less rational than Deana's—by second grade, I spoke English just as well as my native-born classmates. Still, it's been equally severe at times. I once skipped a fifth-grade class field trip because I knew it would involve unstructured time without teachers, and I was worried about navigating the social free-for-all. The summer after I graduated high school, I almost had a panic attack when I realized college would involve attending lots of parties, which I imagined as nightmarish gauntlets filled with subtle social cues and unspoken expectations. (I had failed to factor in alcohol, anxiety's great equalizer.)

But becoming an observer of people, just like Deana and Daniel did, helped me get through the social interactions of my young adulthood. I had always been interested in people and current events, but one reason I took up journalism in high school is that I knew it would force me, a painfully shy brooder, out of my comfort zone. For my high school paper, I interviewed a TV producer and a girl who had struggled with anorexia. Interviewing people not only lessened my unease around strangers, it provided me with a structured way to interact with them. (Next time you're at an awkward cocktail party, try interviewing whoever's nearby.)

Nora Ephron, the journalist-turned-filmmaker, found this to be a practically universal trait among reporters, herself included: "I always seem to find myself at a perfectly wonderful event where everyone else is having a marvelous time, laughing merrily, eating, drinking, having sex in the back room, and I am standing on the side taking notes on it all," she wrote in her aptly named essay collection, *Wallflower at the Orgy*.

For some people, it's more orgasmic to study the orgy than it is to take part in it. We're just weird that way.

## MARY

"You're a summer," said Mary Duffy, a septuagenarian former plus-size model, as we sat down to eat (allegedly) the best hamburgers in New York City in a diner the size of a modest Subaru. But first, she wanted to do my colors. "Summer has medium-brown to blond hair, fair skin without a lot of yellow, and light eyes. If you had a hot date, if you put on a seafoam jacket, or a seafoam dress, and a pale-yellow scarf, you would knock them off their socks."

I thanked her, pondered where I could get a seafoam jacket in 2019, and gently tried to pivot the conversation to learning more about her past as one of the first-ever plus-size models and the owner of the first plus-size modeling agency.

But no.

"We have to finish you," Mary insisted. There are three things every woman should know: her colors (mine is the aforementioned summer), her shape, and her style "personality."

"You're an H!" Mary cried, drawing a letter "H" in the air. By this, I take it, she's describing my sturdy Slavic policewoman's torso. "That's the easiest figure to dress," she assured me. "You look great in pants that are narrow as hell."

Mary leapt up, pointed to her butt, and explained something about tapered jeans that I didn't quite understand. Behind us, raw beef sizzled on a grill.

She sat down and continued my analysis. "I would say personality, you're a classic. You're happier looking appropriate than being totally comfortable or dramatic. I'm dramatic. The dramatic has to take off the last piece of jewelry and the cuckoo clock before leaving the house."

"So you're a classic, H, summer," she said, contentedly. "Congratulations! Avoid beige."

She turned to the waiter and, finally, ordered a cheeseburger. No bun, she was doing Atkins.

Mary had recently received a notification from Classmates.com telling her that the number one word that her classmates used to describe her was "ambitious." She wishes she wasn't so transparent, but as her father always said, "Mary, you're about as obvious as a sledgehammer over the head."

Her mother, meanwhile, thought the young Mary should funnel her ambitions toward weight loss. She slipped seven-year-old Mary little pieces of her amphetamine diet pills, and by the time Mary was eleven, she had her own prescription. When Mary's mother said, "Don't come home till you lose weight," Mary left and stayed away for ten years.

Mary went to college, but afterward she rejected the idea, predominant at the time, that a woman should focus on buffing up her looks so she can marry well. *I'm not going to stay thin so I can marry rich and live in a colonial house like everyone else,* she thought to herself.

She was running an art gallery in Boston when an acquaintance told her that Jordan Marsh, the now-defunct department store, was looking for large-size models, and that she recommended Mary.

Mary came in just after a horrible snowstorm, wearing all white. "I'm Mary Duffy," she said.

The woman booking the models said, "Oh my god, you're beautiful."

Mary turned around to see who she was talking to.

Eventually Mary met a woman who had started what is believed to be the first plus-size modeling agency, Big Beauties, and who was looking to sell it. So in 1979, Mary bought it. With Big Beauties/Little Women—Mary added petites—Mary became one of the only women trying to make plus-size modeling *a thing.*

"It was a tiny little business when I bought it from her, and in two or three years...it went from Mary Who and Big What to 'When are you next going to be in Paris, darling?'" she told me.

Demographic trends worked in Mary's favor. In the early 1980s, baby-boomer women were graduating from college and having families, and the plus-size and petite among them had few choices. "One reason that there was such a stigma to being larger is that they were dressed in some *shmata,*" Mary said.

Having bought the agency, Mary began recruiting models. Some of the models Mary found had experienced rough upbringings and were insecure about their weight. Others were, just like standard-size models, quite privileged and full of themselves. One especially vocal subset was extremely religious. There, Mary's practicality triumphed. "We had a lot of clients who were Jewish, and I said, 'Put a lid on it, girls!'" Mary said. "You don't have to say an Our Father before every snapshot."

Mary was often her own PR woman and staged fashion shows whenever the agency needed a boost of buzz. On Fridays, Mary would sometimes serve her models champagne and pizza. To help them bond, yes—but also because some clients were slow to pay, and she needed to give their paychecks some extra time to clear.

This was before the plus-sized model Ashley Graham graced the cover of *Sports Illustrated*. This is before bootylicious and body positivity and Dove campaigns and Sir Mix-a-Lot. A lot of people, in other words, didn't get what Mary was doing. "Fat models, are you kidding me?" is a refrain she heard a lot. When Mary had open calls for models, women would show up thinking that anyone could be a plus-size model, even if they weren't pretty. And Mary's mother never did come around. When she finally garnered press coverage, Mary remembers her mother saying, "Who cares? You're on the front page for being fat."

But what I got from Mary, between all the quips and the manic stories from diamond-draped 1980s New York, is a certain sincerity that comes through when she looks back on her life.

In college and high school, she noticed that many women had low self-esteem. Women would do anything to stay attractive so they could boost their marriage prospects and lead the kind of life that was "expected" by society. Mary felt called to give them another option, to let full-figured women live a life that's unexpected, if that's what they wanted.

If she had been naturally skinny, Mary reasoned, she probably wouldn't have had much of a career—or at least, not such a significant one. This way, she made a difference. More than being thin, she said, "I wanted to make the world better for other women."

What I heard from Mary was what I heard over and over again from nonconformists: they were driven by a desire to improve the lot of others. After being picked on, marginalized, and sometimes outright insulted, they reflected their hurt feelings back as positive change. In small ways, making life better for others helped nonconformists ameliorate their own exclusion.

## VIVIENNE, PART II

As she sat in the back of the old Suburban with the gun in her hand, Vivienne began questioning her choice to end it all. A revelation pierced the clouds of her mind. Though it was true she wasn't happy, she also started to think that happiness, maybe, wasn't the point.

She was reminded of her father, who always encouraged his children to lead a "life of substance." Vivienne decided that night that her goal should be improving other people's lives. She put the gun down and called her parents to tell them where she was really living.

She took a job at an abalone farm, living in the back of a rotting building with a caved-in roof. After a few months, she re-enrolled in school. She flipped a coin to choose between majors—neuroscience or economics—and neuroscience won. Taking seven classes per quarter, she finished her degree in one year and graduated with honors.

For years after she finished college, however, something still pestered Vivienne's psyche. She continued to feel ill at ease, wracked by insomnia and social anxiety.

In 2004, she met an attractive PhD student named Norma Chang, and they fell in love and moved in together. "I have a deep, dark secret," she told Norma. "Maybe someday I'll share it."

About three years later, as they were getting ready for bed one fall evening, Vivienne said, "My secret is that I wish I were a woman." That night, Vivienne slept soundly for the first time in twenty years.

Vivienne told Norma she would only transition if Norma would stay with her; Norma was more important.

Outwardly, Norma was Vivienne's rock, but internally, she reeled. Vivienne had never given her any previous indication she longed to live as a female. But she made up her mind. "Vivienne is the one I love," Norma told *Oprah* magazine later, "the one with whom I have chosen to spend the rest of my life."

They got married, Norma in a dress and Vivienne in a tuxedo.

Vivienne changed her name from the male name she had been given as a child, and the couple mashed their last names together to form "Ming."

She and Norma went to Goodwill to buy a single dress, and that was the first time Vivienne ever existed openly in the world. Vivienne got Norma pregnant the old-fashioned way, before beginning a series of injections that would change her hormone makeup to resemble that of an adult female. She then underwent an arduous series of surgeries. Some procedures sculpted her penis into a vagina, others shaved away her strong jawline to reveal a daintier, more girlish chin.

But she stuck to her mission of shining a light on social problems. She earned a PhD in computational neuroscience and founded a series of companies focused on health and education issues, such as an app that helps parents of diabetic kids track blood sugar levels.

"I find that the world is full of problems that ought to get more attention than they do," she told me one spring day in 2018. For one of her projects, Vivienne looked at a database of millions of professional profiles to calculate "the cost of being different," as she calls it. For example, after comparing software developers named "Joe" and "José," she found that José would need a master's degree or higher to get promoted, while Joe could do it with no degree at all, she explained in the *Financial Times*. Meanwhile, female software engineers need a master's degree to compete with men who have BAs. "This translates into a tax of $100,000–$300,000 for a chance at the same career outcomes," she wrote. To help bridge this disparity, Vivienne has developed software that can help companies dig up unconventional developers, like those who don't have degrees but might be worth hiring anyway for their great work.

She seems to still suffer from a great deal of impostor syndrome. Over the course of several phone calls, she described variations on wanting to "crawl under a bed," at times. The reason she's able to cope is that she keeps her focus on her projects and the greater mission of maximizing human potential, rather than on herself.

"When people say a nasty thing to me," she says, she just thinks to herself, "it's not about me, it's about making a difference."

## ALLIE

Like the individuals who looked at their problems from an outside perspective, finding a mission larger than themselves helped non-conformists like Vivienne and Mary remain focused on their goals, rather than their insecurities.

Research supports the idea that helping others can mitigate feelings of social anxiety. In one study of people with social anxiety, a group of participants who performed random acts of kindness, such as donating to charity or mowing someone's lawn, had a greater reduction in their anxious feelings than control groups who simply interacted more socially or those who just wrote down what they did that day. The authors of that study suspected that the acts of kindness created kind of a virtuous circle: they made the outside world seem more positive to the participants, which in turn made the participants feel more inclined to interact with other people.

Finding a larger purpose is also what helped Allie Knight, a thin, red-haired thirty-two-year-old, when she was struggling as one of the less than 7 percent of truck drivers who are female.

The trucking life, for Allie, doubled as an escape from a failing marriage and dead-end job in customer service. She signed up for a trucking program in Fort Worth, Texas, passed her written test, and within a week, she was assigned to a driving trainer. For three weeks, she would share the 10-by-10-foot metal cab of an International Prostar truck with a perfect stranger. They would sleep inches from each other on bunk beds and subsist on the fast food they grabbed whenever they made a delivery.

Right away, Allie saw problems. The trainer was several decades her senior, and to her, some of his habits seemed plain wrong. He kept his empty soda cans in laundry bags, which he dangled from the ceiling of their tiny sleeping quarters. She told me that rather than take regular restroom breaks, he peed in a Welch's

White Grape Juice bottle he stowed in the bunk space. Among the man's favorite conversation topics was Jesus—specifically, how Allie should find him. Whenever she made a mistake, which since she was just starting out was often, her trainer would laugh and mock her. "Oh, this little girl thinks she can drive," she remembers him saying. (The trucking company did not return a request for comment.)

It irritated Allie that the worst clichés about male-dominated industries were coming true. Whenever her trainer launched into a rant that felt sexist, Allie would grow silent and numb. "I'm done with this conversation," she'd say. She would climb onto her tiny mattress and wait for the eighteen wheels below to rock her to sleep.

Allie briefly considered switching to a smaller type of truck—one that didn't require spending time with a trainer. But she had dreamed of driving the biggest thing possible ever since she got her driver's license at sixteen and ran her finger up the DMV form to class A—"for vehicles over 26,001 pounds." *What do I have to do to drive that thing?* she wondered. She decided to stick with it.

One freezing day in 2014, Allie was gazing out the passenger-side window of the truck when she noticed it had started snowing. As the snowflakes began their downward drift, the low winter sun waltzed between the passing trees. The scene was so beautiful, she thought if she could just share the moment with others, she could show them why trucking is a great calling, in spite of everything.

Not long after, she posted a video of herself sitting in the cab of her truck, nervously mugging for the camera in a white t-shirt and glasses. "I'm in New York, like waaaaay upstate," she told her yet-to-materialize followers in a goofy singsong. She explained that she would be posting videos from the road, and she invited her audience to tell her if they turned out to be "crap." "Or if you like it!" she added more cheerily. "If you think these are neat. If you like my voice and how terrible it sounds."

"We'll go from here, we'll see how these work," she said, waving to the camera and signing off.

They worked surprisingly well. After that day, Allie uploaded hundreds more videos to her YouTube channel, sharing tips, driver's-side views, and insights into the trucking life. The videos became Allie's larger purpose, a way of helping other new drivers navigate the same challenges she was living and working through. At one point, she reached more than sixty thousand subscribers.

Allie discovered there were quite a few other "little girls"—and Latino guys, and Asian women, and so forth—who want to drive the biggest thing on the lot. Young drivers, or those thinking about joining the industry, wrote to thank her for her honest, whimsical look inside the industry. ("Great video . . . girl has a lot of great information," read one YouTube comment.)

One young female driver wrote her to say she was about to start riding with a trainer, and she was feeling nervous. "What is it like to share a truck with a perfect stranger?" the woman asked.

"Make sure you ask questions," Allie said in her response video. "And remember, this too shall pass."

## AYINDE

A young man named Ayinde Alleyne devised another interesting strategy to cope with his fierce little sting of otherness: he changed the way he thought—and subsequently talked—about it.

Ayinde grew up in a two-bedroom apartment in the Bronx, in the Parkchester neighborhood. His father worked six days a week as an auto mechanic, and his mother was a homemaker, a teacher, and later a secretary. The income of his parents, immigrants from Trinidad and Tobago, never exceeded $30,000 a year.

Ayinde is quiet and studious. As he answered my questions, he sounded like he was in the final rounds of a high-stakes game show, taking a little pause and saying "Uh-huh," before offering his measured answer. He's always loved to push himself. As an eighth-grader, he applied to intensive high schools that would drive him, as he put it, "to be the best version of me possible." When he was accepted to an elite prep school, his advisor at a diversity-access program he attended pressed him to go. The advisor told him it would be challenging—perhaps even in ways Ayinde wouldn't be able to handle at first.

Ayinde discovered what his advisor meant in his first days at the school. He was surrounded by mostly white faces. Soon he would learn that many of those faces belonged to bodies that lived in penthouses and were ferried around by private drivers. As students do in the first days of school, they talked about how they spent their summer vacations. The other kids mentioned jaunts to Europe. Computer camp, at the very least. Ayinde's family, meanwhile, had never taken a vacation. When his turn came, he confessed that he didn't go anywhere.

"Don't your parents ever get tired of working?" he remembers the kids asking.

At first, Ayinde didn't feel frustrated, just isolated. His classmates' everyday occurrences were his distant dreams. The frustration would come later, when he began to feel that many of his classmates weren't even trying to empathize with him. Some kids complained when Ayinde received a scholarship to cover the cost of the school's $275 prom ticket, which he wouldn't have been able to afford otherwise. They would rather have seen him stay home.

Ayinde eventually found a group of fellow outcasts who welcomed him. But during his freshman and sophomore years, he found he couldn't infiltrate most cliques because he couldn't afford to take part in their shared activities—going to the Hamptons on weekends, or even buying fast food every day. He was confounded by questions like, "Where are you going to summer camp?" Like so many other outsiders, Ayinde needed a way to respond "Nowhere," without further singling himself out as the One Poor Kid.

In their book, *Extreme,* Emma Barrett and Paul Martin examined people who push the limits of human endurance—polar explorers, K2 climbers, and so forth—to figure out what bound them together. (The book's cover was blurbed by *Man vs. Wild*'s Bear Grylls, if that gives you a sense.) Here's one charming anecdote in the book from Sir Ranulph "Ran" Fiennes, who trekked across the Antarctic:

> The renewed assault from the ultraviolet burns further damaged my lips, from which blood and pus leaked into the chin cover of my face mask... The scabs always grew together overnight, and when I woke the act of tearing my lips apart (in order to speak and drink) opened up all the raw places. Breakfast consisted of porridge oats in a gravy of blood.

A major trait that helps in such grueling circumstances, Barrett and Martin write, is "hardiness," which they define as a commitment to seeing life as meaningful and interesting; a belief that you can influence events; and a tendency to view even negative events as an opportunity to grow. About half of this mental toughness is passed down from one's parents, they write, but the other half is determined by personality and environment. (And one of the most significant environmental contributors to hardiness is the presence of supportive family members and friends, just as we saw with Julia the NASCAR driver.) The hardy individuals wrote their own scripts about how well their lives were going, even when they were facing mounting setbacks and eating blood-oats.

Research shows that greater well-being and self-confidence tend to come with these so-called "redemptive" narratives, which are a way of telling yourself more edifying stories about what's happening to you. As Joan Didion put it, "We tell ourselves stories in order to live." But the *kinds* of stories you tell yourself matter. There are narratives about yourself in which your life can still get better, and there are those in which it will keep getting worse. There are stories where you are the victim, always put upon, and those where you are the hero, chopping through the brambles. There's the tale in which your boss's criticism means he hates you, and one in which he is trying to help you by being forthright. There's a reason why Drake sings, "Started from the bottom, now we're here," rather than "Didn't it suck back when I was at the bottom? I wish that had never happened." Telling a better story about yourself, both to yourself and others, can change the way you view your circumstances.

One psychologist told me that a useful tactic for constructing these positive narratives could even be to lie to yourself a little bit. If you were bullied because you were frankly kind of a loser, just tell yourself it was because the other kids were intimidated by how awesome you were. That can give you the cognitive boost of a positive story, even if the story was, in actuality, a little dispiriting.

Ayinde came up with a new story to tell about his socioeconomic status. For example, when he spent summers at home instead of at the Hamptons, he figured he at least got to spend more time with his parents. He might mine that for an uplifting anecdote if someone asked—and it would likely be too unexciting to prompt many follotrailw-ups.

I asked Ayinde to teach me how to do this. I was also too poor to go to sleepaway camp as a kid. But people in my circles can't seem to resist sharing fond memories of various expensive enrichment activities they took part in as children. One news website has a perennially popular article titled "You Are How You Camped," as though dropping five thousand dollars for your preteen to kayak is a baseline of human experience. When people ask me what I did during summers in middle school, I'm usually too embarrassed to reveal the truth, which is that I watched TV alone all day. For years, my "interesting fact" at get-to-know-you sessions was that I don't like Radiohead, the band everyone likes, simply because I had no interesting facts, because interesting facts are for rich people.

And I understand the discomfort of being on the other side of that exchange. When I lived in L.A., where college degrees are less common than in the pointy-headed media world, I sparked many an awkward silence by asking people I had just met, "Where did you go to college?" We assume people on equal footing with us had identical trajectories, and revealing the differences can be painful.

Here's Ayinde's advice for that situation: Is there anything that happened while you were home, not at camp, that was interesting or nice? Or is there something you're planning to do next summer? You could say something like, "No, I didn't get a chance to go to camp this summer, but I'm hoping to hike the Appalachian Trail after I graduate."

These types of verbal pivots allow you to create a narrative that staves off your interrogators without making you feel insecure about your differences. It's uplifting, but it's also true. And it underscores that your story is still being told.

"The past is something that you can't change," Ayinde told me. "But what you do now, you have control over."

## EMMA, PART III

One day when I was visiting my family in North Texas, I drove out to a small town near Fort Worth, where Emma Gingerich, the woman who grew up Amish, now lives.

She's now in her early thirties, has an MBA, and loves hockey and football. Her hair is dyed black and she often wears striking makeup that accentuates her absinthe green eyes. For a while after college, she thought of moving to Washington state, but Texas pulled her in, like tree roots growing over an unsuspecting stone.

There are still some elements of Amish culture that appeal to Emma. Behind her house, there's a small garden where she grows tomatoes, green beans, lettuce, eggplant, zucchini, cucumbers, and cabbage. She would love to live closer to her family so she could see her nieces and nephews grow up. But that's not an option. The visits she's paid to her family have so far been tense. When she returned home to visit six months after she left, her parents made it clear they saw a change in her. "You look like the world and you live like the world," her father said, according to Emma's memoir. When she returned another time, for her brother's wedding, none of her former friends spoke to her. She felt awkward and left early.

When I arrived at her house, Emma led me into her darkened living room. The first time I met her, years before, she seemed nervous, but now she looked sad. She told me she's had to work on her communication skills, on how to say things so that people hear her and understand her. Not just the words, but the meaning behind them.

She initially moved our interview because she had to go help her younger brother leave the Amish. It came as a surprise, as she didn't expect any of her siblings to follow in her footsteps. She wanted to help him get his learner's permit and buy some modern clothes that fit. She didn't want it to be as terrifying for him as it was for her. She wanted to protect him, she said, from "bad people."

Bad like the man who had raped her soon after her escape. And like another man who had assaulted her just a few months prior to our conversation.

Here's how she described the more recent incident. She had been considering making a career change. She got connected with a man who said he might have a job for her, and he invited her to a business meeting in another city she asked me not to name.

They were out with a group, but the man kept trying to get her alone. After the group left, one by one, to return to their hotel rooms, the man told Emma to stay and drink with him. Before long, she says, he grabbed her hand, put it against his crotch, and said, "Do you want this?"

She decidedly did not want it, but he insisted on walking her back to her hotel. He insisted on stopping by her hotel room to use the restroom. There, she says, he threatened that if she didn't stop saying "no," he would force himself on her.

Older men had determined almost every facet of Emma's life as a child; they made all the rules. A good woman, she was taught, was submissive. It was the rule, the norm. Breaking the rules meant shunning—sanctioned, systematized ostracism. Typically, people are shunned for six weeks, after which they can beg for forgiveness and, potentially, be invited back into the church. Those who don't own up to their wrongdoings might be kicked out entirely.

Emma had already been ousted from her group, though. She wasn't going to be submissive any longer.

She gathered all her strength and told the man, "Get your fucking clothes on right now and leave."

After she returned home from the business trip, she reported the man to the police. (Calls I made to the man and his lawyer were not returned.) Hit by a wave of crashing fatigue, she fell into bed and went to sleep for the first time in two days.

The next morning, she tried to get to work but found herself unable to remember the route she had driven hundreds of times before. She kept making wrong turns, and people honked at her. She called her manager in tears. "I just wanna die, this is so difficult," she sobbed. "I can't get to work, I'm going to be late, and I don't know where I'm at."

Her boss told her to go to the emergency room. There, she was diagnosed with severe anxiety and PTSD.

At this point in the interview, Emma started laughing—a nervous habit she has whenever something intensely sad happens. "It's almost like I can't handle the emotion of it or the actual feelings, the sadness," she explained.

Growing up, she wasn't supposed to reveal her emotions. Even smiling in church was frowned upon. Amish women were meek; they didn't question things. There was nothing to be protected from, so there was no need to protect yourself. "I think that, because I experienced that as my childhood, I've never been able to get away or know how to stand up for myself and fight back versus just try to please," she said. Despite the agony she felt after the horrible balloon procedure, she told her parents it was helping her, because that's what she felt like they wanted to hear.

The hardest part of not being Amish has been learning how to be less of a people-pleaser. "I have learned to take care of myself first and not worry about how the other person's going to feel," she said. "That has been absolutely the hardest struggle for me."

During our last interview, Emma told me she had been dating off and on. She would try to find men who were career-oriented, but nice; who were dominant, but who would respect her boundaries. Some of the men she met made jabs at her Amish background in ways she found uncomfortable—much like making fun of your sibling and having your sibling made fun of are two very different things. "I don't want somebody who, before you even meet me, you already have this idea of what my life was like, when you don't," she explained to me. She is the Amish girl who left...but she is not *just* the Amish girl who left.

Ultimately, Emma decided to take control of her story. She would be direct about her situation with new men she met, and not let them project their own ideas onto her. She came up with her own redemptive narrative. With one guy she was on a date with recently, she decided to lay everything out right away. "I was raised Amish," she told him. But then she quickly pivoted to how her background made her who she is. "Today I am very driven," she told him. "I'm focused on what I want in my life, and I don't let the past hold me back."

"And it actually worked," she told me, a smile sneaking across her serious face.

He wasn't like the others. He heard her.

# CHAPTER 11

# Change Yourself

## CURT

You wouldn't immediately notice Curt's arm, but if you did, it might prompt a double take. As a result of a birth injury, it's slightly shortened and slightly pink. It's not much of a physical limitation: he can cook gourmet dinners, drive, and sail. But our arms are right there; you can't help but see them. It's not a major difference, but it's enough of one. His arm is not the only reason Curt grew up feeling shy and self-conscious, but it contributed.

Curt was raised in Indiana in a conservative, Baptist home—the "earth-is-only-four-thousand-years-old kind," he says—and he was homeschooled for a few years before being placed into a private Christian school that had thirty kids per grade. When everyone entered the awkward morass of middle school, his was more awkward than most. Suddenly, the easy comity of early childhood morphed into something more fraught and punishing. He remembers his two best friends, who were both named Evan, both inexplicably ending their friendship with him at the same time. Once, when he overheard a girl talking about an upcoming Halloween party, she turned to him and said, "Just in case you heard that, you're not invited."

In order to improve his college prospects, Curt convinced his parents to allow him to transfer to a large public high school. The problem there, however, was that most people in his class of 450 students already knew each other, and Curt had never met so many new people at once. This giant group of teenagers did as teenagers do: they were extremely body conscious, they weren't accustomed to the look of Curt's arm, and they weren't tactful in how they asked about it. Rumors circulated that Curt had polio. One boy sidled up to him in the middle of class and asked, "So what's up with your hand? Is it just totally dead and withered or what?" A girl once accidentally bumped into his arm, then ran out of the room crying. At senior prom, his date ditched him for another boy. Curt ended up going to church a lot and playing *Counter-Strike* by himself.

When it was time for college, Curt earned a scholarship to nearby Purdue University, but when he visited, he found himself too intimidated by the frat houses and jocks. *I'm not gonna fit in again,* he thought. *This is going to be a repeat of high school.*

Then he visited a much smaller, private engineering college, where he met a bunch of nerdy kids building a giant air cannon. *Those* were his people. *Everybody here is a weirdo,* he thought. It would be easier, he decided, to fit in with a bunch of kids who didn't fit in anywhere themselves.

Curt was right. He joined the other computer nerds, rarely going to parties but drinking in his dorm room plenty. (He had shed his Baptist beliefs at that point.) The mostly male campus was so unconcerned about appearances and popularity, in fact, that its hygiene levels were among the most horrific Curt had ever seen. At one point, the situation became so fragrant that the students were given tokens that said "Take a shower" and "Do your laundry" to hand to one another. (This little factoid is in part why Curt asked me not to name the school.)

Curt found that in this quirky, geeky utopia, he was no longer "the smart kid." Unlike in high school, many students were more scientifically gifted than he was, but they tended to be socially awkward. Curt decided that in order to distinguish himself, he would try to craft a new identity as a naturally sociable extrovert.

"I always thought people who were outgoing were happier," he told me. "They seem like they're having more fun. I wanted to be that person, and I'm painfully logical, so I thought, 'I'll make myself do it.'"

First, he wanted something he could tell random strangers who asked about his arm, so he made up a story that sounded much cooler than the birth injury he had actually suffered. The new story involved a pit bull and chair throwing, and he made sure to tell it so bombastically that no one would question its veracity.

Then, he began committing himself to things he didn't really want to do, but which would push him to be more extroverted. He decided to study abroad in Japan, a decision he was terrified by. Every time he thought about backing out, he reminded himself that the deposit was already spent.

Not long after, he signed up to give a presentation before an audience of four hundred, then began convincing himself he loved speaking in front of other people. Whenever fear flooded his mind, he would tell himself, *"You love public speaking, remember?"*

Somehow, this strategy cured Curt of his shyness. He still finds prolonged social interactions to be slightly exhausting, but he now regularly gives talks for his job as a computer scientist.

Years ago, before he got married, he decided to join some online dating apps, despite his occasional fear that he wasn't very "dateable." He made a joke about his arm in his dating profile: "If the ability to do the monkey bars is one of your criteria for a potential partner, you should probably pass me up." Some women didn't even notice it until the second date.

Curt would also make an effort to go out by himself and meet new people—typically every introvert's nightmare. He would find a bar that's slow, then talk to the bartender. One time, the bartender's friends came in, and he wound up hanging out with them all night. These solo journeys are how he's ended up, on occasion, at house parties with complete strangers, the belle of a ball he didn't even know about when the evening began.

Curt acknowledges that this strategy of melting down your personality like chocolate and remodeling it into a soaring new centerpiece...might not work for everyone. But if people want to change something about themselves and are willing to try, he thinks they should. "I was totally uncomfortable," he said, "until I suddenly wasn't."

Hippocrates, the Greek physician and namesake of the "oath," believed that people's personalities were governed by the amounts of phlegm, blood, black bile, and yellow bile that flowed through their bodies. Depending on the levels of these fluids, people could be classified as melancholic, or anxious introverts; phlegmatic, or relaxed introverts; sanguine, or relaxed extroverts; and choleric, or anxious extroverts. Notions of bile and humors, of course, have long since been discarded by modern science. And now, as the psychologist Richard Wiseman put it in his book *The As If Principle,* it appears the idea that our personalities are immutably biologically programmed is also not quite true. The book's title comes from the idea that you can behave "as if" you are the person you want to be. Pretty soon, you might find that it *is* you. This means that if you're an introvert—or disorganized, or not punctual, or quick to judgment—you don't have to stay that way forever.

Of course, not all people who are different should or can change their personalities. They should not have to contend with discrimination, no matter what their disposition is like. But while we work at ending prejudice, we can also be living the lives that we want. In some cases, like Curt's, a personality change can be helpful, especially when the change leads to more friendships and social connections, rather than further isolation.

Few people are as ready and willing to transform their entire personalities as Curt was. But research suggests that personalities are fairly flexible, and for those who are interested in changing themselves, change is not only possible, it can happen rather quickly.

Many researchers have now found that adults can change the five traits that make up personality: extroversion, openness to experience, emotional stability, agreeableness, and conscientiousness. Changing a trait primarily requires acting in ways that embody that trait, just as Curt did, rather than simply thinking about it. For example, in one study, putting more effort into homework led students to become more conscientious—a reversal of the popular idea that conscientious students put more effort into their homework.

A personality change can occur across a variety of other domains and ages. Gigi Vorgan, coauthor of the book *Snap!: Change Your Personality in 30 Days,* gives the example of an elderly couple in which the wife, Audrey, wants to move across the country, but the husband, Howard, isn't sure about the idea. Howard could start using strategies to slowly increase his level of "openness," such as going to a new restaurant. "Ideally, with time, these improved behaviors and thinking patterns will transition into new habits," Vorgan told the *Wall Street Journal.*

George Kelly, a prominent 1950s psychologist, helped his clients change by asking them to perform "roles" that represented new personality traits. A person who wanted to be more extroverted might, like Curt did, sign up to speak in front of people or go to bars to talk to strangers. After a few weeks, many people began to think of the roles as their real selves. "Many of Kelly's clients reported that the new role seemed as though it had always been their real self and that it was only now that they were becoming fully aware of it," Wiseman writes.

Geraldine Downey, a Columbia psychologist who studies social rejection, has found that socially excluded people who want to become part of a group are better off if they assume that other people will like them. They should behave *as if* they are the popular kid. Going into social interactions expecting the worst—as I and many other weird kids often did—tends to be a self-fulfilling prophecy.

In one study, people were able to become more extroverted or conscientious over the course of four months just by listing the ways they'd like to change and what steps they would take to get there. So, someone who wanted to become more extroverted might write down, "Call Andrew and ask him to lunch on Tuesday." After enough lunches with Andrew (and presumably with others, too), people became the extroverts they hoped to be.

Therapy can help with this process. Take neuroticism, a trait responsible for anxiety and rumination. Neuroticism tends to decline naturally with age. But one review of studies found that a month of therapy—any kind of therapy—reduced neuroticism by about half the amount you might expect to see it naturally decline over the course of your entire life. Bizarrely, even psychoanalytic therapists—who generally think personality is set in childhood— were able to help people change their personalities. The individuals' personalities remained different for at least a year after the therapy took place.

After neuroticism, extroversion was the next most changeable personality trait, according to this research. Coincidentally, neuroticism and extroversion are the two factors that play a major role in the kind of social anxiety Curt and others experienced. Change those two elements of personality, and you can extinguish much of your self-doubt.

Brent Roberts, a psychologist at the University of Illinois at Urbana-Champaign and the lead author on that review of studies, was himself a little surprised that such a short burst of therapy could have such dramatic effects. He thinks it might be that when a person reaches their nadir and realizes they want to change, there's something beneficial about having a warm, comforting presence there to support them. "[The therapist] sends an unambiguous message to you that you're a valued person," he said. Having someone in our corner, even if it's because we pay them by the fifty-minute hour, appears to be one of the reasons therapy works. "Change is hard," Roberts said. "It takes work, but it can happen."


TODD, PART II

One way to revamp your social life is to simply make more friends. Hardened introverts might be relieved to know that there's a ceiling to how many friends you can really have. "Dunbar's number" is the amount of individuals that can realistically make up a social group—about 150, in the view of its namesake, the British anthropologist Robin Dunbar. That's roughly how many casual friends, whom you see at least once a year, a person can maintain. But within that are concentric circles of bros, homies, and confidants. The innermost circle is a pack of three to five very best friends and family members. Then there's a "sympathy group" of about twelve to fifteen, who wouldn't necessarily give you a kidney, but would give you a lift to the airport.

But for many people, it's reaching anything close to this number, not exceeding it, that's the true problem. Making friends requires self-disclosure—revealing morsels about yourself, not just small talk—and time. (Indeed, people who engage in small talk—conversations about the news, pets, or sports—actually grow less close over time, one study by University of Kansas professor Jeffrey Hall found.) However, neither soul-baring honesty nor free time is an especially plentiful commodity these days.

Hall has found it takes about eighty to a hundred hours to turn an acquaintance into a real friend, and more than two hundred hours to really wriggle your way into someone's "sympathy group." Even the least intimate type of friendship, "casual" friendship, only formed after forty to sixty hours spent together. In other words, friendship requires the equivalent of working several weeks at a full-time job. Perhaps the reason we hear more about "best friends" from children, rather than adults, is that children simply have more time on their hands.

But still, it's worth making an effort to expand your circle of support. For a look at why, we turn back to Todd, the tech worker who admitted to having no friends.

About three years after our initial phone call, I reconnected with Todd, whom we met at the very beginning of this book. He told me that the last time we spoke, he was happy to be largely friendless. But very soon after our call, his life of lonely self-reliance began to crumble.

Todd was never starved for human contact, exactly. He was married with a son. In fact, romantic relationships were about the only kind that came easily to him. After a largely celibate high school experience, in college he found he could get girlfriends relatively easily. The girlfriends, then, were the source of his friendships: when he was dating someone, he would just hang out with her friends. Between relationships, there was "lots of alone time," he said. He learned bartending and got into photography. But because of the lack of companionship in his life, he dealt with stress primarily by reaching out to women. Women who weren't his wife.

When his job got frustrating, Todd had few people to turn to. If he had an especially bad day at work, he would text a female friend and go to a long lunch or early happy hour with her. His wife, meanwhile, became more like a roommate to him, and their marriage began to deaden. Mostly, Todd engaged in what people call "emotional cheating." The unspoken deal was that he would provide emotional support for his female friends, and they would flirt with him and make him feel desirable. After these get-togethers, they would exchange racy pictures or sext each other. And he did have one actual affair.

"It was not actually solving any problems," he told me. "It was pushing them into the future."

When his wife found out about the affair, Todd thought she was going to kick him out. While they tried to mend the relationship, Todd realized something. His wife had lots of friends who were calling her every day to check on her. Meanwhile, he had literally no one. The women he had so relied upon to make himself feel better had ghosted when he needed them most.

Todd found himself in therapy, which drove home the point that he really needed to make platonic friends. Like Curt, he decided to change his personality so he could be happier in the world.

He opted to take a four-year-old's approach, in which you stumble upon random life-forms and ask outright to be their friend. Except Todd was nearly forty. When a former colleague moved to his city from across the country, Todd invited him and his wife out for dinner. The man agreed, and on the winds of this success Todd decided to forge ahead with his new life of companionship.

The hardest part, Todd said, was "having any idea what the fuck to do with the person at all. I hadn't gone out with people in a non-romantic way in my adult life."

He considered taking them to the driving range, but he had never played golf. Taking a cue from some sitcoms he'd seen, he'd ask people to get coffee. He realized there was a guy he had chatted with casually in church a few times, and he asked him out for drinks. Now they get drinks every Thursday.

Along the way, he had some surprising insights about friendship conventions—the kinds of breakthroughs you have when you're performing an otherwise ordinary human skill for the first time in four decades. For example, if you invited someone to do something one time, and they don't invite you back for a while, it's okay to invite them again. In other words, just because you don't alternate the role of initiator doesn't mean you aren't really friends. Todd realized that in the past, he had let a lot of friendships lapse simply because he made plans twice in a row, and he figured he shouldn't make the effort a third time.

He also had to find a balance between seeing people in person and keeping in touch between in-person get-togethers—something I immediately realized I myself completely don't do. "Like how often do people spend time with friends, and how often do they contact their friends, and what do they contact them about?" he asked me. (It was rhetorical, but I had literally no idea. When my friends call me I assume someone has died, and I spend the phone call getting progressively more confused about the purpose of the call as it slowly dawns on me that there has been no death, and they are simply in line at Trader Joe's.) But this seems like an important element of friendship. In his study, Hall found that "keeping abreast of friends' daily lives by catclehing up and joking around" brings friends closer together, even if they don't spend extra time with one another.

Todd created a reminder on his phone that says, "Text a guy friend and ask them how their day is," which sounds like something a serial killer would do, but frankly, it has worked for Todd. "I'm learning to be a human being," Todd explained.

He estimates he now has about five or six "good friends," up from maybe one a few years ago. It's not quite Dunbar's number, but he considers it a clear improvement on his life before. When he's struggling with a friendship situation, he asks his wife, a true social butterfly, for advice.

Within these friendships, he's deviated from his past role as an amateur anthropologist. He opens up on occasion. Once, a new friend, a fellow dad from his son's daycare, told Todd, "I'm sorry if I'm off, but my wife and I are having problems."

"So I told him what went on in my marriage," Todd said. "That meant a lot to him, and we built a friendship off of these wonderful conversations."

The near-divorce from his wife is the thing that pushed Todd to finally take the friend-making plunge, he thinks. In high school, he could easily avoid connecting with other people because he could always go home and play video games. But, he realized, "If I don't suck it up and find some positive method of dealing with all my needs...I am only going to be able to see my son on alternating weekends."

When he first explained that, I thought it sounded a little calculating. How would his friends feel, knowing they were the only things standing between him, his wife, and a divorce lawyer? But friendship can be so difficult, and so time-consuming, that maybe this is just what the initial stage looks like: admitting human connection is something you need, like vegetables and water, because it's good for you. Eventually, you come to like it. Or maybe even to crave it.

The first time I picked my skin until I bled, I was eight or nine, in some horrible after-school center, feeling left out and not sure how to fix the situation. Instead, I grabbed hold of my cuticle and tugged it with the full force of my resentment. When the blood came, it startled me, but it also gave me something to do. *I can't talk right now, I have to go ask for a Band-Aid.* No one wanted to talk to me anyway, but they couldn't have even if they wanted to, since I had an emergency on my hands. Literally.

I've done this same thing, mostly subconsciously, ever since. I do it mostly when I'm feeling anxious, but some days I seem to be in a constant state of having just picked, picking, or about to pick my skin. I usually only realize it has happened when I feel a warm trickle next to my nail bed or look down and see red finger-prints on my computer keyboard. Many of my shirts have crimson streaks near the hems, evidence of where I've pulled them on or off my body with my mangled fingers.

I realize the irony: when I feel uncomfortable in my skin, I peel it away. I've come to realize the embarrassment of picking doesn't dissuade me from doing it. Instead, it creates an excuse, a reason why things didn't go the way they should have. It wasn't my fault, I can say to myself. I was bleeding. Who can function when they're bleeding?

When my boyfriend picked me up from visiting Deana, I told him to drive me straight to the emergency room. My thumb was oozing, and I could no longer ignore the pain.

At two in the morning, I was seen by a doctor who gave me a handout that told me to try to reduce my anxiety. Several more doctors' visits later, I was diagnosed with both a viral and staph in-fection. It took months to clear up.

As my thumb healed, I decided to try to make some personality changes of my own, through a social-anxiety app I had heard about called Joyable. The hope was that it would help me stop picking my skin, but also more generally help me feel calmer and more confident. I was ready, in short, to be free of the feeling that I was the worst person alive, and that everyone would soon discover this.

The app involved setting goals and doing experiments that would be likely to provoke anxiety. Then I would process how the experiments made me feel both through the app and through weekly calls with the not-a-licensed-therapist that Joyable assigned to me, whom I'll call Chloe.

The first step was an introductory call with Chloe, who had a voice so soothing it will one day be implanted in robot nannies, once those get advanced enough. Before she said anything, Chloe would ask me if it's okay, as in, "If it's okay with you, can I share a tip that might help?"

Chloe told me that everyone experiences social anxiety; it's what makes us human. I told her about the specific elements of my anxiety I'd like to change. I would like to dwell less on whether I've said something that might have sounded dumb, to feel more relaxed about certain work situations, and to not get as upset when I feel socially excluded. I would also like to let up on my poor thumbs.

The early exercises went something like this: I would put forth an anxious thought, or "cognitive distortion." ("X person hates me," or the like.) Then I'd have to come up with a thought that was more realistic than that one. ("They were just busy, that's why they were short with me.") I told Chloe that I do this all the time, even without Joyable. The problem is that I never believe the replacement thought. You can't lie to yourself if you're not a very good liar.

The key, she said, was to come up with an alternate thought that's more believable. So, something like, "Maybe they *were* annoyed with me, but they still like me."

This entire process is codified in what Joyable calls the "three Cs"—catch the thought that's making you anxious, check that thought, and change the thought to something that's "more accurate," which is likely to be something less anxiety-inducing.

Once, Chloe asked me how I would remember my new, less anxious thought, and when I said I had no idea, she told me to write a note to myself on a sticky note on my computer.

"Chloe," I said, "if I wrote 'So-and-so likes me' on my computer, and so-and-so sees it, so-and-so would probably stop liking me."

That made Chloe laugh hard. (See, how could anyone not like me?!) She told me just to write something a little more ambiguous, someplace more private. I liked the phrase she suggested—"Look for the gray areas"—and I wrote it on my whiteboard at home. Perhaps it was my brief dalliance with religion, but I liked having a reassuring truth to look to every day.

I found that my scheduled calls with Chloe would often occur at unexpectedly helpful times. Once, for example, she called right after a source had yelled at me for attempting to get the other side of a story. It's a necessary and standard part of any journalist's job, but not one that always sits well with our sources, who sometimes want us to take their perspective at face value.

When Chloe asked if there were any cognitive distortions I was applying to the interaction, I explained that the source had actually been upset with me—it's not like I imagined it.

There was a long pause.

"Would it be okay if I offered a suggestion?" Chloe asked.

"Sure," I said.

"You're personalizing this," she said. "You're making this about you, not the situation."

She had a good point. I was just doing my job. I'm (fortunately) far from the only journalist who has ever had to get both sides of a story. But I hadn't considered that not everything unpleasant that happens in the world is my personal fault. It was a comforting resolution, at least for that day.

Joyable, I realized, was mostly a process of filing your anxious thoughts into different thought folders, where they may still exist, but at least they'll be organized. This one is personalizing the situation, that one is black-or-white thinking. I wasn't sure if it was working yet, but at the very least, it was nice to tell someone about the random, petty things that come up in my day—even an unlicensed therapist.

Eventually, the week came when I was to do a "challenge" out in the world. I chose the challenge of going to a networking happy hour—an experience that makes me itch with nervousness—and to do so without drinking, my usual crutch when talking with large groups of new people.

I came, I had Diet Coke, I conquered—sort of. In truth, it was a little tedious. The shop talk was dull, the personal-brand management was tense, and I felt even less agreeable about it all than I normally do.

Afterward, though, I felt a little proud. I often suffer from the common writer's fallacy that every life experience should be impeccably amusing. We only watch the best TV shows and read the best books and go to the best parties. We only leave the house because we're expected to be somewhere or so we can brag about being there later. But some things are just kind of boring, and networking is one of them. If I had been drinking, it would have only slightly dulled the pain, anyway.

When Chloe called, I told her about this minor victory. She congratulated me and asked me how I did it.

I explained that I had approached the evening as an experiment—*Would I be able to survive this social interaction sober?*—and wondered aloud to her if it was a good idea to game-ify my awkwardness in this way.

"Maybe," she said, "this is a first step."

The app was not always a panacea. A few months into my time with Joyable, someone close to me said something really awful to me. I can't revisit it here, but it happened just before Chloe was scheduled to call, and I mentioned it to her. Though she offered some good, alternate ways to think about the situation, her tips didn't really work that time. The wound was too deep. My brain felt like a runaway train; there was nothing I could do to steady it on its tracks.

I told Chloe that my boyfriend naturally takes criticism in the Joyable-approved way. "When you criticize him, he seems to say, 'That's interesting! I'll assess your viewpoint along with all the other evidence,'" I said.

She laughed again. "That's rare, though," she said.

Toward the very end of my time with Joyable, I noticed some small changes in myself. I began to recognize the Joyable cognitive distortions in other people, and was occasionally able to help them calm down. Once, I could tell a friend was exaggerating how bleak a situation was simply because she, herself, was feeling extremely anxious about it. In reality, the strength of our emotions doesn't necessarily reflect the force of an event. I was able to gently talk my friend down, the way Chloe would reassure me.

I took an assessment at the beginning and end of my time with Joyable, and though my use of "avoidance" actions—like procrastinating or skin picking—got better, my "spin" score—how socially anxious I felt—remained basically the same. Of course, it's probably too much to expect all your anxious thoughts to be KonMari-ed into neat little triangles of reframed uplift within just a few months. Like a messy sock drawer, social anxiety was still going to happen to me on occasion. But I was grateful to learn some tools for managing it, both through Joyable and through some of the strategies employed by the people in this book. The emotional troughs seem less deep when you know others have climbed out of them, and that you might one day, too.

# PART FOUR

# TO STAY DIFFERENT, OR TO FIND YOUR OWN KIND?

# CHAPTER 12

# Staying

Michael Ain, the surgeon with dwarfism, specialized in surgery on children of short stature, fusing spines and straightening bowed legs under the round glare of an operating light. But there's one kind of surgery he avoided doing if patients' only complaint was their height: limb lengthening, the controversial procedure in which the bones are broken and spaced apart so they grow back longer. "Listen," Michael would tell children of short stature, in his thick Long Island accent. "This is the way God blessed you, and you need to make the most of it."

When he was twelve, Michael declined to get the operation himself. Why go through the pain, the risk, the months lost to recovery, he thought, just to be a few inches taller?

Michael's take on the surgery highlights an interesting distinction between Little People in the United States and those in other countries. One 2012 study, for instance, compared the experience of Little People in Spain to that of Little People in the U.S. In Spain, Little People's support organizations are relatively newer and more supportive of limb-lengthening surgery. The main Spanish organization in the study even promoted finding a medical "solution" to achondroplasia, a condition that causes dwarfism. In America, meanwhile, support groups tended to celebrate the identity of Little People and work to abolish things like "midget wrestling." "[The American nonprofit] organizes a large annual conference with the aim of increasing contact among individuals with dwarfism," the study authors write, "while [the Spanish group] organizes more technical conferences with medical experts to assist affected individuals and their families."

Accordingly, limb-lengthening surgery was more popular among the Spanish Little People, according to the study. In the U.S., meanwhile, Little People drew their strength from being around other Little People—who, for the most part, hadn't had the surgery.

In Spain, the authors theorized, Little People are viewed more like what researchers call "deviants," or outsiders who don't join forces with their own kind, preferring instead to try to integrate into the larger population. In the U.S., meanwhile, Little People are more like "classical minorities"—outsiders who proudly link arms with others in their group to fight off discrimination from the broader world. It's not just Little People that make this choice: Some deaf people learn sign language; others get cochlear implants. Some overweight people love their size; others labor desperately to lose weight.

Both paths—uniting with other outsiders or going your own way—are equally valid, and which to pursue is a matter of individual preference. The psychologist Nyla Branscombe and her colleagues write that a more independent coping strategy—say, getting limb-lengthening surgery—might help the individual, but it doesn't really help the marginalized group they're part of. Drawing closer to the stigmatized group, meanwhile, might ultimately help the group, but in the process, it could attract even more discrimination and hostility to the individual.

However, as Branscombe and the other authors of the limb-lengthening study point out, it's easier to have a positive self-concept as a Little Person if you rally around fellow Little People, rather than get the surgery. "When the option of concealing the dwarfing condition prevails, it may be rather difficult for the affected young person to develop a positive self-concept as a person with dwarfism," they write, "especially if he or she knows that most of the people like him/her conceal the stigmatized characteristic through a long and arduous surgical process." It's hard to feel good about something you're trying to hide.

Michael, for what it's worth, has no shame about his height. In fact, it infuriates him that it's considered socially acceptable to ridicule someone because of their stature. The m-word, midget, "curls the back of my hair," he told me. He'd rather see society change than change himself. (He once went so far as to reprimand a seven-year-old who stared at him in an airport.)

As I interviewed different types of outsiders, it became clear that many had grappled with the decision of whether to try to blend in, or whether to stay noticeably different. As the Little People of America activist Colleen Gioffreda put it to the Associated Press in 2001, in voicing opposition to limb-lengthening surgery, "Do you just go along with the crowd or teach people difference is okay?"

She seemed to have meant it rhetorically, but it's an important choice, with major ramifications for a person's identity.

The one time I had a chance to join forces with another Russian in childhood, I passed, fearing the stigma of belonging to a weird group would be worse than being without a group at all. In seventh grade, I briefly attended a Dallas-area middle school that had the social dynamics of an overcrowded prison. At one point, we got a kid directly from Russia. I discovered this in gym class, when some of the popular kids began relentlessly teasing a round boy with a heavy accent.

The boy—whom I'll call Feodogroup r, because I don't remember his name—had come over with his family just a few months prior. He spoke in broken English, and I rarely saw him during the day because he was in the regular classes while I was in "pre-AP" with the rest of the nerds. Gym, though, was the grand bazaar, the place where all the kids were pelted equally with harassment and dodgeballs, regardless of class or creed.

While the teacher was taking attendance, Feodor slid his polyester-clad thighs a few inches in my direction. We commenced what I can only imagine is the conversation covert CIA agents have when they encounter each other in the field.

"Olga?" he whispered in our shared mother tongue. "Are you Russian?"

"Shut up!" I hissed in English. "Of course I am."

He made entreaties toward friendship, and I considered it. It could be nice, this, uh, Soviet union. I'd finally have someone to sit with at lunch. Though I was not the thirteen-year-old version of sexually attracted to him, I could have made him my boyfriend—thus leveling up to the clique of "ugly girls with boyfriends," who had so far rejected me for failing to meet their terms of membership.

But Feodor and I would need at least one other person to form a proper middle school posse. And who would we recruit? The Chinese girls had already made it clear they wanted nothing to do with me, and that was, realistically, the next most welcoming immigrant group. There was one Iranian kid, but he wore acid-washed jeans, and it was not one of the two fashion eras during which that was acceptable (early 1990s and 2010s). No, I thought. I had already shimmied one rung up the ladder and dug in my nails. There was no way I was slipping back down.

*God be with you, Feodor,* I thought. For the rest of the year, I ignored him.

I didn't meet many Russians my age until fourteen years later, when I was at an outdoor concert in Silver Spring, Maryland, and was introduced by some friends to a compact Jewish man wearing a polo shirt. I had interacted with so few Russians in my life that when he told me his name, I almost didn't understand him. "Anka?" I asked.

Only later did I realize he was saying the Americanized version of the word Russians pronounce Ahn-TOHN, like a big, radioactive kick drum.

Anton and I learned we had both come over as children. We both had Jewish fathers and *shiksa* moms—all the guilt and none of the praise. We both had siblings that were ten years younger and born in the U.S. We both grew up with few other Russians around.

A few weeks after the concert, Anton invited me to happy hour, and all we talked about was being Russian in the U.S. Anton had made Russian friends before, but for me, he was like a gulp of cold water after a life of wandering in the desert.w

I couldn't help but compare notes with him. "Does your dad think there are no gay people in Russia?" I asked.

"Yes!" he said. "Did you ever pretend you were from some other country because pretty much anywhere sounds better to Americans than Russia?"

"Oh my *god* yes," I said. We carried on this way, as though on an especially strange Tinder date, for hours. The process was so emotionally overwhelming that when we left the bar, he forgot his briefcase.

For a while, I thought my rapport with Anton meant it was time to make more Russian-American friends, and to try to become more Russian, in general. There are now nearly a million of us here in America, after all. I thought maybe that together, we could sift through all the baggage of our lives and make sense of what it means to be "us." I wanted to determine whether I should try to fight my way back into the Russian tribe or just accept the fact that I was just like any other American, and would probably remain that way forever.

But when I met up with other Russians, I was surprised at how little we had in common. When I first moved to L.A., I lived next to a house full of recent Eastern European immigrants who all clung together in a cologne-drenched gang. But because my Russian is so rusty and they didn't obsessively listen to Slate podcasts, I didn't have much to talk with them about.

Years later, I had dinner with one woman—ironically also named Olga—who was extremely nice and smart. But she grew up in L.A., which has a large Russian population. When I dropped hints about my fish-out-of-water trauma, she didn't pick them up. To her, being Russian was cool, being "Olga" was cool. She seemed to consider the topic as banal as a long discussion about oatmeal varietals. When the waitress came to collect our check, she looked at the names on our credit cards and asked if we were playing a prank on her.

I even went to Russia a few years ago without my parents in

an attempt to learn more about my identity. I felt anything but at home. My vocabulary had degraded so much I accidentally dropped some swear words in a fancy bakery and struggled to explain to a family friend why I couldn't come to his house. At one point, I ducked into a bar near my childhood home, wiping away tears of frustration and ordering in English.

Certain elements of Russian culture have, at times, made me wary of espousing my nationality. Not long ago, I interviewed a group of Russian conservatives. They were a boisterous group who generously allowed me to observe their political arguments before hugging it out over an enormous meal. One of them asked me to date her son.

But I felt unsettled by my encounter with one of them in particular. In the middle of the interview, the woman went on a long, racist tirade. At one point, she brought her beloved cat into the room and placed him on the couch, where he began proudly licking his genitals. As I grew hotter and increasingly tired and uncomfortable, she grew more opinionated about "ze blyecks." The cat, meanwhile, more aggressively licked his own gonads. I cut the interview short, desperate to get some air. *How is it that someone who is supposed to be so close to me culturally,* I thought, *could be so incredibly far?*

Ultimately, Anton and I chose slightly different tribes. He married a smart young consultant who moved to the U.S. from Moscow just a few years ago. My partner, meanwhile, is a man whose family has been in the U.S. since the 1600s.

I've stopped trying to befriend people just because they're Russian. To assume we'll relate is to compress foreigners' personalities to a caricature—the offense for which I had always resented certain Americans. I might return to Russia again, but if I do I'll probably speak English.

When, for another story, I interviewed the president of HIAS, the refugee aid society that brought my family to the U.S., I surprised myself by awkwardly prefacing our conversation with a "thank you." I was grateful that HIAS had brought us here. I was—dare I say—*proud to be an American.* I've been an American almost my whole life, and no matter how much I dabble in Russian culture, I'm going to remain one for good.

## ROBERT

Social psychology is one of the most left-leaning professions in the United States. Studies and polls put the number of right-of-center social psychologists at around 6 percent, at most. Robert Mather, an assistant dean and professor of psychology at the University of Central Oklahoma, is, therefore, one of the few conservative social psychologists on earth.

Robert grew up in Chickasha, Oklahoma, the son of two college professors. His parents were both Republicans and he also became one, absorbing the ambient conservatism around him. His neighbors were Republican, Oklahoma was Republican, and when he arrived at Westminster College, a private school in central Missouri, he found it was predominantly Republican, too. He liked the party's emphasis on fiscal responsibility and reduced government regulation.

It was when he decided to pursue social psychology in grad school that he realized his classes were suddenly devoid of conservatives, even at the University of Central Oklahoma. His professors were also liberal, but Robert didn't let on that he disagreed with them. "That would have been career suicide," he said.

Robert went on to earn his PhD at Texas Tech University in Lubbock, Texas, and there, too, he stood out. One day, he was wearing a "College Republicans" t-shirt he had left over from his undergrad days. Another student saw him and said, "That's hilarious, that's an awesome joke." Some classes devolved into mass trashings of Ronald Reagan or George H. W. Bush. Once, he says, a fellow grad student sent out an email to the entire department—who were all Texas state employees—suggesting that everyone go watch the rabidly liberal Michael Moore film *Fahrenheit 9/11* together.

Robert thinks there are so few conservatives in the field because the topics social psychologists study—racism, discrimination, and the like—tend to be liberal topics, and conservative approaches to studies are often shut down by the liberal majority in the field. He worked on one study that sought to explore why whites were more likely than African Americans to get fatally hit by a car during the daytime, while African Americans were more likely than whites to be fatally struck by cars at night. Robert's study, which used a driving simulation, found this is because of the visual contrast between a person's skin tone and their surroundings, not because of racial bias. When he submitted the paper to journals, "I've never gotten reviews back that were so angry," he told me. "They said it was a dangerous idea." (Indeed, research also suggests that conservative psychologists, few though they might be, believe their field is hostile to their views. And in some cases, they're right: close to 38 percent of social psychologists admit to being reluctant to choose a conservative future colleague.)

Robert gets emails from people looking for conservative therapists, as well as messages from right-leaning faculty on other campuses searching for a friendly ear. "A combination of extremists and people who don't have a voice," he calls them.

But he has no intention of leaving either social psychology or the Republican Party. Lately, Robert's approach to comments about "evil Republicans" has largely been to ignore them. In his grad school days, he spoke out a few times, but his desire to do that has ebbed. "Committee meetings drag on anyway, and if we fight about things that don't matter, we'll be there forever," he said.

He's well liked in his field; he stays that way because, he says, he "keeps politics out of everything." He likes liberals—how self-reflective and compassionate they are—and seems reluctant to offend them.

That's despite the fact that now, there's a big, loud elephant in the room: Trump. The morning after the 2016 election, one of Robert's colleagues came in to Robert's office, closed the door, and said, "It's happening. The Nazis are taking over. I can't fathom how anyone would vote for this person—all these racists!"

"Wait." The man paused. "Who did you vote for?" he asked

Robert.

Robert responded that he voted for Trump.

The man left without saying another word.

It might have been the right thing to do, Robert says. He has liberal relatives, but they simply don't argue about politics when they get together.

Robert's abstention from political talk is shrewd, in a way. People assume he's liberal; they assume he's one of them. Why disturb that notion unless absolutely necessary? I don't usually tell people I'm Russian unless they demand to know. If you're getting away with being weird, why ruin it for yourself?

Robert and I both decided to remain surrounded by people different from us. But some people just don't wish to cope with the daily discomfort of being weird. For them, seeking out their own tribe is the only way forward.

# CHAPTER 13

# Leaving

In May of 2018, I returned to McKinney, the Dallas suburb where I attended high school, to meet with a man who left home in order to be with people who *are* just like him. The previous year, Paul Chabot had moved to McKinney from California, his home, to be among like-minded Republicans. And now, he was encouraging other people to do the same thing, through an organization he founded called Conservative Move.

Conservative Move is situated near a subdivision whose McMansions are so polished, they make other suburbs look like the Fyre Festival. There's no ocean nearby. There aren't snow-capped mountains to hike. If you like Ethiopian food, you're in for at least a half-hour drive. But if you want to live in a safe, cloistered polworld, with masterful wainscoting, it's perfect. When I visited, the organization was based inside a Keller Williams Realty building that, like nearly everything else in McKinney, is supposed to look like it was designed by artisans centuries ago but instead was designed by a guy wearing Dockers circa 2007. The foyer has a rug that's meant to look like hardwood. A sign for Paul's organization shows a family hugging and staring at a white house with dormer windows. "Helping families move right," it promises.

Paul led me upstairs so we could talk. His Californianism reveals itself when he says the word "McKinney." Texans tend to pinch the "i" sound, but Paul lets it just roll out of his mouth, so that it nearly rhymes with "uncanny." "I don't have a cowboy hat or cowboy boots," he joked.

Paul is in his mid-forties, but with his thick hair and easygoing affect, he could pass for younger. He wouldn't be out of place in a JCPenney catalog, but instead of hawking polo shirts, he'd be extolling the virtues of the free market.

Paul grew up in Riverside, about fifty miles east of Los Angeles, in what is sometimes enterprisingly called "the Inland Empire." It wasn't a charmed childhood. His parents divorced when he was in the third grade, and the family was so poor that Paul had three paper routes. By twelve, he was in rehab for pot and booze. Paul's parents weren't very political—his father had only voted once, for Barry Goldwater—but some early experiences sparked Paul's interest in policy.

When he was sixteen, Paul became a Sheriff Explorer Scout, which is like a Boy Scout who specializes in learning about law enforcement. His five years in that program, and later as a reserve deputy, opened his eyes to an underworld of child abuse and domestic violence. Then in college, he joined a fraternity that an advisor called "the most diverse" on campus.

"It actually bothered me a little bit because we were compartmentalizing people on that, and I just saw us as a great brotherhood," Paul told me. Regardless, the experience "really elevated me to understanding how to work with diverse people." (If you have noticed that Paul speaks a little like a politician, it might be because he ran for Congress twice.) Finally, he served in the military, including a tour in Iraq in 2008, and with that came the admiration for veterans and military might that are more closely associated with the Republican Party.

Paul and his wife were in some ways the typical California parents. On weekends, sure, they could sometimes enjoy the beach and the mountains. But there were drawbacks that, to them, outweighed the natural beauty. They didn't like the schools in the area, so they put their kids in pricey private schools. Paul ran his own company doing counterterrorism consulting, and his wife would commute hours on clogged highways. Nobody went to PTA meetings; they were too busy fighting traffic. People in California are "house broke," he says—if they can afford a house, that's all they can afford. In California, unions "control everything." The state has "decriminalized drugs"; it's letting criminals off the hook with what he considers to be lenient sentences. Meanwhile, the state hikes gas taxes, further sticking it to the poor commuters.

The Inland Empire seems to be Paul's favorite case study. In 1977, he points out, the city of San Bernardino was designated an "All-America City," an award given by the National Civic League for good citizenship. Since then, he says, the city has opened lots of drug rehabs and halfway homes—nice in theory, but "as a dad with kids, do I want a house right next to me to be [filled] with four felons that just got out of prison?" He couldn't take his kids to the nearby mountains, because, he says, they were covered in graffiti and trash. "San Bernardino today," he said, "it is the second poorest city only behind Detroit. They have on average I think thirteen police officers on duty in a city of two hundred thousand. Over 50 percent of the population is on welfare. Gang violence, drugs, crimes, out of control. Many parts of it look like a third-world country, and that is happening to a lot of other cities throughout California." In Paul's view, Democratic policies are what have caused this hellscape.

Some elements of his dystopic view seem slightly exaggerated. San Bernardino was indeed the second-poorest "large city" in 2010. But since then, its economic picture has improved: unemployment in the county has fallen from 14 percent to less than 4 percent. The city of San Bernardino's police department web page says it has "225 sworn officers," and in 2011, just after the recession, 46 percent of San Bernardino did receive some type of government aid. But that includes food stamps and the state's Medicaid insurance program, not simply welfare.

Nevertheless, in 2016, the second time Paul ran for Congress—as a Republican—and lost—to the Democrat—Paul and his wife threw up their hands. *We cannot help people who don't want to help themselves,* they thought. They decided to head for greener—which is to say redder—pastures.

Conservative areas, Paul says, are more likely to have the three ingredients of a quality life: good schools, low crime, and good-paying jobs. In McKinney, Paul felt like he "moved back to America." It was California the way he remembered it. His neighbors brought him baked goods when he moved in. People tried to help him unload his moving van, which he would never have allowed in California, lest someone run off with his television. Here, the PTA has "like ten vice presidents." His four kids ride bikes in the streets—and they don't have to worry about locking them up. There's always a new church being built in McKinney, and, wouldn't you know it, Paul's neighbor is his pastor. The brain-searing heat of North Texas—it was supposed to be 104 the following day—was not that different from summers in the Inland Empire, he said.

Paul said he always had a mix of liberal and conservative friends, but he feels at home in Texas now that he's among fellow Republicans. (Or at least, the majority of the county's residents are.) "I'm not here to change Texas," he told me, crescendoing. "I'm here to be a Texan." He's even created a political action committee called Keep Texas Red PAC. The premise: don't let liberals ruin Texas like they ruined California.

Even the process of setting up Conservative Move proved Paul's case to himself. It took him six months to set up a business in California, he said, but just two weeks to create Conservative Move in Texas.

Conservative Move can refer its clients to real-estate agents in different states, but 90 percent of the people who contact them are interested in Texas. Number two is Idaho. Some people want to move to Waco, where the TV show *Fixer Upper* was set, but McKinney is the main event.

Sure, people could just find a real-estate agent on their own, but they're inspired by Paul's story. They sympathize with the reasons Paul left. He said the company had three thousand leads in its system at various points in the process. Some are years away from moving to McKinney. They contact Conservative Move every month to say, "I'm coming as soon as I retire."

Derek Baker, an eighth-generation Texan, is the company's lead agent in the state. He graduated from the evangelical Liberty University before working for conservative members of Congress and for the House Republican Study Committee. Derek carries a concealed handgun with him almost everywhere he goes. (He's never had to use it, but he's twice had to flash it at someone—and that "did the trick," he said.) "Once he told me his conservative credentials, we knew he was the right person for the job," Paul said happily.

Paul said people have claimed he's trying to create a "white utopia," which he finds insulting, because if you'll recall from the fraternity story, he doesn't "look at people by color." (But if he did, he would approximate that over 50 percent of those flying out to explore moving to Texas from California "have a Latino surname.")

Some people seek out Conservative Move because they home-school and feel "threatened" by their liberal states. Conveniently enough, Derek also homeschools. He can help them find the right church. He can rescue them from a blue state and show them a house with a pool for less than $400,000.

But another major force pulling conservatives to McKinney is their desire to stop feeling like outcasts. People tell Derek that they can't even admit to their California neighbors that they're Republican. "In California," Derek told me, most of his clients "can't even talk about politics. They get shouted down, they get called names, they get called racist and other things." Other than an inability to buy a house, without fail, Derek says, his clients come because they feel ostracized and unwelcome in liberal enclaves.paul

Paul's project is, in a way, facilitating what the journalist Bill Bishop called *The Big Sort*. It's the idea, described in his 2008 book by the same name, that Americans are increasingly moving to places where everyone is just like them. In 1976, Bishop points out, less than a quarter of Americans lived in counties that one presidential candidate won in a landslide. By 2004—when the playwright Arthur Miller asked, "How can the polls be neck and neck when I don't know one Bush supporter?"—nearly half of all voters lived in a landslide county. What happened was that evangelicals moved to other evangelical strongholds, and Godless college-educated people moved to places with tiny apartments and injera bread. In 2014, 50 percent of "consistently conservative" people told the Pew Research Center that they want to live near people who share their political views, as did 35 percent of "consistent" liberals.

Paul acknowledges that sorting along racial, ethnic, and even ideological lines happens, but he genuinely believes the conservative way is better for America's future. It's how we can avoid becoming Europe, which, I take it, would be terrible. "When they look at the more Open Society George Soros model, that's more like a European Union," he said. "It's not so much an American way of looking at things."

If you still don't believe him, he urges you to come see McKinney for yourself. "We tell them to do it all the time, catch a Southwest flight dirt cheap at Sacramento, land here at Love Field [Airport] and just come here and just get lost."

*Where is there to lose yourself in McKinney?* I thought.

The following day, Paul introduced me to two of his recent clients, a couple in their mid-twenties named Kurtis and Crystal. They had moved to McKinney from Long Beach, California, where they lived across from the beach and near all the shops and restaurants they could want, all within walking distance. The problem?

"Our apartment was the size of this room," Crystal said, glancing around the small conference room we were sitting in. They paid $1,500 a month for 500 square feet and no air-conditioning.

Kurtis spent three hours driving to and from work every day, bumper to bumper on the 405. He's an accountant, so during tax season he would wake at 5 a.m. and get home at 8:30 p.m., then do it all over again the next day.

Crystal, who was in school for social work, would sometimes have her friends over, and their bleeding hearts clashed with Kurtis's more conservative sensibilities. Kurtis told them he doesn't believe in global warming. "How dare you!" the friends would say. When Kurtis said he was voting for Trump, people called him a racist.

Kurtis was against sanctuary cities, the high taxes in California, and all the restrictions on gun ownership. "Homeless people need to get a job," he added. "We shouldn't be patting them on the back, telling them it's okay to be homeless."

Crystal, meanwhile, didn't like how her social-work program downplayed religion. She said she was told not to talk about religion with her clients or to share her views on abortion or homosexuality.

They were secret conservatives, feeling like they couldn't even talk about their beliefs. "It's like I couldn't walk around with my ideas," Kurtis said.

The turning point was when they got married in Mexico and came back to a tiny apartment, to the grind of work, to the insanity of Southern California traffic. Termites invaded their apartment, and their landlord asked them to move. *There has to be more,* they thought.

That's when they began thinking more seriously about Texas. Kurtis had always admired the state's conservative values, and when he heard Paul Chabot being interviewed on a local radio show he likes, Paul's talk of what Kurtis called "the homeless problem" in California and "crime going up because they've let a lot of criminals out" resonated. He got home and emailed Paul immediately.

The couple flew out to McKinney in August. The scorching weather wasn't *so* bad, they thought. Instead, they noticed the lack of trash on the streets and the absence of homeless people, the manicured lawns. "It just looked like a well-taken-care-of city," Kurtis said.

Derek, the real-estate agent, was like a father figure to them. He'd tell them when to bid and when not to, write contracts up for them late at night. After three bidding wars, they bought a four-bedroom, three-bathroom house with a pool and wrap-around deck for $325,000, a fraction of what they would have paid in Long Beach. Their decision, if it was ever in question, was thoroughly validated.

Some adjustments have been necessary, of course. Kurtis was a little surprised to find drinking is somewhat frowned upon here. Not long after his arrival, Kurtis was told by a grocery-store clerk that he couldn't buy beer on Sunday mornings. They hadn't been going out as much, so they hadn't made many friends. One young couple they met moved to Austin.

Still, they say, here, they can do all the same things they did in California, "minus the beach and the mountains." (Which, to me, seems like the entire point of California, if you don't count the mind-blowing restaurants, which McKinney is also not strong on.)

Already, Kurtis and Crystal feel more ideologically accepted. Right away, people here ask them what church they go to. At her first job here, there was a morning prayer, and Crystal seemed to find it refreshing. There were few Priuses or Obama bumper stickers around. Kurtis wore a "Trump" t-shirt outside, and no one honked angrily. They saved up their empty cans and bottles, then drove around in vain looking for a recycling center, which are ubiquitous in California. Eventually, they gave up and tossed it all in the garbage. "I guess we don't recycle in Texas!" Kurtis said.

In Kurtis, I saw a mirror image of my own journey out of McKinney to Washington for college, where all the worldly things I had always craved were at my fingertips. A girl in my college orientation program was the niece of Helen Thomas, the legendary White House reporter. I had never so much as smoked a cigarette, but right away I became a regular at hookah bars. I choked down sushi and pretended to love it. It was all so new, but also so familiar to the image of myself I had always held in my heart. It was thrilling.

During our interview, I found myself smiling along with Kurtis and Crystal at the cozy sensation of being understood for the first time. (In my own hometown, no less!) Finding your own kind can feel like sinking into a warm bath on a cold day, with every inch of skin soothed by how good it feels.

When the interview was done, they asked me if I was thinking of moving back to McKinney, too. I almost didn't have the heart to tell them no. Almost.

# CHAPTER 14

# In Between

Mary Duffy, the plus-size modeling agent, built a career on being proud of being overweight and recruiting other women who felt the same way. But even she seemed of two minds when it came to her uniqueness: On one hand, she was grateful for her natural curviness. On the other, she seemed to dwell on thinness.

In the old days, she told me, it drove her crazy when her models would try to lose weight to fit societal norms. She would often think to herself, *I'm so pretty that I can even gain weight and they'll still pay me three hundred dollars an hour to stand in front of a camera.* She devised one-liners to lob at people who made fun of her models because of their weight: *"Mattel made the Barbie and God made the rest of us."*

"I'm Irish," she explained. "If you're purposely rude to me, I can't be completely happy until I've thrown you into a month of therapy."

And yet. When I walked into her apartment, practically the first thing she said was, "You're thin as a pencil!" She asked me whether I was "naturally" that way or if I watch what I eat.

As a young adult, Mary would buy the smallest size she could fit in and would use water pills and lingerie in order to squeeze into it. As she showed me old images of herself in catalogs, she stopped to point to her size-16 frame and say, "My God, I was a large woman."

Being different can bring about a great deal of ambivalence. Not even those who achieved success *because* of their difference, as Mary did, were able to escape an occasional inkling that life as someone more traditional might have been better. And many still don't fit perfectly in one group or the other, instead finding themselves in between two different tribes.

This is especially the case when a person's difference is the result of physical appearance, which can be altered with surgery, but which is so fundamental to identity. *"That's you!"* people say, when they spot you in photos. How could you want to be someone other than yourself, even if the physical manifestation of "you" is not what society prefers?

I encountered these kinds of conflicting feelings about difference when I spoke with Ariel Henley, a writer with a facial disfigurement. Ariel was born with Crouzon syndrome, a disorder in which a fetus's skull bones don't fuse properly, resulting in a visibly deformed head and wide-set, bulging eyes. Ariel has undergone many surgeries, but her facial difference is still visible. Her eyes are slightly farther apart than most people's, and one is slanted downward. Her disfigurement is the subject of much of her writing.

As a child, she would cry when she saw pictures of herself. She'd beg her doctors, "Fix me," as she described in a *Narratively* essay. When she was interviewed by French journalists as a little girl and they compared her face to a work by Picasso, she tore the magazine to shreds.

But when doctors did "fix her," so to speak—when they performed the extensive surgeries that added cheekbones, changed her nose, and moved her jaw forward—it wasn't always the transformation she was hoping for.

In seventh grade, she and her twin sister, who also has Crouzon, had surgeries that completely altered their appearance. When she returned to school, people kept asking Ariel what happened to her. Some asked if she'd been in a car accident—or worse. "You look like a bomb exploded on your face," one boy said. When she was five, another surgery made Ariel ask her mother for her "old face back."

Today, Ariel's view of her condition is somewhat mixed. She says she wouldn't want to have been born "normal," given the chance. But she also wouldn't wish the painful experiences that often come with Crouzon on anyone.

Many transgender women just want to blend, or to not be perceivable as transgender. At the very least, many wish to be seen and treated as cis women would. But, Jess Herbst admits, "I'll really never have that, because I'm always going to be *that transgender person*." Being one of the only trans people in her area, she sometimes feels like the sign at the mall that lays out a map of all the stores. When people wonder "Where's Sears?," they can come ask Jess.

People ask her if she has a penis, and if so, if she's getting rid of it; they ask her if her breasts and hair are real; if she likes men or women romantically.

"I don't get upset," she said. "And the more people ask me the questions that other trans people do not want to answer means [other trans people] don't get asked those questions."

Her attitude surprised me. I assumed that if you were different, you wouldn't want people constantly pointing it out.

"It's just at some point when you wake up and there's four news trucks in that circle driveway," she said, gesturing out her window, and "the next thing you know you're on the BBC and you're on the radio in Ireland, Australia, Spain.... It was kind of like there's no hiding, there's no pretending that people don't know. And I might as well make the best of it I can for myself and for the community."

Because ultimately, making the community better will help her, too. Maybe after all the questions have been asked and answered, she won't be considered unusual anymore. Maybe no trans people will be. "You're not going to want to be here because I'm not going to be a story," she said. "That's really what we're looking for."

When I met Vivienne for the first time, she was smiling serenely. There was no trace—physical or emotional—of the troubled college student who nearly committed suicide. Her surgical procedures worked so well that no one would ever suspect she wasn't assigned female at birth. She often gets catcalled by men. The only thing she misses about presenting as a man, she says, is peeing standing up. "When the world is your toilet, you have a certain power," she told me with a smirk. That, and the fact that after she transitioned, people stopped asking her math questions, she says. As frustrating as it is, sometimes being underestimated by venture capitalists allows Vivienne to outmaneuver them.

Still, still! Though she no longer feels like the "gorilla in a tutu" she felt she resembled before her operations, Vivienne struggles with the nagging sense that she doesn't belong. If she's invited to speak at events, she hides out in her hotel room. She feels anxious talking one-on-one. "It's so evocative of feelings I had when I was younger. It's not like the gender fairy came and fixed everything," she told me when we met up one summer. "I still have an instinct to duck out of the way when I see someone, unless I have a tactical plan to discuss something with them. Why would anyone be interested in talking to me? I feel like I'm inflicting myself on other people."

"You don't spend thirty years of your life learning how not to connect with people and change that overnight," she added.

And yet, she is constantly called upon to explain her life story, to represent transgender people, to answer endless questions about herself. (She has been profiled a few times before, and I can only imagine what it's like to trot out the worst moments of your childhood to journalist after journalist over BLTs.) Even if she wasn't so pretty, and so smart, she would still never get to be just an average, unassuming woman. Her background is just too splashy of an angle.

It sounded like she was on the path toward accepting all that. "I'm my kids' mom. I'm a scientist out in the world. I'm an entrepreneur who has had real success. I genuinely feel 'me,'" Vivienne explained, the sun glinting off her blond curls. "I'm Vivienne

Ming, the weird woman with the weird name. I'm comfortable with being a big outlier. It's not just okay, it's the right thing to be different."

In her book about parenting while trans, the writer Jennifer Finney Boylan explained how she ended up with the parental moniker "Maddy," which is halfway between the feminine "mom" she was transitioning to and the masculine "dad" she was when her kids were born. "Let's call you 'Maddy,'" one of her children said. "That's like, half Mommy, and half Daddy."

To be sure, both Jess and Vivienne are real women; they're not between genders. But their experiences reflect the fact that gender transition is not always a smooth flip between identities. There are still elements to their lives that cis women never have to contend with.

There is, for example, the role of explainer, guide, and activist that trans people are often thrust into. It's as if by the very nature of their existence, trans people are "pro" something. "I didn't want to be a revolutionary," Boylan writes. "A lot of the time, more than anything, I just wanted to be like everybody else. I still want that, sometimes."

As Audre Lorde writes in *Sister Outsider,* "oppressed groups"— people of color, older people, women, and the working class— are often forced to be the gap-bridgers with what she calls "the oppressor." "Whenever the need for some pretense of communication arises, those who profit from our oppression call upon us to share our knowledge with them...I am responsible for educating teachers who dismiss my children's culture in school...Women are expected to educate men. Lesbians and gay men are expected to educate the heterosexual world." Until the world fully understands and accepts these "other" groups, they will forever be explaining themselves.

Merle Miller, a gay writer and editor, was also pressed into the roles of unlikely revolutionary and unwitting explainer. It started when, in the September 1970 issue of *Harper's,* the writer Joseph Epstein wrote a long screed against homosexuality. Epstein dwelled on how gay men seemed, to him, to be hopelessly weird. *"They are different from the rest of us,"* he wrote, in searing italics. He would wish homosexuality off the face of the earth if he could. "Nothing [my four sons] could ever do would make me sadder than if any of them were to become homosexual. For then I should know them condemned to a permanent n****rdom among men, their lives, whatever adjustment they might make to their condition, to be lived out as part of the pain of the earth." Again, it was 1970. To give you a sense of how recent this was, the first personal computers were released within the decade.

Not long after the *Harper's* article came out, Merle Miller had lunch with two editors at *The New York Times Magazine,* and Epstein's piece came up. Miller was by then already an established journalist and author—though not always a progressive one, judging by a 1953 issue of *Pageant* magazine I dug up in which he denounces "career girls." When Miller revealed during the lunch that he, himself, is gay, one of the *Times* editors asked Miller to write a reaction piece.

Miller's piece would play a crucial role in LGBT history. Called "What It Means to Be a Homosexual," it was among the first major works of journalism in which the author himself comes out. "I did not encounter the word faggot until I got to Manhattan," he writes. "I'll tell you this, though. It's not true, that saying about sticks and stones; it's words that break your bones."

As Emily Greenhouse described in 2012 in *The New Yorker,* Miller at first resisted writing something personally revelatory, but "it seems to have spilled out from his pen, his typewriter, a reasoned and reasonably furious demand for respect."

The piece attracted more than two thousand letters, many of them, as Miller's obituary reads, "from other homosexuals thanking him for helping to restore their self-respect." Miller seemed compelled to use his personal story to steer history in a more humane direction. (Fittingly, Miller's essay was later published as a book called *On Being Different.*)

Not only was Miller reluctant to tell his personal story, he also seemed not entirely ready to embrace his difference. "If I had been given a choice (but who is?), I would prefer to have been straight," he writes. At points in the piece, he wonders to himself if homosexuality is, indeed, contagious.

But writing the article also seemed to bring him some relief, or perhaps even some contentment, in his role of uncertain navigator. "It is a very clear day in late December, and the sun is shining on the pine trees outside my studio," Miller wrote. "The air is extraordinarily clear, and the sky is the color it gets only at this time of year, dark, almost navy blue. On such a day I would not choose to be any one else or any place else."

Toward the end of this project, I became less sure about whether my family *were*, in fact, outsiders in West Texas, where I spent my early childhood. Or rather, whether we maybe started out as outsiders, but did not end up that way. Did people really only hire my father for translation out of practical concerns? Or was there an element of wanting to reach out and learn? There was the family who used his services to adopt a baby girl from Russia. Perhaps less nobly, another man had my dad translate his correspondence with a mail-order bride. If they hated Russians, why would they want them living in their home? And the proselytizing was persistent—proselytizing usually is—but if they hated Russians, why would they want them in their Heaven?

When I was researching this book, I spent some time interviewing my parents about Midland. My dad harped on it. He mocked a hypocritical Bible-school teacher we knew ("Did you know I saw him in the car with his mistress?") and berated his *petit-bourgeois* former bosses, one of whom banned him from walking across the hall to talk to my mom during work hours.

As my dad and I shook our heads and chuckled, I noticed my mom sitting there silently. We were used to this. Unlike my dad and I, who have a tendency to narrate every minor twist of our boring lives—ask him about the time he accidentally handed a fifty-dollar bill to a cashier—my mom reacts to things on an as-needed basis. Send her a sixteen-paragraph email, and she'll write back, "Got it, thanks."

"I liked them," she said, finally. "I miss the Midland people."

My taciturn, agnostic mother loved the warm, in-your-face Christians. She liked how they, knowing we were new and friendless, included us in every barbecue and Christmas dinner. The bless-your-hearts had a certain fakeness, yes, but to my mom, their attempts at friendship were enough. It was the effort that counted; it was the effort that said, "We see that you're refugees with beet-based foods. We're going to pretend that, despite your strange accents and mannerisms, you're just like us."

Russians, to my mother, were too cold and impersonal. She dreaded even going to the store in Leningrad, since by being so bold as to enter any establishment in the U.S.S.R. you were signing up to be barked at by a sales clerk. In Midland, meanwhile, she literally felt she had more freedom—to shop, to socialize. Rudeness was a quality West Texans neither possessed nor understood.

Yes, Midlanders at times asked nosy questions, but my mom appreciated their interest. When she fumbled her English, they were patient. If she'd never had Mexican food, they would take her out for it that very day.

My mom's own boss, whom she didn't get along with, wrote her a glowing, superlative recommendation when we moved away, because that's just the kind of thing you did for folks. When my mom went into labor with my brother, a coworker of hers somehow got word, left work in the middle of the day, and raced to the hospital to sit by my mom's side. She cut my brother's umbilical cord. Once, a distant acquaintance invited us to his *family reunion,* where we caught catfish and ate ice cream that ran down our arms in the heat.

"I think in Midland," she said, "those were my kind of people. They were truly my friends."

She even felt more comfortable in Midland than she did in the Dallas suburbs, where weirdos of all stripes are more plentiful. I was surprised by this, since they are culturally similar places. These days McKinney is somewhat of a Sunbelt boomtown, but when we moved there, it was small and sleepy, just like Midland.

But I suspect Midland's extreme geographic isolation worked to its advantage, in this regard. While newcomers to Dallas might find various weekend activities or social groups to join, arriving in Midland is like docking to the International Space Station. No one discriminates against the Russians or Japanese or Americans up there, in space. You are in an inhospitable, difficult, boring environment. You are relying on each other to live. For entertainment, people my parents knew in Midland would invite everyone from the office—it was usually a small office—directly to their backyards. *That was the extent of the entertainment available.* You enjoyed whoever was around, weird or otherwise, because whoever was around was all there was.

Midland, despite its cultural tightness, was itself a weird place. It was a brotherhood of loners. It was unusual in that it made a home for whatever weirdos, exhausted from a long journey, landed bemusedly on its dusty steppe. There was no other choice.

### DEANA, PART II

I met Deana one summer day at a—perhaps *the*—hip coffee shop in Wichita Falls, where she, too, was now living and working as a psychologist. Deana doesn't try that hard to fit in anymore. People can accept her or not, it's up to them. She still has a Slavic inflection to her voice, but her bright red hair and button-down shirt made her look more like the frontwoman of a punk band than a traditional Russian lady.

She told me her background actually helps her with her therapy clients these days. Many people feel "like the outsiders in their current context," she said. "They feel isolated and alone." The obstacles she's overcome allow her to connect with her clients' struggles. For instance, if someone is gay and grew up in a homophobic family, she can empathize with them because of her experience with anti-Semitism.

Pursuing her graduate degree wasn't easy for Deana. She has ADHD, and people had always told her she was dumb. It didn't help that many of those people didn't speak the same language she did, and therefore couldn't tell how smart she was. But Deana's mother died just before she had to decide whether to pursue her PhD, and she figured, "Well, my mom is dead, what else do I have to lose?"

Meanwhile, Deana's connections with Russian culture grew more tenuous. At one point, Deana met another Russian woman at a university she attended during her training. She tried to speak to her in their mother tongue, but the woman told Deana, with a look of judgment on her face, that she had an American accent. Deana felt a little bit offended.

Later, Deana's half sister found her through a Russian social network called *Odnoklasniki,* or "Classmates," and through her, Deana got connected with her birth father. The man told Deana he wanted to Skype with her nearly every day, and that he wanted her to come visit him for a month. When Deana said she was too busy to do that and, besides, she didn't feel comfortable enough speaking Russian anymore, he grew upset. Then he started lobbying her to move back to Russia and get married. "He didn't seem to understand that education is how women empower themselves," she explained. It was all too much. She told him she needed space, and they lost contact.

After she graduated, Deana decided to stay in Wichita Falls, since her husband and brothers are all nearby. With her mom gone, she feels like the matriarch of the family. The place is more diverse than the tiny town she originally landed in, at least. She still describes herself as a Russian-Jewish woman living in Texas. Not a Texan.

Throughout all this, I was struck by how functional she seemed, despite all the things that made her weird. Dead mom? PhD in a second language? Living deep in Trump country as a strong feminist? Deana seemed unbothered by it all.

If there are any scars left from the ordeal, it's that she can be, at times, a little hypervigilant. Once, she was leaving a grocery store wearing shorts (it was hot; it's always hot), and came upon three men hanging out by their truck. They ogled her pretty openly, so

Deana turned to her husband and said, "Why would they gawk?!" loud enough so they could hear.

"I'm not just some piece of meat," she told me, indignantly. "I'm not a T-bone."

It can seem, if you don't know her, like a little bit of an overreaction.

But the thing is, *I'm kind of defensive too.* So many of my stories about being wronged by Americans involve long descriptions of their tone and the look in their eye, because really, their actual words weren't that bad. They probably didn't even mean anything by it, but I'm bundling together my off-brand Nikes and the time I pronounced it "JACK-uzzi" and the time everyone laughed because I didn't know what an airplane hangar was, and wrapping it in the prosciutto of their innocuous comment, and baking it all in the oven of my immigrant shame, until out pops a hot little oozing nugget of offense taken. When you're an outsider, you never really know when you've finally been allowed in. You're constantly throwing your hands up in front of your face, probing for the invisible barrier between you and everyone else.

Deana seems to take this all in stride. There was something about meeting her, specifically—a person who is more foreign than I am living in a place that's more "Texas" than McKinney—that gave me strength. I felt like I had finally met the Russian kid I was always missing in high school. *"You see?"* her presence assured me. *"It's okay to be like us."* Maybe I don't need to have gone to Yale and summer camp. Maybe I can just be like me.

Toward the end of our time together, we climbed into Deana's white CRV, where she likes to listen to Ozzy Osbourne, Led Zeppelin, and AC/DC as she cruises the sun-bleached highways. She drove to her office, a route that took us past a brick building labeled simply "Downtown Pharmacy," another building that looked abandoned, and a shop called "Sam's Dollar Saver." When we arrived, I was greeted by her supervisor, who had the kind of swirly mustache you see on men who are about to tie someone to the railroad tracks. It looked like we had stepped out of soy-latte land and into Westworld.

The room where she practiced psychotherapy, though, was trendy and modern, with a salt lamp from Tibet and a fancy hourglass from Walmart. She pays attention to whether the client sits on the big blue couch or the chair next to it—it could say something about what they feel their place in the world should be. Deana sat down in a small computer chair.

She took a Wonder Woman mug off a nearby shelf—a gift from a client. She and the client called each other Wonder Woman in order to pump each other up during difficult times.

Deana told me she had seen the *Wonder Woman* movie recently and was happy to see that the main character was played by Gal Gadot, a Jewish actress.

Then, out of nowhere, she began to cry.

"I wish my grandma could have seen this movie with me," she said, wiping away tears.

When Deana left Belarus, she was numb to the fact that she would probably never see her grandmother again. After her family arrived in Texas, Deana was depressed and her grandma was on morphine for her cancer pain. They didn't talk on the phone much. Deana would often sleep late, and her mother told her not to bother her grandma at odd hours. Deana didn't really get a chance to say goodbye. "I wish my grandma was there when I graduated with my PhD," she said softly. "Knowing that I've inherited that grit that my grandmother had, it just makes me so proud."

"I never felt like an outsider with her," she continued. "It's hard to find that kind of support. It's hard to open up, be real and honest. Whenever you open up, you invite hurt."

At this point, I was crying too, thinking about the last real conversation I had with my own grandmother, who raised me until I was three. My parents and I were visiting her in her tiny apartment in Saint Petersburg a few years ago, before her mental faculties began to deteriorate. She was in her usual, bizarrely high spirits. When my parents and I got up to leave, she looked me dead in the eye in a way that said, "This is the last time." Outside, my parents asked me why I was crying, and I mumbled something about not being able to find an Uber. But really, it was because I feared that I would never see her, at least not in that way, ever again. And the weirder you are, the fewer and more precious are the people who truly accept you.

Deana and I cried for our Soviet grandmas for a few silent minutes. Then we gathered ourselves and walked out into this foreign land.

# Acknowledgments

I'm fortunate to have so many people in my life who have helped enormously with this project.

I'm so thankful to my agent, Howard Yoon, who tirelessly shepherded, shaped, and cheer-led this idea from the beginning. Without him this book would not exist. My wonderful editor, Brant Rumble, had such sharp insights all along the way and is perhaps the fastest, and kindest, email answerer on the East Coast. He made the book so much better and the process so much less stressful. The Hachette copy editors are also the most gracious yet exacting readers, as are Michael Gaynor and Laura Bullard, who checked parts of this book.

Many people read early drafts, and their feedback was invaluable. I'm so thankful to Anton Tripolskii, Nicole Deterding, Anastasia Kolobrodova, Bethany Allen-Ebrahimian, and Marissa Chmiola for chugging through a Word document version of this and offering their take. Richard Rushfield is an extraordinary friend and mentor who also read the book and kept me going.

The entire Atlantic team is the smartest and most generous bunch around. I'm so grateful to Jeff Goldberg and Adrienne LaFrance for giving me so many opportunities, for believing in me, and for letting me take book leave. Denise Wills, Paul Bisceglio, Swati Sharma, Kate Julian, Ross Andersen, Julie Beck, and Rachel Gutman all have made and continue to make me a better writer and thinker every day. Before that, the *Washington Post* and USC Annenberg took a chance on a weird immigrant kid. Dan Beyers, Dion Hayes, K.C. Cole, Alan Mittelstaedt, and Marc Cooper gave me a voice and taught me how to use it.

So few things I do, including this, would be possible without Rich, the best partner in life and love. From reading early drafts to driving me across the country, he did so much to help me finish this project, and I'm eternally grateful to him.

My parents gamely sat for interviews and fact-checked the parts that related to them. I appreciate them so much for immigrating to America and for everything else they've done for me.

Finally, I have so much admiration and gratitude for the people who appear in this book. Their patience and vulnerability are commendable. They opened up their lives to me and to my readers, all in the service of making weirdos feel a little less alone. I hope their stories inspire others; I know they inspired me.

# Notes

**7 "those phony 'traditions'":** Lamb, S., *The Not Good Enough Mother* (Boston: Beacon Press, 2019), 81.

**13 "sometimes lascivious":** Mercer, W., *Orthopaedic Surgery* (London: Edward Arnold, 1959).

**15 "In a 2018 survey":** Cigna, "Cigna U.S. Loneliness Index," May 2018, https://www.multivu.com/players/English/8294451-cigna -us-loneliness-survey/.

**16 "women in their cohort":** Bostwick, V. K., & Weinberg, B. A., "Nevertheless She Persisted? Gender Peer Effects in Doctoral STEM Programs" (September 2018), NBER Working Paper Series, 25028.

**16 "smoking fifteen cigarettes":** Holt-Lunstad, J., Smith, T., & Bradley Layton, J. B., "Social Relationships and Mortality Risk: A Meta-Analytic Review," *PLoS Medicine* (July 27, 2010): 7.

**16 "deadlier than obesity":** Holt-Lunstad, J., Baker, M., Harris, T., Stephenson, D., & Smith, T. B., "Loneliness and Social Isolation as Risk Factors for Mortality: A Meta-Analytic Review," *Perspectives on Psychological Science* (2015): 2, 10, 227–37.

**16 "risk of dementia":** Holwerda, T. J., Deeg, D. J., Beekman, A. T., van Tilburg, T. G., Stek, M. L., Jonker, C., & Schoevers, R. A., "Feelings of Loneliness, but Not Social Isolation, Predict Dementia Onset: Results from the Amsterdam Study of the Elderly (AMSTEL)," *Journal of Neurology, Neurosurgery & Psychiatry* 85, no. 2 (2012): 135–42.

**16 "*more* segregated by race":** Ferguson, J-P., and Rembrand, K., "Firm Turnover and the Return of Racial Establishment Segregation," *American Sociological Review* 83, no. 3 (2018): 445–74.

**16 "also on the rise":** Fry, R., & Taylor, P., "The Rise of Residential Segregation by Income," Pew Research Center, August 2012, http://www .pewsocialtrends.org/2012/08/01/the-rise-of-residential-segregation-by -income/.

**16 "match them perfectly":** Chandler, A., "Why Richer People Spend More Time with Their Friends," *Atlantic,* May 9, 2016, https://www.theatlantic.com/business/archive/2016/05/friendship-privilege-income/481884/.

**16 "different sexual orientation":** Najle, M., & Jones, R., "American Democracy in Crisis: The Fate of Pluralism in a Divided Nation," PRRI, February 19, 2019, https://www.prri.org/research/american-democracy-in-crisis-the-fate-of-pluralism-in-a-divided-nation/.

**16 "Eventually, the man left":** Pinsker, J., "The 'Hidden Mechanisms' That Help Those Born Rich to Excel in Elite Jobs," *Atlantic,* February 26, 2019, https://www.theatlantic.com/entertainment/archive/2019/02/class-ceiling-laurison-friedman-elite-jobs/582175/.

**17 "Shanto Iyengar and Masha Krupenkin":** Iyengar, S. & Krupenkin, M., "The Strengthening of Partisan Affect," *Political Psychology* 39 (2018): 201–18.

**17 "the overall labor force":** Deming, D., "The Growing Importance of Social Skills in the Labor Market" (2017), NBER Working Paper Series, 21473.

**22 "fell again after the 1920s":** Google Ngram search.

**22 "called *Weird Maryland*":** Lake, M., Moran, M., & Sceurman, M., *Weird Maryland: Your Travel Guide to Maryland's Local Legends and Best Kept Secrets* (New York: Sterling, 2006).

**22 "Keep Austin Weird":** Yardley, J., "Austin Journal: A Slogan Battle Keeps Austin Weird," *New York Times,* December 8, 2002, https://www.nytimes.com/2002/12/08/us/austin-journal-a-sloganbattle-keeps-austin-weird.html.

**22 "breeding ground for weirdos":** Yonan, J., "Can Austin Stay Weird?," *Washington Post,* March 27, 2011.

**23 "disagree with the group":** Schachter, S., "Deviation, Rejection, and Communication," *The Journal of Abnormal and Social Psychology* 46, no. 2 (1951): 190–207.

**23 "less energy as a result":** Kaufman, L., "Utilities Turn Their Customers Green, with Envy," *New York Times,* January 30, 2009, https://www.nytimes.com/2009/01/31/science/earth/31compete.html.

**23 "In a 2014 study":** Kitayama, S., King, A., Hsu, M., Liberzon, I., & Yoon, C., "Dopamine-System Genes and Cultural Acquisition: The Norm Sensitivity Hypothesis," *Current Opinion in Psychology* 8 (April 2016): 167–74.

**24 "Edith Wharton describes":** Wharton, E., *The Age of Innocence* (New York: Vintage Books, 2012).

**25 "individual begin to diverge":** Revillard, A., "Social Norms (1):

Norms and Deviance," https://annerevillard.files.wordpress.com/2015/04
/its02-social-norms-1.pdf.

**25 "would be under the law":** Durkheim, É., *The Rules of Sociological
Method* (New York: Macmillan Press, 1895/1982).

**26 "commit 'fatalistic' suicide":** Gelfand, M. J., *Rule Makers, Rule
Breakers: How Tight and Loose Cultures Wire Our World* (New York: Scribner), 193.

**25 "just a few years ago":** Harrington, J. R., Boski, P., & Gelfand, M. J.,
"Culture and National Well-Being: Should Societies Emphasize Freedom
or Constraint?," *PLoS One* 10, no. 6 (June 5, 2015).

**28 "*Pool as a Negotiated Order*":** Scott, S., "Reclothing the Emperor:
The Swimming Pool as a Negotiated Order," *Symbolic Interaction* 32
(2011): 123–45.

**30 "Betsy Levy Paluck discovered":** Paluck, E. L., "Reducing Intergroup Prejudice and Conflict Using the Media: A Field Experiment in
Rwanda," *Journal of Personality and Social Psychology* 96, no. 3 (2009):
574–87.

**32 "*New York Times* wrote in 1951":** Boal, S., "Revelations—
1900–1951," *New York Times,* August 26, 1951, https://timesmachine
.nytimes.com/timesmachine/1951/08/26/88454413.pdf.

**32 "bloomers and stockings":** "The 1900s Victorian Bathing Suit," *Vic-
toriana Magazine,* http://www.victoriana.com/Fashion/victorian-bathing
-suit.html.

**32 "license in women's dress":** Horwood, C., "'Girls Who Arouse Dangerous Passions': Women and Bathing, 1900–39," *Women's History Review*
9, no. 4 (2000): 653–73.

**32 "women in burqinis":** Minganti, P. K., "Burqinis, Bikinis and
Bodies: Encounters in Public Pools Italy and Sweden," in *Islamic Fashion and Anti-fashion: New Perspectives from Europe and North America,*
eds. E. Tarlo & A. Moors, Annelies (London: Bloomsbury, 2013),
33–55.

**32 "to the water's edge":** Toussaint, K., "This Woman's One-piece Bathing
Suit Got Her Arrested in 1907," *Boston Globe,* July 2, 2015, https://
www.boston.com/news/history/2015/07/02/this-womans-one-piece
-bathing-suit-got-her-arrested-in-1907.

**32 "*How to Swim* in 1918":** Kellerman, A., *How to Swim* (New York:
George H. Doran, 1918), 45.

**32 "to the *Boston Sunday Globe*":** Toussaint, "This Woman's One-piece
Bathing Suit Got Her Arrested in 1907."

**34 "factories are disappearing":** Miller, C. C., "Why Men Don't Want
the Jobs Done Mostly by Women," *New York Times,* January 4, 2017,

https://www.nytimes.com/2017/01/04/upshot/why-men-dont-want-the
-jobs-done-mostly-by-women.html.

**34 "*New York Times* in 2017":** Miller, "Why Men Don't Want the Jobs Done Mostly by Women."

**34 "shaving their genitals":** Chur-Hansen, A., "Preferences for Female and Male Nurses: the Role of Age, Gender and Previous Experience— Year 2000 Compared with 1984," *Journal of Advanced Nursing* 37, no. 2 (January 2002): 192–98.

**34 "A 2002 sociological study":** Sargent, P., "Under the Glass: Conversations with Men in Early Childhood Education," *Young Children* 57, no. 6 (November 2002).

**35 "just over 2 percent":** Bureau of Labor Statistics, "Employed Persons by Detailed Occupation, Sex, Race, and Hispanic or Latino Ethnicity," 2018, https://www.bls.gov/cps/cpsaat11.htm.

**37 "top NASCAR series":** Hembree, M., "For Most Female Racecar Drivers, Breaking Through Asphalt Ceiling Proves Elusive," *USA Today*, May 15, 2018, https://www.usatoday.com/story/sports/nascar/2018/05/15/women -auto-racing-danica-patrick-nascar-indycar-nhra/528855002/.

**40 "One journalist, Bob Pockrass":** Pockrass, B., "Furniture Row Racing's Demise Highlights NASCAR's Competitive Problems," ESPN, September 4, 2018, http://www.espn.com/racing/nascar/story/_/id/24578901/nascar -cup-series-end-furniture-row-racing-bad-nascar.

**40 "on TV these days":** Sigalos, M., "Here's What Went Wrong with NASCAR," CNBC.com, July 7, 2018, https://www.cnbc.com/2018/06 /28/nascar-america-formula-one.html.

**41 "Julia and Danica Patrick":** Associated Press, "Danica 2.0? NASCAR Searching for More Female Drivers," February 13, 2018, https://www .usatoday.com/story/sports/nascar/2018/02/13/danica-2-0-nascar-searching -for-more-female-drivers/110386844/.

**42 "that study concluded":** Jacobs, T., "And the Oscar Goes to…an American," *Pacific Standard*, February 6, 2017, https://psmag.com/news /and-the-oscar-goes-to-an-american, and Steffens, N. K., Haslam, S. A., Ryan, M. K., & Millard, K., "Genius Begins at Home: Shared Social Identity Enhances the Recognition of Creative Performance," *British Journal of Psychology* 108, no. 4 (February 2017): 721–36.

**42 "friendships and romantic relationships":** Hutson, M., "You're Just Like Me!" *Atlantic*, January/February 2015, https://www.theatlantic.com /magazine/archive/2015/01/youre-just-like-me/383502/.

**42 "emotions, attention, and reasoning":** Parkinson, C., Kleinbaum, A. M., & Wheatley, T., "Similar Neural Responses Predict Friendship," *Nature Communications* 9 (2018).

**42 "hundreds of different variables":** Bahns, A. J., Crandall, C. S., Gillath, O., & Preacher, K. J., "Similarity in Relationships as Niche Construction: Choice, Stability, and Influence Within Dyads in a Free Choice Environment," *Journal of Personality and Social Psychology* 112, no. 2 (February 2017): 329–55.

**42 "acknowledged in a news release":** University of Kansas, "Study Finds Our Desire for 'Like-Minded Others' Is Hard-Wired," February 23, 2016, https://news.ku.edu/2016/02/19/new-study-finds-our-desire-minded-others-hard-wired-controls-friend-and-partner.

**45 "with President Reagan":** NCSJ, "March on Washington 1987," http://sovietjewry.org/march_on_washington.php.

**45 "even mentioned arms control":** Shipler, D., "Summit Aftermath: In the Private Talks, Humor and a Deep Disagreement," *New York Times,* December 12, 1987, https://www.nytimes.com/1987/12/12/world/summit-aftermath-in-the-private-talks-humor-and-a-deep-disagreement.html.

**45 "report several years ago":** Kliger, S., "Russian-Jewish Immigrants in the U.S.: Social Portrait, Challenges, and AJC Involvement," accessed in 2015, http://www.ajcrussian.org/site/apps/nlnet/content2.aspx?c=chLMK3PKLsF&b=7718799&ct=11713359.

**51 "fines and jail time":** Article 19, "Russia: Federal Laws Introducing Ban of Propaganda of Non-traditional Sexual Relationships," 2013, https://www.article19.org/data/files/medialibrary/37129/13-06-27-russia-LA.pdf.

**51 "considered homosexuality acceptable":** Pew Research Center, "The Global Divide on Homosexuality," June 4, 2013, http://www.pewglobal.org/2013/06/04/the-global-divide-on-homosexuality/.

**51 "Russians attend church regularly":** Pew Research Center, "Russians Return to Religion, but Not to Church," February 10, 2014, http://www.pewforum.org/2014/02/10/russians-return-to-religion-but-not-to-church/.

**51 "capitalizes on illiberal sentiments":** Khazan, O., "Why Is Russia So Homophobic?," *Atlantic,* June 12, 2013, https://www.theatlantic.com/international/archive/2013/06/why-is-russia-so-homophobic/276817/.

**51 "that are more homogeneous":** Jetten, J., Hogg, M. A., & Mullin, B. A., "In-Group Variability and Motivation to Reduce Subjective Uncertainty," *Group Dynamics: Theory, Research, and Practice* 4, no. 2 (2000): 184–98.

**52 "them more tolerant toward difference":** Cohen, G. L., Sherman, D. K., Bastardi, A., Hsu, L., McGoey, M., & Ross, L., "Bridging the Partisan Divide: Self-Affirmation Reduces Ideological Closed-Mindedness and Inflexibility in Negotiation," *Journal of Personality and Social Psychology* 93, no. 3 (2007): 415–30.

52 "countries like Finland or Sweden": Uz, I., "The Index of Cultural Tightness and Looseness Among 68 Countries," *Journal of Cross-Cultural Psychology* 46, no. 3 (2015): 319–35.

53 "as is the Netherlands": Gelfand, M. J., *Rule Makers, Rule Breakers: How Tight and Loose Cultures Wire Our World* (New York: Scribner, 2018), 199.

53 "positive bodily exploration": Rough, B., "How the Dutch Do Sex Ed," *Atlantic,* August 27, 2018, https://www.theatlantic.com/family /archive/2018/08/the-benefits-of-starting-sex-ed-at-age-4/568225/.

53 "in a major 2011 study": Gelfand, M. J., Raver, J. L., Nishii, L., Leslie, L. M., Lun, J., Lim, B. C., Duan, L.,…Yamaguchi, S., "Differences Between Tight and Loose Cultures: A 33-Nation Study," *Science,* May 27, 2011, 332, 1,100–1,104.

53 "ads do the opposite": Kim, H., & Markus, H. R., "Deviance or Uniqueness, Harmony or Conformity? A Cultural Analysis," *Journal of Personality and Social Psychology* 77, no. 4 (1999): 785–800.

53 "societies tend to be loose": Gelfand, M. J., "Culture's Constraints: International Differences in the Strength of Social Norms," *Current Directions in Psychological Science* 21, no. 6 (December 2012): 420–24.

54 "where life is loose": Greenfield, P. M., "The Changing Psychology of Culture from 1800 Through 2000," *Psychological Science* 24, no. 9 (September 2013): 1722–31.

54 "and Hawaii is loose": Harrington, J. R., & Gelfand, M. J., "Tightness-Looseness Across the 50 United States," *Proceedings of the National Academy of Sciences* 111, no. 22 (June 3, 2014): 7990–95.

54 "cultures similar to their own": Chua, R. Y. J., Roth, Y., & Lemoine, J.-F., "The Impact of Culture on Creativity: How Cultural Tightness and Cultural Distance Affect Global Innovation Crowdsourcing Work," *Administrative Science Quarterly* 60, no. 2 (June 2015): 189–227.

54 "anxieties in their people": Pelto, P. J., "The Difference Between 'Tight' and 'Loose' Societies," *Transaction* 5 (1968): 37–40.

55 "index of D+44—meaning": The Cook Political Report, Partisan Voting Index, Districts of the 115th Congress, https://www.docdroid.net /JZXMmxl/arranged-by-pvi-rank-1.pdf#page=9.

56 "a character call Wichita Falls": Shield, R. R., "The Improbable Rise of Redneck Rock by Jan Reid," *Ethnomusicology* 22, no. 2 (May 1978): 358.

56 "*Texas Monthly* ranked": Hauptman, W., "Will the World Flock to Wichita Falls?," *New York Times Magazine,* August 7, 1988, https://www .nytimes.com/1988/08/07/magazine/will-the-world-flock-to-wichita-falls .html.

**60 "for exchanging racy letters":** Stryker, S., *Transgender History: The Roots of Today's Revolution* (New York: Seal Press, 2017), 69–83.

**61 "dressing rooms and resting rooms":** Kogan, T., "How Did Bathrooms Get to Be Separated by Gender in the First Place?," *Guardian*, June 11, 2016, https://www.theguardian.com/commentisfree/2016/jun/11/gender-bathrooms-transgender-men-women-restrooms.

**61 "basic safety and privacy":** Berman, M., Larimer, S., & Horwitz, S., "North Carolina, Justice Dept. File Dueling Lawsuits over Transgender Rights," *Washington Post*, May 9, 2016, https://www.washingtonpost.com/news/post-nation/wp/2016/05/09/north-carolina-justice-dept-face-monday-deadline-for-bathroom-bill/?utm_term=.3d7afb1cfe7d.

**61 "gender identity in her remarks":** Macon, A., "New Hope Mayor Jess Herbst Testifies Against Bathroom Bill," *D Magazine*, July 21, 2017, https://www.dmagazine.com/frontburner/2017/07/new-hope-mayor-jess-herbst-testifies-against-bathroom-bill/.

**65 "than more blue-collar jobs":** Cook, G., "A Powerful Force That Shapes All of Our Decisions," *Scientific American*, September 11, 2018, https://www.scientificamerican.com/article/a-powerful-force-that-shapes-all-of-our-decisions/.

**66 "then she came out, too":** King, D., "Anna Planning and Zoning Commission Chair Announces She's Transgender," *Anna-Melissa Tribune*, March 7, 2017, http://www.amtrib.com/news/20170307/anna-planning-and-zoning-commission-chair-announces-shes-transgender.

**67 "a *D Magazine* reporter":** Crain, Z., "Modern Family," *D Magazine*, June 2017, https://www.dmagazine.com/publications/d-magazine/2017/june/texas-first-transgender-mayor-jess-herbst-new-hope/.

**69 "other equality-promoting policies":** Phelan, J. E., & Rudman, L. A., "System Justification Beliefs, Affirmative Action, and Resistance to Equal Opportunity Organizations," *Social Cognition* 29, no. 3 (2011): 376–90.

**69 "when they affect us personally":** Gavac, S., Murrar, S., & Brauer, M., "Group Perception and Social Norms," in *Social Psychology: How Other People Influence Our Thoughts and Actions*, ed. R. Summers (Santa Barbara, CA: ABC-CLIO, Inc., 2016), 333–60.

**70 "the Gare d'Orsay in Paris":** Tajfel, H., *Human Groups and Social Categories: Studies in Social Psychology* (Cambridge, UK: Cambridge University Press, 1981), 1.

**70 "drive rifts between people":** Obituary: Henri Tajfel, *British Journal of Social Psychology* 21, no. 3 (September 1982): 185–88.

**70 "at Claremont Graduate University":** Hogg, M. A., "Social Identity Theory," in *Understanding Peace and Conflict Through Social Identity*

*Theory: Contemporary Global Perspectives,* eds. S. McKeown, R. Haji, & N. Ferguson (New York: Springer, 2016), 3–17.

71 **"'group X' and 'group W'"**: Billig, M., & Tajfel, H., "Social Categorization and Similarity in Intergroup Behaviour," *European Journal of Social Psychology* 3, no. 1 (1973): 27–52.

71 **"book, *Human Groups & Social Categories*"**: Tajfel, H., *Human Groups and Social Categories: Studies in Social Psychology* (Cambridge, UK: Cambridge University Press, 1981), 141.

72 **"by machetes. Lawrence Sugiyama"**: Sugiyama, L. S., "Illness, Injury, and Disability Among Shiwiar Forager-Horticulturalists: Implications of Health-Risk Buffering for the Evolution of Human Life History," *American Journal of Physical Anthropology* 123, no. 4 (2004): 371–89.

72 **"Daniel Fessler in a 2006 study"**: Navarrete, C. D., & Fessler, D. M., "Disease Avoidance and Ethnocentrism: The Effects of Disease Vulnerability and Disgust Sensitivity on Intergroup Attitudes," *Evolution and Human Behavior* 27, no. 4 (2006): 270–82.

73 **"hunter-gatherers and remained wary"**: "The Truth About Migration: How Evolution Made Us Xenophobes," *New Scientist,* April 6, 2016, https://www.newscientist.com/article/mg23030680-800-the-truth-about-migration-how-evolution-made-us-xenophobes/.

73 **"of anyone else"**: Gifford, A., "Peter J. Richerson and Robert Boyd, Not by Genes Alone: How Culture Transformed Human Evolution," *Journal of Bioeconomics* 10, no. 2 (August 2008): 193–98.

73 **"even in recent centuries"**: Wheeler G. C., & Westermarck, E., *The Tribe, and Intertribal Relations in Australia…With a Prefatory Note by E.A. Westermarck* (London: John Murray, 1910), https://archive.org/details/tribeintertribal00wheeuoft/page/14.

73 **"found a beached whale"**: Grey, G., *Journals of Two Expeditions of Discovery in North-west and Western Australia During the Years 1837, 38 and 39 under the Authority of Her Majesty's Government* (London: T. and W. Boone, 1841).

74 **"troubling habits: eating pickles"**: Ziegelman, J., "Immigrant Identities, Preserved in Vinegar?," *New York Times,* August 3, 2011, https://www.nytimes.com/2011/08/04/opinion/immigrant-identities-preserved-in-vinegar.html.

75 **"side they were on"**: Gooden, P., *May We Borrow Your Language?: How English Steals Words from All over the World* (London: Head of Zeus, 2016).

75 **"an *Irish Times* article"**: O'Faolain, N., "What to Do in the Face of Sectarian Hatred?," *Irish Times,* February 2, 1998, https://www.irishtimes.com/opinion/what-to-do-in-the-face-of-sectarian-hatred-1.131048.

**75 "*Not Fit for Our Society*":** Schrag, P., *Not Fit for Our Society: Immigration and Nativism in America* (Oakland, CA: University of California Press, 2010), 7.

**75 "character and intelligence":** Lodge, H. C., "Lynch Law and Unrestricted Immigration," *The North American Review* 152 (1891).

**75 "characters, and paupers—to":** Dingley, F. L., "European Emigration: Studies in Europe of Emigration Moving out of Europe, Especially That Flowing to the United States," Department of State, 1890, https://play.google.com/books/reader?id=dWlMAAAAYAAJ&hl=en&pg=GBS.PA208-IA1.

**75 "'is rapidly increasing,' Lodge wrote":** Lodge, H. C., "Lynch Law and Unrestricted Immigration," 1891.

**76 "and 'worthless race types'":** Schrag, *Not Fit for Our Society*, 76.

**76 "letter's author? Adolf Hitler":** Schrag, *Not Fit for Our Society*, 76.

**76 "public attitudes toward immigration":** Fetzer, J. S., *Public Attitudes Toward Immigration in the United States, France, and Germany* (Cambridge, UK: Cambridge University Press, 2001), 33.

**76 "followers vandalized Jewish stores":** Schrag, *Not Fit for Our Society*, 36.

**76 "advocated 'liquidating'":** Irwin, T., *Inside the Christian Front* (Washington, DC: American Council on Public Affairs, 1940), http://www.ajcarchives.org/AJC_DATA/Files/THR-CF7.PDF.

**76 "that said 'No Japs Welcome'":** Fetzer, *Public Attitudes*, 39.

**77 "official language of the U.S.":** Fetzer, *Public Attitudes*, 42.

**77 "In Detroit in 1982":** Wu, F. H., "Why Vincent Chin Matters," *New York Times*, June 22, 2012, https://www.nytimes.com/2012/06/23/opinion/why-vincent-chin-matters.html.

**77 "dominant WASP norm":** Fetzer, *Public Attitudes*, 44.

**77 "Betty Friedan called it":** Friedan, B., *The Feminine Mystique* (New York: W. W. Norton & Company, 1963), 274.

**78 "sympathizing with the Reds":** Coontz, S., *A Strange Stirring: "The Feminine Mystique" and American Women at the Dawn of the 1960s* (New York: Basic Books, 2011), 54.

**78 "not truly male":** Coontz, *A Strange Stirring*, 71.

**78 "soon wear themselves out":** Coontz, *A Strange Stirring*, 68.

**78 "risked being ostracized":** Coontz, *A Strange Stirring*, 12.

**78 "writes, were pitied":** Coontz, *A Strange Stirring*, 75.

**79 "*Sex Today in Wedded Life*":** O'Neill, T., "7 Tips for Keeping Your Man (from the 1950s)," *Mental Floss*, August 14, 2013, https://theweek.com/articles/461207/7-tips-keeping-man-from-1950s.

**79 "the perfect follower":** Coontz, *A Strange Stirring*, 15.

**79 "the standard procedure":** Cornell, B., *Betty Cornell's Teen-Age Popularity Guide* (Prentice-Hall, Inc., 1953).

**79 "*How to Pick a Mate*":** Adams, C. R., & Packard, V. O., *How to Pick a Mate, the Guide to a Happy Marriage* (New York: Dutton, 1946), 83, https://archive.org/details/howtopickmategui00adamrich/page/96.

**79 "according to Adams":** Adams & Packard, *How to Pick a Mate,* 96.

**80 "want to be on the move":** Adams & Packard, *How to Pick a Mate,* 99.

**80 "shave their armpits":** Brown, H. G., *Sex and the Single Girl* (Bernard Geis Associates, 1962).

**80 "describe in their study":** Anand, R., & Winters, M.-F., "A Retrospective View of Corporate Diversity Training from 1964 to the Present," *Academy of Management Learning and Education* 7, no. 3 (2008): 356–72.

**81 "tribe. Several studies":** McCutcheon, R., Bloomfield, M., Dahoun, T.,…& Howes, O., "Amygdala Reactivity in Ethnic Minorities and Its Relationship to the Social Environment: An fMRI Study," *Psychological Medicine* 48, no. 12 (2018), and Hart, A. J., Whalen, P. J., Shin, L. M., McInerney, S. C., Fischer, H., & Rauch, S. L., "Differential Response in the Human Amygdala to Racial Outgroup vs Ingroup Face Stimuli," *Neuroreport* 11, no. 11 (August 2000): 2351–55.

**81 "preparation for a fight":** Javanbakht, A., & Saab, L., "The Science of Fright: Why We Love to Be Scared," *The Conversation,* October 26, 2017, https://theconversation.com/the-science-of-fright-why-we-loveto-bescared-85885?xid=PS_smithsonian.

**81 "sex as they get older":** Telzer, E. H., Flannery, J., Humphreys, K. L., Goff, B., Gabard-Durman, L., Gee, D. G., & Tottenham, N., "The Cooties Effect: Amygdala Reactivity to Opposite- Versus Same-sex Faces Declines from Childhood to Adolescence," *Journal of Cognitive Neuroscience* 27, no. 9 (April 7, 2015): 1685–96.

**81 "exhibits less empathy":** Meyer, M. L., Masten, C. L., Ma, Y., Wang, C., Shi, Z., Eisenberger, N. I., & Han, S., "Empathy for the Social Suffering of Friends and Strangers Recruits Distinct Patterns of Brain Activation," *Social Cognitive and Affective Neuroscience* 8, no. 4 (2013): 446–54.

**81 "outside our own":** Cikara, M., Bruneau, E., & Saxe, R., "Us and Them: Intergroup Failures of Empathy," *Current Directions in Psychological Science* 20, no. 3 (2017): 149–53.

**81 "rival sports teams":** Hein, G., Silani, G., Preuschoff, K., Batson, C. D., & Singer, T., "Neural Responses to Ingroup and Outgroup Members' Suffering Predict Individual Differences in Costly Helping," *Neuron* 68, no. 1 (October 2010): 149.

**82 "were of their same race":** Avenanti, A., Sirigu, A., & Aglioti, S. M., "Racial Bias Reduces Empathic Sensorimotor Resonance with Other -Race Pain," *Current Biology* 20, no. 11 (June 2010): 1018–22, and Xu, X., Zuo, X., Wang, X., & Han, S., "Do You Feel My Pain? Racial Group Membership Modulates Empathic Neural Responses," *Journal of Neuroscience* 29, no. 26 (2009): 8525–29.

**82 "more like schadenfreude":** Molenberghs, P., "The Neuroscience of In-Group Bias," *Neuroscience and Biobehavioral Reviews* 37, no. 8 (September 2013): 1530–36.

**82 "an overflowing toilet":** Harris, L. T., & Fiske, S. T., "Dehumanizing the Lowest of the Low: Neuroimaging Responses to Extreme Out -Groups," *Psychological Science* 17, no. 10 (October 2006): 847–53.

**82 "their same unique trait":** Nelson, L. J., & Miller, D. T., "The Distinctiveness Effect in Social Categorization: You Are What Makes You Unusual," *Psychological Science* 6, no. 4 (1995): 246–49.

**82 "In a 2002 article":** Fiske, S. T., "What We Know Now About Bias and Intergroup Conflict, the Problem of the Century," *Current Directions in Psychological Science* 11, no. 4 (August 2002): 123–28.

**82 "seem fair-minded":** Molenberghs, P., "The Neuroscience of In -Group Bias," *Neuroscience and Biobehavioral Reviews* 37, no. 8 (September 2013): 1530–36.

**83 "wrote in 2016":** The Conversation, Gelfand, M., Jackson, J. C., Harrington, J. R., "Trump Culture: Threat, Fear and the Tightening of the American Mind," *Scientific American,* April 27, 2016, https://www.scientificamerican.com/article/trump-culture-threat-fear-and-the-tightening-of-the-american-mind/#.

**83 "support for Trump":** Lopez, G., "The Past Year of Research Has Made It Very Clear: Trump Won Because of Racial Resentment," Vox, December 15, 2017, https://www.vox.com/identities/2017/12/15/16781222/trump-racism-economic-anxiety-study.

**83 "*The Atlantic* in 2018":** Khazan, O., "People Voted for Trump Because They Were Anxious, Not Poor," *Atlantic,* April 23, 2018, https://www.theatlantic.com/science/archive/2018/04/existential-anxiety-not-poverty-motivates-trump-support/558674/.

**83 "*Wall Street Journal* analysis":** Adamy, J., & Overberg, P., "Counties That Experienced Rapid Diversification Voted Heavily for Donald Trump," *Wall Street Journal,* November 9, 2016, https://www.wsj.com/articles/counties-that-experienced-rapid-diversification-voted-heavily-for-donald-trump-1478741076.

**84 "one-third Latino":** Hansen, N., "Despite National Tensions, Arcadia Embraces Diversity," *La Crosse Tribune,* April 9, 2017, https://

/lacrossetribune.com/news/local/despite-national-tensions-arcadia-embr
aces-diversity/article_a1b9a828-5a2f-5b40-b15b-2bf57e01fd55.html.

**84 "6 percent Latino":** United States Census, "Race and Hispanic or
Latino Origin," 2010, https://factfinder.census.gov/faces/tableservices/jsf
/pages /productview.xhtml?src=CF.

**85 "John Kimmel proposed":** Hubbuch, C., "Latinos Look for Answers:
Arcadia Mayor's Immigration Proposals Spur Anger, Confusion," *Lee Newspapers,* August 20, 2006, https://lacrossetribune.com/news/latinos-look-for
-answers-arcadia-mayor-s-immigration-proposals-spur/article_55fd8931-7
0fb-545f-b522-bea6644932b5.html.

**85 "proposals were scrapped":** Adamy, J., & Overberg, P., "Places Most Unsettled by Rapid Demographic Change Are Drawn to Donald Trump," *Wall
Street Journal,* November 1, 2016, https://www.wsj.com/articles/places-most
-unsettled-by-rapid-demographic-change-go-for-donald-trump-14780109
40.

**85 "being arrested and deported":** Schlicht, K., "Arcadia Reacts to Immigration Arrests," WEAU, February 24, 2010, https://www.weau.com
/home/headlines/85260222.html.

**85 "newcomers 'a blessing'":** Hansen, N., "In the Era of Trump, Arcadia
Celebrates Growing Diversity," *Winona Daily News,* April 9, 2017, https:/
/www.winonadailynews.com/news/local/in-the-era-of-trump-arcadia-cele
brates-growing-diversity/article_39d5bb78-fdd1-5bb2-bea4-f1b0d4b055
4f.html.

**85 "would bring crime":** Gillespie, S., "Clinton Failed to Grasp Dis-
content in the Heartland," *Star Tribune,* November 14, 2016, http:/
/www.startribune.com/postmortemclinton-failed-to-grasp-discontent-in
-the-heartland/401182675/.

**86 "be an American":** Hainmueller, J., & Hopkins, D. J., "Public Attitudes Toward Immigration," *Annual Review of Political Science* 17 (2014):
225–50.

**86 "Several studies show that":** Chandler, C. R., & Tsai, Y-M., "Social
Factors Influencing Immigration Attitudes: An Analysis of Data from
the General Social Survey," *Social Science Journal* 38, no. 2 (June 2001):
177–88; Hainmueller, J., & Hopkins, D. J., "The Hidden American
Immigration Consensus: A Conjoint Analysis of Attitudes Toward Immigrants," *American Journal of Political Science* 59, no. 3 (2014): 529–48;
Newman, B. J., Hartman, T. K., & Taber, C. S., "Foreign Language
Exposure, Cultural Threat, and Opposition to Immigration," *Political Psychology* 33, no. 5 (2012): 635–57.

**86 "on time each day":** MacBride, E., "Jens Hainmueller: What Drives
Anti-Immigration Attitudes?," Insights by Stanford Business, January 5,

2015, https://www.gsb.stanford.edu/insights/jens-hainmueller-what-drives
-anti-immigration-attitudes.

**86 "in their study on this topic":** Hainmueller & Hopkins, "Public Attitudes," 225–50.

**86 "described in a 2010 paper":** Hopkins, D. J., "Politicized Places:
Explaining Where and When Immigrants Provoke Local Opposition,"
*American Political Science Review* 104, no. 1 (February 2010): 40–60.

**86 "generalize those negative attributes":** Rubin, M., "The Dispro-
portionate Influence of Negative Encounters with Out-Group Members on Prejudice," Mark Rubin's Social Psychology Research, https:
//sites.google.com/site/markrubinsocialpsychresearch/positive-and-neg
ative-experiences-with-members-of-other-groups.

**87 "*Wall Street Journal* that year":** Adamy, J., & Overberg, P., "Places
Most Unsettled by Rapid Demographic Change Are Drawn to Donald
Trump," *Wall Street Journal,* November 1, 2016, https://www.wsj.com
/articles/places-most-unsettled-by-rapid-demographic-change-go-for-don
ald-trump-1478010940.

**87 "*Milwaukee Journal Sentinel* in 2016":** Romell, R., "In Western
Wisconsin, Trump Voters Want Change," *Milwaukee Journal Sentinel,*
November 27, 2016, https://www.jsonline.com/story/news/politics
/elections/2016/11/26/western-wisconsin-trump-voters-want-change/94
436384/.

**87 "backlash spread with them":** Schrag, *Not Fit for Our Society,* 185.

**90 "Amish 'going high'":** Gingerich, E. J., *Runaway Amish Girl: The
Great Escape* (Aledo, TX: Progressive Rising Phoenix Press, 2014), 132.

**93 "to try a different life":** Khazan, O., "Escaping the Amish for a Connected World," *Atlantic,* February 17, 2016, https://www.theatlantic.com
/technology/archive/2016/02/escaping-the-amish-fora-connectedworld/
463116/.

**94 "groups cohere more firmly":** Jetten, J., & Hornsey, M. J., "Deviance
and Dissent in Groups," *Annual Review of Psychology* 65 (June 7, 2013):
461–85.

**95 "Nobel, Murray found":** Murray, D. R., "Direct and Indirect Implications of Pathogen Prevalence for Scientific and Technological Innovation," *Journal of Cross-Cultural Psychology* 45, no. 6 (April 30, 2014):
971–85.

**96 "2016 *Atlantic* article":** Khazan, O., "Why Pregnancy Makes Women
Xenophobic," *Atlantic,* January 14, 2016, https://www.theatlantic.com
/science/archive/2016/01/the-disease-theory-of-xenophobia/423975/.

**96 "countries are less likely":** Schaller, M., & Murray, D. R., "Pathogens,
Personality, and Culture: Disease Prevalence Predicts Worldwide Variability

in Sociosexuality, Extraversion, and Openness to Experience," *Journal of Personality and Social Psychology* 95, no. 1 (2008): 212–21.

**97 "further along in their pregnancies":** Navarrete, C. D., Fessler, D. M. T., & Eng, S. J., "Elevated Ethnocentrism in the First Trimester of Pregnancy," *Evolution and Human Behavior* 28, no. 1 (2007): 60–65.

**97 "greater levels of religiosity":** Fincher, C. L., & Thornhill, R., "Parasite-Stress Promotes In-Group Assortative Sociality: The Cases of Strong Family Ties and Heightened Religiosity," *Behavioral and Brain Sciences* 35, no. 2 (April 2012): 61–79.

**97 "supported this connection":** Tybur, J. M., Merriman, L. A., Hooper, A. E., McDonald, M. M., & Navarrete, C. D., "Extending the Behavioral Immune System to Political Psychology: Are Political Conservatism and Disgust Sensitivity Really Related?," *Evolutionary Psychology* 8, no. 4 (October 2010).

**97 "tough on crime, anti-gay":** McAuliffe, K., "Disgust Made Us Human," *Aeon,* June 6, 2016, https://aeon.co/essays/how-disgust-made -humans-cooperate-to-build-civilisations.

**97 "politically conservative":** McAuliffe, K., "The Yuck Factor," *Atlantic,* March 2019, https://www.theatlantic.com/magazine/archive/2019/03 /the-yuck-factor/580465/.

**97 "disease-bearing outside groups out":** Liuzza, M. T., Lindholm, T., Hawley, C. B., Gustafsson Senden, M., Ekström, I., Olsson, M. J., & Olofsson, J. K., "Body Odour Disgust Sensitivity Predicts Authoritarian Attitudes," *Royal Society Open Science* 5, no. 2 (February 28, 2018).

**97 "Ebola-infected outsiders away":** Beall, A. T., Hofer, M. K., & Schaller, M., "Infections and Elections: Did an Ebola Outbreak Influence the 2014 U.S. Federal Elections (and If So, How)?," *Psychological Science* 27, no. 5 (May 2016): 595–605.

**97 "claimed illegal immigrants":** CNN, *Lou Dobbs Tonight,* "Border Insecurity; Criminal Illegal Aliens; Deadly Imports; Illegal Alien Amnesty," CNN.com, April 14, 2005, http://edition.cnn.com/TRANSCRIPTS /0504/14/ldt.01.html.

**98 "unlike themselves, one study":** Uz, I., "The Index of Cultural Tightness and Looseness Among 68 Countries," *Journal of Cross-Cultural Psychology* 46, no. 3 (2015): 319–35.

**98 "are fast-growing:"** The Church of Jesus Christ of Latter-day Saints, "Grown of the Church," https://www.mormonnewsroom.org/topic /church-growth.

**98 "is basically stagnant":** Unitarian Universalist Association, "Aggregate Data from Unitarian Universalist Association (UUA) Congregations," https://www.uua.org/data/demographics/uua-statistics.

**98 "in his book *Sapiens*":** Harari, Y. N., *Sapiens: A Brief History of Humankind* (New York: HarperCollins, 2014).

**99 "form of social security":** Hruschka, D. J., & Henrich, J., "Institutions, Parasites and the Persistence of In-Group Preferences," *PLoS One* 8, no. 5 (May 21, 2013).

**99 "slew of critical commentaries":** Fincher, C. L., & Thornhill, R., "Parasite-Stress Promotes In-Group Assortative Sociality: The Cases of Strong Family Ties and Heightened Religiosity," *Behavioral and Brain Sciences* 35, no. 2 (April 2012): 61–79.

**100 "happen to be less extroverted":** Napolioni, V., Murray, D. R., Comings, D. E., Peters, W. R., Gade-Andavolu, R., & MacMurray, J., "Interaction Between Infectious Diseases and Personality Traits: ACP1*C as a Potential Mediator," *Infection, Genetics and Evolution* 26 (August 2014): 267–73.

**100 "protects us from pathogens":** Gassen, J., Prokosch, M. L., Makhanova, A., Eimerbrink, M. J., White, J. D., Proffitt Leyva, R. P., Peterman, J. L.,…Hill, S.E., "Behavioral Immune System Activity Predicts Downregulation of Chronic Basal Inflammation," *PLoS One* 13, no. 9 (September 20, 2018).

**101 "One week in 1995":** Williams, K. D., Bernieri, F. J., Faulkner, S. L., Gada-Jain, N., & Grahe, J. E., "The Scarlet Letter Study: Five Days of Social Ostracism," *Journal of Personal and Interpersonal Loss* 5, no. 1 (2000): 19–63.

**102 "three minutes of ostracism":** Neubert, A. P., "Professor: Pain of Ostracism Can Be Deep, Long-Lasting," Purdue University News Service, May 10, 2011, https://www.purdue.edu/newsroom/research/2011/110510 WilliamsOstracism.html.

**102 "third of kids are bullied":** Jacobson, L., "Survey: One-Third of Students Report Being Bullied," Education Dive, September 24, 2018, https://www.educationdive.com/news/survey-one-third-of-students-report-being-bullied/532795/.

**102 "post-bullying syndrome":** Baggaley, K., "How Being Bullied Affects Your Adulthood," Slate, June 20, 2016, http://www.slate.com/articles/health_and_science/medical_examiner/2016/06/the_lasting_effects_of_childhood_bullying_are_surprisingly_not_all_detrimental.html.

**102 "explained by childhood bullying":** Bowes, L., Joinson, C., Wolke, D., & Lewis, G., "Peer Victimisation During Adolescence and Its Impact on Depression in Early Adulthood: Prospective Cohort Study in the United Kingdom," *BMJ* 350 (2015).

**103 "she cleaned houses":** Gingerich, *Runaway Amish Girl,* 70.

**104 "her use of technology":** Khazan, O., "Escaping the Amish for a Connected World," *Atlantic,* February 17, 2016, https://www.theatlantic.com/technology/archive/2016/02/escaping-the-amish-for-a-connected-world/463116/.

**110 "perpetuating a cycle of loneliness":** Masi, C., Chen, H.-Y., Hawkley, L., & Cacioppo, J., "A Meta-Analysis of Interventions to Reduce Loneliness," *Personality and Social Psychology Review* 15, no. 3 (2010): 219–66.

**110 "end of a crocheted sweater":** Cacioppo, J. T., Fowler, J. H., & Christakis, N. A., "Alone in the Crowd: The Structure and Spread of Loneliness in a Large Social Network," *Journal of Personality and Social Psychology* 97, no. 6 (2010): 977–91.

**111 "have more heart attacks":** Quinn, B., "Loneliness Linked to 30% Increase in Heart Disease and Stroke Risk," *Guardian,* April 19, 2016, https://www.theguardian.com/science/2016/apr/19/loneliness-linked-to-30-increase-in-heart-disease-and-stroke-risk.

**111 "worse cancer outcomes":** Reinberg, S., "Loneliness May Sabotage Breast Cancer Survival, Study Finds," CBS News, December 31, 2016, https://www.cbsnews.com/news/loneliness-may-sabotage-breast-cancer-survival-study-finds/.

**111 "likely to develop dementia":** Holwerda, T. J., Deeg, D. J., Beekman, A. T., Van Tilburg, T. G., Stek, M. L., Jonker, C., & Schoevers, R. A., "Feelings of Loneliness, but Not Social Isolation, Predict Dementia Onset: Results from the Amsterdam Study of the Elderly (AMSTEL)," *Journal of Neurology, Neurosurgery, and Psychiatry* 85, no. 2 (2014): 135–42.

**111 "prone to viral infections":** Cohen, S., Doyle, W. J., Skoner, D. P., Rabin, B. S., & Gwaltney, J. J. M., "Social Ties and Susceptibility to the Common Cold," *JAMA: The Journal of the American Medical Association* 277, no. 24 (June 25, 1997).

**112 "being discriminated against":** Pascoe, E. A., & Richman, L. S., "Perceived Discrimination and Health: A Meta-Analytic Review," *Psychological Bulletin* 135, no. 4 (July 2009): 531–54.

**112 "women are more likely":** Eltoukhi, H. M., Modi, M. N., Weston, M., Armstrong, A. Y., & Stewart, E. A., "The Health Disparities of Uterine Fibroid Tumors for African American Women: A Public Health Issue," *American Journal of Obstetrics and Gynecology* 210, no. 3 (March 2014): 194–99.

**112 "*Atlantic* article, several studies":** Khazan, O., "Being Black in America Can Be Hazardous to Your Health," *Atlantic,* July/August 2018,

https://www.theatlantic.com/magazine/archive/2018/07/being-black-in
-america-can-be-hazardous-to-your-health/561740/.

**113 "diabetes twenty-five years later":** Thomas, J., Thomas, D. J., Pearson, T., Klag, M., & Mead, L., "Cardiovascular Disease in African American and White Physicians: The Meharry Cohort and Meharry-Hopkins Cohort Studies," *Journal of Health Care for the Poor and Underserved* 8, no. 3 (August 1997): 270–83.

**113 "amused contempt and pity":** Du Bois, W. E. B., *The Souls of Black Folk: With Related Readings* (Chicago: A.C. McClurg, 1903).

**114 "very unsettling indeed":** Hohman, Z. P., Gaffney, A. M., & Hogg, M. A., "Who Am I If I Am Not Like My Group? Self-uncertainty and Feeling Peripheral in a Group," *Journal of Experimental Social Psychology* 72 (September 2017): 125–32.

**114 "yes, they really do":** Pickett, C. L., Bonner, B. L., & Coleman, J. M.,"Motivated Self-stereotyping: Heightened Assimilation and Differentiation Needs Result in Increased Levels of Positive and Negative Self-stereotyping," *Journal of Personality and Social Psychology* 82, no. 4 (April 2002): 543–62.

**114 "will overcome hatred":** Piketty, T., "Le Tout-Sécuritaire Ne Suffira Pas," *Le Monde,* November 24, 2015, http://piketty.blog.lemonde.fr /2015/11/24/le-tout-securitaire-ne-suffira-pas-2/.

**115 "Esteban Klor, found":** Benmelech, E., & Klor, E. F., "What Explains the Flow of Foreign Fighters to ISIS?," National Bureau of Economic Research, 2016.

**115 "canceled their asylum applications":** Forsell, T., "Thousands of Iraqi Refugees Leave Finland Voluntarily," Reuters, February 12, 2016, https:// www.reuters.com/article/us-europe-migrants-finland-idUSKCN0VL0UE.

**115 "The majority of Finns":** Pew Research Center, "Being Christian in Western Europe," May 29, 2018, http://www.pewforum.org/2018/05/29 /being-christian-in-western-europe/.

**115 "keeping our women safe":** Faiola, A., "Fear and Paranoia Lead Finns to Form Vigilante Groups That 'Protect Women' from Asylum Seekers," *Washington Post,* January 31, 2016, https://www.washingtonpost.com/world /europe/fear-and-paranoia-lead-finns-to-form-vigilante-groups-that-protect -women-from-asylum-seekers/2016/01/23/c16f8646-b943-11e5-85cd-5a d59bc19432_story.html.

**115 "uncomfortable in either culture":** Long, H., "Who's Joining ISIS? It Might Surprise You…" CNN, December 15, 2015, https://money.cnn.com /2015/12/15/news/economy/isis-recruitcharacteristics/index.html.

**116 "extremism to support its cause":** Lyons-Padilla, S., Gelfand, M. J., Mirahmadi, H., Farooq, M., & van Egmond, M., "Belonging Nowhere:

Marginalization & Radicalization Risk Among Muslim Immigrants," *Behavioral Science & Policy* 1, no. 2 (2015): 1–12.

**116 "groups that excluded them":** Ellemers, N., "The Group Self," *Science* 336 (2012): 6083.

**116 "bullied as a child":** Bates, C., "I Was a Neo-Nazi. Then I Fell in Love with a Black Woman," BBC, August 29, 2017, https://www.bbc.com/news/magazine-40779377.

**116 "cognitive skills and self-awareness":** Olds, J., & Schwartz, R. S., *The Lonely American: Drifting Apart in the Twenty-first Century* (Boston: Beacon Press, 2010), 72–73.

**116 "Across several studies":** Hogg, M. A., "From Uncertainty to Extremism: Social Categorization and Identity Processes," *Current Directions in Psychological Science* 23, no. 5 (October 15, 2014): 338–42.

**116 "becoming 'somebody' again":** Kruglanski, A., Jasko, K., Webber, D., Chernikova, M., & Molinario, E., "The Making of Violent Extremists," *Review of General Psychology* 22, no. 1 (March 2018): 107–20.

**117 "Kathleen Blee told PBS":** Couch, C., "Recovering from Hate," PBS Nova, July 29, 2015, https://www.pbs.org/wgbh/nova/article/hatred/.

**117 "most private moments":** Ratcliffe, R. G., "'Our Daughters' Used as the Bathroom Bill's Protection," *Texas Monthly,* August 1, 2017, https://www.texasmonthly.com/burka-blog/daughters-used-bathroom-bills-protection/.

**118 "a 2016 study found":** Seelman, K. L., "Transgender Adults' Access to College Bathrooms and Housing and the Relationship to Suicidality," *Journal of Homosexuality* 63, no. 10 (2016): 1378–99.

**118 "high rate of suicide":** Johns, M. M., Lowry, R., Andrzejewski, J., Barrios, L. C., Demissie, Z., McManus, T., Rasberry, C. N.,…Underwood, J. M., "Transgender Identity and Experiences of Violence Victimization, Substance Use, Suicide Risk, and Sexual Risk Behaviors Among High School Students—19 States and Large Urban School Districts, 2017," *Morbidity and Mortality Weekly Report* 68, no. 3 (2019): 67–71.

**118 "in 2013":** Herman, J., "Gendered Restrooms and Minority Stress: The Public Regulation of Gender and Its Impact on Transgender People's Lives," The Williams Institute, UCLA School of Law, June 2013, https://williamsinstitute.law.ucla.edu/research/transgender-issues/hermanjpmss-june2013/.

**118 "*Transgender Health* in 2016":** Rood, B. A., Reisner, S. L., Pantalone, D. W., Surace, F. I., Puckett, J. A., Pantalone, D.,…Maroney, M. R., "Expecting Rejection: Understanding the Minority Stress Experiences of Transgender and Gender-Nonconforming Individuals," *Transgender Health* 1, no. 1 (2016): 151–64.

**118 "compared to straight people":** Bränström, R.,"Minority Stress Factors as Mediators of Sexual Orientation Disparities in Mental Health Treatment: A Longitudinal Population-Based Study," *Journal of Epidemiology and Community Health* 71, no. 5 (2017): 446–52.

**118 "Another paper":** Sattler, F. A., Wagner, U., & Christiansen, H., "Effects of Minority Stress, Group-Level Coping, and Social Support on Mental Health of German Gay Men," *PLoS One* 11, no. 3 (March 2016).

**119 "language get more headaches":** Woodford, M. R., Howell, M. L., Silverschanz, P., & Yu, L., "'That's So Gay!': Examining the Covariates of Hearing This Expression Among Gay, Lesbian, and Bisexual College Students," *Journal of American College Health* 60, no. 6 (2012): 429–34.

**119 "controlling for HIV status":** Lick, D. J., Durso, L. E., & Johnson, K. L., "Minority Stress and Physical Health Among Sexual Minorities," *Perspectives on Psychological Science* 8, no. 5 (September 2013): 521–48.

**119 "were in the closet":** Cole, S. W., Kemeny, M. E., Taylor, S. E., Visscher, B. R., & Fahey, J. L., "Accelerated Course of Human Immunodeficiency Virus Infection in Gay Men Who Conceal Their Homosexual Identity," *Psychosomatic Medicine* 58, no. 3 (1996): 219–31.

**119 "cortisol, a stress hormone":** Huebner, D. M., & Davis, M. C., "Gay and Bisexual Men Who Disclose Their Sexual Orientations in the Workplace Have Higher Workday Levels of Salivary Cortisol and Negative Affect," *Annals of Behavioral Medicine* 30, no. 3 (2005): 260–67.

**122 "attend services regularly":** Pew Research Center, "Religious Belief and National Belonging in Central and Eastern Europe," May 10, 2017, http://www.pewforum.org/2017/05/10/religious-belief-and-national-belonging-in-central-and-eastern-europe/.

**122 "State Department report":** U.S. Department of State, "Bulgaria 2015 International Religious Freedom Report," https://www.state.gov/documents/organization/256385.pdf.

**128 "large, amorphous crowd":** Leonardelli, G. J., Pickett, C. L., & Brewer, M. B., "Optimal Distinctiveness Theory: A Framework for Social Identity, Social Cognition, and Intergroup Relations," *Advances in Experimental Social Psychology* 43 (2010): 63–113.

**133 "In a study":** Kim, S. H., Vincent, L. C., & Goncalo, J. A., "Outside Advantage: Can Social Rejection Fuel Creative Thought?," *Journal of Experimental Psychology General* 142, no. 3 (2013): 605–11.

**134 "'odd or peculiar' as children":** Ludwig, A. M., *The Price of Greatness: Resolving the Creativity and Madness Controversy* (New York: Guilford Press, 1995), 48.

**134 "be considered 'different' in adulthood":** Ludwig, *The Price of Greatness*, 65.

**134 "In his 1962 study":** MacKinnon, D. W., "The Nature and Nurture of Creative Talent," *American Psychologist* 17, no. 7 (1962): 484–95.

**135 "*Los Angeles Times* later":** McCulloh, T. H., "Chay Yew Mines Dark Side of Asian Life in 'Porcelain,'" *Los Angeles Times,* January 10, 1993, http://articles.latimes.com/1993-01-10/entertainment/ca-1621_1_chay-yew.

**136 "points of view at once":** Tadmor, C. T., & Tetlock, P. E., "Bi-culturalism: A Model of the Effects of Second-Culture Exposure on Acculturation and Integrative Complexity," *Journal of Cross Cultural Psychology* 37, no. 2 (2006): 173–90.

**136 "better communicators overall":** Fan, S. P., Liberman, Z., Keysar, B., & Kinzler, K. D., "The Exposure Advantage: Early Exposure to a Multilingual Environment Promotes Effective Communication," *Psychological Science* 26, no. 7 (2015): 1090–97.

**136 "word and conceptual problems":** Maddux, W. W., & Galinsky, A. D., "Cultural Borders and Mental Barriers: The Relationship Between Living Abroad and Creativity," *Journal of Personality and Social Psychology* 96, no. 5 (2009): 1047–61.

**136 "two generations later":** Simonton, D. K., "Foreign Influence and National Achievement: The Impact of Open Milieus on Japanese Civilization," *Journal of Personality and Social Psychology* 72, no. 1 (1997).

**136 "originality in their thinking":** Saad, C. S., Damian, R. I., Moons, W. G., Robins, R. W., & Benet-Martinez, V., "Multiculturalism and Creativity: Effects of Cultural Context, Bicultural Identity, and Ideational Fluency," *Social Psychological and Personality Science* 4, no. 3 (May 2013): 369–75.

**137 "Americans to start businesses":** Wiens, J., & Stangler, D., "The Economic Case for Welcoming Immigrant Entrepreneurs," Kauffman Foundation, September 8, 2015, https://www.kauffman.org/what-we-do/resources/entrepreneurship-policy-digest/the-economic-case-for-welcoming-immigrant-entrepreneurs.

**137 "hold high-quality patents":** Nunn, R., O'Donnell, J., & Shambaugh, J., "A Dozen Facts About Immigration," Brookings, October 9, 2018, https://www.brookings.edu/research/a-dozen-facts-about-immigration/.

**137 "become highly educated":** Nunn, R., et al., "A Dozen Facts About Immigration."

**137 "looseness of repression":** Weeks, D., & James, J., *Eccentrics: A Study of Sanity and Strangeness* (New York: Villard, 1995), 65.

**137 "than cloister yourself":** Leung, A. K., & Chiu, C., "Multicultural Experience, Idea Receptiveness, and Creativity," *Journal of Cross Cultural Psychology* 41, 5-6 (2010): 723–41.

137 **"unconventional knowledge"**: Saad, C. S., et al., "Multiculturalism and Creativity," 369–75.

137 **"think of a Citibank ad"**: Vimeo, https://vimeo.com/59026239.

138 **"upward, instead of down"**: Ritter, S. M., Damian, R. I., Simonton, D. K., van Baaren, R. B., Strick, M., Derks, J., & Dijksterhuis, A., "Diversifying Experiences Enhance Cognitive Flexibility," *Journal of Experimental Social Psychology* 48, no. 4 (2012): 961–64.

138 **"Damian has a theory"**: Goclowska, M. A., Damian, R. I., & Mor, S., "The Diversifying Experience Model: Taking a Broader Conceptual View of the Multiculturalism-Creativity Link," *Journal of Cross-Cultural Psychology* 49, no. 2 (January 18, 2018): 303–22.

140 **"boost the creativity"**: Van Dyne & Saavedra, "A Naturalistic Minority Influence Experiment," *British Journal of Social Psychology* 35, no. 1 (1996): 151–67.

140 **"Across several studies"**: Nemeth, C., Brown, K., & Rogers, J., "Devil's Advocate Versus Authentic Dissent: Stimulating Quantity and Quality," *European Journal of Social Psychology* 31, no. 6 (2001): 707–20.

140 **"even just to think harder"**: Van Dyne & Saavedra, "A Naturalistic Minority Influence Experiment," 151–67.

140 **"In a 2001 study"**: De Dreu, C. K. W., & West, M. A., "Minority Dissent and Team Innovation: The Importance of Participation in Decision Making," *Journal of Applied Psychology* 86, no. 6 (2001): 1191–1201.

141 **"money after bad"**: Greitemeyer, T., Schulz-Hardt, S., & Frey, D., "The Effects of Authentic and Contrived Dissent on Escalation of Commitment in Group Decision Making," *European Journal of Social Psychology* 39, no. 4 (2009): 639–47.

141 **"famous 1951 experiment"**: Asch, S. E., "Effects of Group Pressure upon the Modification and Distortion of Judgment," in *Groups, Leadership and Men,* ed. H. Guetzkow (Oxford: Carnegie Press, 1951).

141 **"being seen as 'peculiar'"**: McLeod, S. A., "Solomon Asch—Conformity Experiment," Simply Psychology, 2018, https://www.simplypsychology.org/asch-conformity.html.

141 **"by up to 80 percent"**: McLeod, "Solomon Asch."

142 **"follow-up Asch studies"**: Monin, B., & O'Connor, K., "Reactions to Defiant Deviants: Deliverance or Defensiveness?," in *Rebels in Groups: Dissent, Deviance, Difference and Defiance in Groups,* eds. J. Jetten & M. Hornsey (Oxford, UK: Wiley-Blackwell, 2011), 267.

142 **"replicated in other studies"**: Nemeth, C., & Goncalo, J., "Rogues and Heroes: Finding Value in Dissent," in *Rebels in Groups: Dissent, Deviance, Difference and Defiance in Groups,* eds. J. Jetten & M. Hornsey (Oxford, UK: Wiley-Blackwell, 2011), 23.

**142 "according to research on persuasion":** Nemeth & Goncalo, "Rogues and Heroes," 21.

**142 "viewpoint more carefully":** Martin, R., & Hewstone, M., "Majority Versus Minority Influence, Message Processing and Attitude Change: The Source-Context-Elaboration Model," *Advances in Experimental Social Psychology* 40 (2008): 237–326.

**142 "Jack Goncalo put it":** Nemeth & Goncalo, "Rogues and Heroes," 22.

**142 "rather than a drawback":** Prislin, R., Davenport, C., & Michalak, J., "Groups in Transition: Differences in the Context of Social Change," in *Rebels in Groups: Dissent, Deviance, Difference and Defiance in Groups,* eds. J. Jetten & M. Hornsey (Oxford, UK: Wiley-Blackwell, 2011), 186.

**142 "become more closed-minded":** Prislin et al., "Groups in Transition," 188.

**143 "more easily later on":** McDaniel, M. A., Dornburg, C. C., & Guynn, M. J., "Disentangling Encoding Versus Retrieval Explanations of the Bizarreness Effect: Implications for Distinctiveness," *Memory & Cognition* 33, no. 2 (March 2005): 270–79.

**143 "in our memory banks":** Schmidt, S. R., "Effects of Humor on Sentence Memory," *Journal of Experimental Psychology: Learning, Memory, and Cognition* 20, no. 4 (July 1994): 953–67.

**143 "in a study":** Hornsey, M. J., Wellauer, R., McIntyre, J. C., & Barlow, F. K., "A Critical Test of the Assumption That Men Prefer Conformist Women and Women Prefer Nonconformist Men," *Personality and Social Psychology Bulletin* 41, no. 6 (June 2015): 755–68.

**143 "satisfaction in dating":** Hornsey et al., "A Critical Test," 755–68.

**144 "two million subscribers":** Morris, B. R., "You've Got Romance! Seeking Love on Line," *New York Times,* August 26, 1999, https://www.nytimes.com/1999/08/26/technology/you-ve-got-romance-seeking-love-on-line.html.

**145 "fifty-nine million members":** Dewey, C., "'We Are Frequently Under Attack': Match.com Says Hackers Are After Its Data," *Washington Post,* October 19, 2015, https://www.washingtonpost.com/news/the-intersect/wp/2015/10/19/we-are-frequently-under-attack-match-com-says-hackers-are-after-its-data/.

**145 "*New York Times* story":** Morris, "You've Got Romance!"

**145 "a *Wall Street Journal*":** Saranow, J., "How Did You Meet? If Answer Is 'Online,' Couples Tend to Lie," *Wall Street Journal,* November 6, 2002, https://www.wsj.com/articles/SB1036533515435168988.

**148 "In an experiment":** Milgram, S., "Behavioral Study of Obedience," *Journal of Abnormal and Social Psychology* 67, no. 4 (1963): 371–78.

**148 "a six-inch stinger—despite":** Jolly, J., "A Shocking Way (Really) to Break Bad Habits," *New York Times,* May 2, 2016, https://well.blogs.nytimes.com/2016/05/02/a-shocking-way-really-to-break-bad-habits/.

**148 "'appliances,' he wrote":** Milgram, "Behavioral Study," 371–78.

**148 "65 percent, of participants":** Monin, B., & O'Connor, K., "Reactions to Defiant Deviants: Deliverance or Defensiveness?," in *Rebels in Groups: Dissent, Deviance, Difference and Defiance in Groups,* eds. J. Jetten & M. Hornsey (Oxford, UK: Wiley-Blackwell, 2011), 261–80.

**148 "describe in a review paper":** Jetten, J., & Hornsey, M. J., "Deviance and Dissent in Groups," *Annual Review of Psychology* 65, no. 1 (June 2013): 461–85.

**148 "In a 2003 study":** Hornsey, M. J., Majkut, L., Terry, D. J., & McKimmie, B. M., "On Being Loud and Proud: Non-Conformity and Counter-Conformity to Group Norms," *British Journal of Social Psychology* 42 (September 2003): 319–35.

**149 "Jetten and Hornsey write":** Jetten & Hornsey, "Deviance and Dissent," 461–85.

**150 "chicken gizzards":** The Jonestown Institute, "Inside Peoples Temple," May 20, 2013, https://jonestown.sdsu.edu/?page_id=14026.

**152 "hunger and harsh weather":** Moore, R., "An Update on the Demographics of Jonestown," The Jonestown Institute, 2017, https://jonestown.sdsu.edu/?page_id=70495.

**152 "had been raped":** Scheeres, J., *A Thousand Lives: The Untold Story of Hope, Deception, and Survival at Jonestown* (New York: Free Press, 2011).

**153 "drinking the poison":** Scheeres, *A Thousand Lives.*

**153 "Ultimately, 907":** The Jonestown Institute, "How Many People Died on November 18?," March 4, 2014, https://jonestown.sdsu.edu/?page_id=35368.

**153 "Just thirty-six people":** The Jonestown Institute, "How Many People Survived November 18?," January 3, 2018, https://jonestown.sdsu.edu/?page_id=35419.

**154 "destiny as individuals":** Scheeres, J., "Escape from Jonestown," Longreads, November 12, 2014, https://longreads.com/2014/11/12/escape-from-jonestown/.

**154 "she had 'double feelings'":** Bahadur, G., "The Jonestown We Don't Know," *New York Review of Books,* December 21, 2018, https://www.nybooks.com/daily/2018/12/21/the-jonestown-we-dont-know/.

**159 "liked Julia's 'marketability'":** NASCAR, "Julia Landauer to Race in the Pinty's Series with Joey McColm and CBRT," July 12, 2018, https:/

/hometracks.nascar.com/2018/07/12/julia-landauer-to-race-in-the-pintys
-series-with-joey-mccolm-and-cbrt/.

171 **"threat overstated—one study":** Strauss, V., "Why Those Annoying 'Helicopter Parents' Aren't So Bad After All," *Washington Post,* October 21, 2015, https://www.washingtonpost.com/news/answer-sheet/wp/2015 /09/09/whythose-annoying-helicopter-parents-arent-so-bad-after-all/?utm _term=.b157399b23f3.

171 **"kind of support":** Fingerman, K. L., Cheng, Y.-P., Wesselmann, E. D., Zarit, S., Furstenberg, F., & Birditt, K. S., "Helicopter Parents and Landing Pad Kids: Intense Parental Support of Grown Children," *Journal of Marriage and Family* 74, no. 4 (August 2012): 880–96.

172 **"to grow up happily":** Pew Research Center, "The Decline of Marriage and Rise of New Families," November 18, 2010, http://www.pewsocial trends.org/2010/11/18/the-decline-of-marriage-and-rise-of-new-families/2 /#ii-overview.

174 **"still single at thirty-eight":** Lenti, S., "Single, Childless and Nearing 40, I Saw One Real Option," CNN, May 13, 2018, https://www.cnn.com /2017/04/25/opinions/ivf-3-7-percent-opinion-lenti/index.html.

178 **"*Popular Music and Society*":** Inglis, I., "Conformity, Status and Innovation: The Accumulation and Utilization of Idiosyncrasy Credits in the Career of the Beatles," *Popular Music and Society* 19, no. 3 (1995): 41–74.

183 **"In one study":** Seery, M. D., Gabriel, S., Lupien, S. P., & Shimizu, M., "Alone Against the Group: A Unanimously Disagreeing Group Leads to Conformity, but Cardiovascular Threat Depends on One's Goals: Cardiovascular Threat from Group Disagreement," *Psychophysiology* 53, no. 8 (August 2016): 1263–71.

187 **"women of color":** National Association for Law Placement, Inc., "Report on Diversity in U.S. Law Firms," 2017, https://www.nalp.org /uploads/2017NALPReportonDiversityinUSLawFirms.pdf.

187 **"*New York Times* described it":** Keh, A., "Smashing a Ceiling and a Lot of Egos," *New York Times,* August 16, 2014, https:/ /www.nytimes.com/2014/08/17/sports/basketball/michele-roberts-nba -unionsnew-leaderconfronts-gender-barriers.html.

188 **"syndrome are by women":** Young, V., *The Secret Thoughts of Successful Women: Why Capable People Suffer from the Impostor Syndrome and How to Thrive in Spite of It* (New York: Crown Business, 2011), 8.

188 **"arrived at Princeton":** Young, *The Secret Thoughts of Successful Women,* 41.

189 **"worked fourteen-hour days":** Young, *The Secret Thoughts of Successful Women,* 73.

**189 "*The Impostor Phenomenon*":** Clance, P. R., *The Impostor Phenomenon: Overcoming the Fear That Haunts Your Success* (Atlanta, GA: Peachtree Publishers, 1985).

**192 "Solomon's sage advice":** Herbert, W., "The (Paradoxical) Wisdom of Solomon," Association for Psychological Science, March 14, 2015, https://www.psychologicalscience.org/news/were-only-human/the-paradoxical-wisdom-of-solomon.html.

**193 "a series of studies":** Grossmann, I., & Kross, E., "Exploring Solomon's Paradox: Self-Distancing Eliminates the Self-Other Asymmetry in Wise Reasoning About Close Relationships in Younger and Older Adults," *Psychological Science* 25, no. 8 (2014): 1571–80.

**193 "Other studies":** Carroll, L., "Quiet Your Anxiety by Talking to Yourself in the Third Person," *Today*, July 31, 2017, https://www.today.com/series/one-small-thing/talking-yourself-third-person-can-calm-emotions-t114420.

**194 "that he once":** Freedom House, "Timeline: 20 Years of Human Rights Abuses in Belarus," https://freedomhouse.org/fair-play-beyond-sports/timeline-20-years-human-rights-abuses-belarus.

**198 "accommodative dilemmas":** Giles, H., and Giles, J., "Ingroups and Outgroups," in Kurylo, A., "Inter/Cultural Communication: Representation and Construction of Culture," 2012, https://www.sagepub.com/sites/default/files/upm-binaries/48648_ch_7.pdf.

**198 "feelings. (One paper":** Ryan, E. B., Kennaley, D. E., Pratt, M. W., & Shumovich, M. A., "Evaluations by Staff, Residents, and Community Seniors of Patronizing Speech in the Nursing Home: Impact of Passive, Assertive, or Humorous Responses," *Psychology and Aging* 15, no. 2 (2000): 272–85.

**200 "*Wallflower at the Orgy*":** Ephron, N., *Wallflower at the Orgy* (New York: Viking, 1970).

**204 "told *Oprah* magazine":** Arnold-Ratliff, K., "How Evan Smith Became Vivienne Ming: An Incredible Story of Self-Discovery," *Oprah Magazine*, October 12, 2013, https://www.huffingtonpost.com/2013/10/12/vivienne-ming-self-discovery-gender-transition_n_3998281.html.

**205 "in the *Financial Times*":** Ming, V., "There Is a Tax on Being Different," *Financial Times*, July 3, 2016, https://www.ft.com/content/1929cd86-3eb6-11e6-8716-a4a71e8140b0.

**206 "In one study":** Trew, J. L., & Alden, L. E., "Kindness Reduces Avoidance Goals in Socially Anxious Individuals," *Motivation and Emotion* 39, no. 6 (2015): 892–907.

**206 "than 7 percent":** Bureau of Labor Statistics, "Employed Persons by

Detailed Occupation, Sex, Race, and Hispanic or Latino Ethnicity," https://www.bls.gov/cps/cpsaat11.htm.

**209 "their book, *Extreme*":** Barrett, E. C., & Martin, P. R., *Extreme: Why Some People Thrive at the Limits* (New York, Oxford University Press, 2016).

**210 "blood-oats. Research":** McAdams, D. P., & Guo, J., "Narrating the Generative Life," *Psychological Science* 26, no. 4 (March 5, 2015): 475–83.

**210 "and self-confidence":** Del Corso, J., & Rehfuss, M. C., "The Role of Narrative in Career Construction Theory," *Journal of Vocational Behaviour* 79, no. 2 (October 2011): 334–39.

**212 "to Emma's memoir":** Gingerich, *Runaway Amish Girl,* 134.

**213 "they made all the rules":** Hostetler, J. A., *Amish Society* (Baltimore, MD: Johns Hopkins University Press, 1968), 151, 167.

**219 "or anxious extroverts":** Wiseman, R., *The As If Principle: The Radically New Approach to Changing Your Life* (New York: Free Press, 2013), 190.

**220 "in one study":** Göllner, R., Damian, R. I., Rose, N., Spengler, M., Trautwein, U., Nagengast, B., & Roberts, B. W., "Is Doing Your Homework Associated with Becoming More Conscientious?," *Journal of Research in Personality* 71 (December 2017): 1–12.

**220 "the *Wall Street Journal*":** Ruffenach, G., "Change Your Personality Later in Life? Yes, It Is Possible," *Wall Street Journal,* April 22, 2018, https://www.wsj.com/articles/change-your-personality-later-in-life-yes-it-is-possible-1524449340.

**220 "Wiseman writes":** Wiseman, *The As If Principle,* 216.

**220 "In one study":** Hudson, N. W., & Fraley, R. C., "Volitional Personality Trait Change: Can People Choose to Change Their Personality Traits?," *Journal of Personality and Social Psychology* 109, no. 3 (2015): 490–507.

**221 "naturally with age":** Chopik, W. J., & Kitayama, S., "Personality Change Across the Life Span: Insights from a Cross-Cultural, Longitudinal Study," *Journal of Personality* 86, no. 3 (June 2018): 508–21.

**221 "review of studies":** Roberts, B. W., Luo, J., Briley, D. A., Chow, P. I., Su, R., & Hill, P. L., "A Systematic Review of Personality Trait Change Through Intervention," *Psychological Bulletin* 143, no. 2 (February 2017): 117–41.

**222 "anthropologist Robin Dunbar":** Konnikova, M., "The Limits of Friendship," *New Yorker,* October 7, 2014, https://www.newyorker.com/science/maria-konnikova/social-media-affect-math-dunbar-number-friendships.

**222 "of about twelve to fifteen":** Dunbar, R., *How Many Friends Does*

*One Person Need?: Dunbar's Number and Other Evolutionary Quirks* (Cam bridge, MA: Harvard University Press, 2010).

**222 "Jeffrey Hall found":** Hall, J. A., "How Many Hours Does It Take to Make a Friend?," *Journal of Social and Personal Relationships* 36, no. 4 (March 15, 2018): 1278–96.

**222 "Hall has found":** Hall, "How Many Hours," 1278–96.

**233 "One 2012 study":** Fernandez, S., Gomez, A., Morales, J. F., & Branscombe, N. R., "Influence of the Social Context on Use of Surgical-Lengthening and Group-Empowering Coping Strategies Among People with Dwarfism," *Rehabilitation Psychology* 57, no. 3 (August 2012): 224–35.

**233 "like 'midget wrestling'":** Little People of America, "Advocacy and Community Outreach," https://www.lpaonline.org/advocacy-and-community -outreach.

**234 "colleagues write":** Branscombe, N. R., Fernandez, S., Gomez, A., & Cronin, T., "Moving Toward or Away from a Group Identity: Different Strategies for Coping with Pervasive Discrimination," in *The Social Cure: Identity, Health, and Well-being*, eds. J. Jetten, C. Haslam, & S. A. Haslam (Hove, UK: Psychology Press, 2012), 115–31.

**235 "Associated Press in 2001":** Payne, P., "Dwarfs Divided over Limb Lengthening," Associated Press, July 29, 2001, http://articles.latimes.com /2001/jul/29/news/mn-27763.

**239 "around 6 percent":** Inbar, Y., & Lammers, J., "Political Diversity in Social and Personality Psychology," *Perspectives on Psychological Science* 7, no. 5 (2012): 496–503.

**240 "worked on one study":** Mather, R. D., & DeLucia, P. R., "Testing for Effects of Racial Attitudes and Visual Contrast on the Speed of a Driver's Response to a Pedestrian," *Transportation Research Part F: Traffic Psychology and Behaviour* 10 (2007): 437–46.

**240 "conservative future colleague":** Inbar, Y., & Lammers, J., "Political Diversity in Social and Personality Psychology," *Perspectives on Psychological Science* 7, no. 5 (2012): 496–503.

**244 "'large city' in 2010":** Mozingo, J., "San Bernardino: Broken City," *Los Angeles Times*, June 14, 2015, http://graphics.latimes.com/san-bernardino/.

**244 "less than 4 percent":** Fred Economic Research, accessed June 9, 2019, https://fred.stlouisfed.org/series/CASANB1URN.

**244 "225 sworn officers":** City of San Bernardino, California, "About SBPD," https://www.ci.san-bernardino.ca.us/cityhall/police_department /about_sbpd/about_sbpd/default.asp.

**244 "of San Bernardino":** Dulaney, J., "San Bernardino Flooded in Welfare Funds," *Los Angeles Daily News*, October 23, 2011, https://www .dailynews.com/2011/10/23/san-bernardino-flooded-inwelfare-funds/.

**246 "called *The Big Sort*":** Bishop, B., *The Big Sort: Why the Clustering of Like-minded America Is Tearing Us Apart* (New York: Houghton Mifflin Harcourt, 2008).

**247 "is just like them":** Badger, E., "Political Migration: A New Business of Moving Out to Fit In," *New York Times,* August 16, 2017, https://www.nytimes.com/2017/08/16/upshot/political-migration-a-new-business-of-moving-out-to-fit-in.html.

**247 "a landslide county":** Bishop, *The Big Sort,* 6.

**247 "35 percent of 'consistent' liberals":** Pew Research Center, "Political Polarization and Personal Life," June 12, 2014, http://www.people-press.org/2014/06/12/section-3-political-polarization-and-personal-life/.

**251 "doctors, 'Fix me'":** Henley, A., "There's a Mathematical Equation That Proves I'm Ugly—Or So I Learned in My Seventh Grade Art Class," Narratively, July 18, 2016, http://narrative.ly/theres-a-mathematical-equation-that-proves-im-ugly-or-so-i-learned-in-my-seventh-grade-art-class/.

**254 "one of her children":** Boylan, J. F., *Stuck in the Middle with You: A Memoir of Parenting in Three Genders* (New York: Crown, 2013), 20, 113.

**254 "the heterosexual world":** Lorde, A., *Sister Outsider: Essays and Speeches* (New York: Crossing Press, 1984), 114.

**255 "'of us,' he wrote":** Epstein, J., "Homo/hetero: The Struggle for Sexual Identity," *Harper's Magazine,* September 1970. https://harpers.org/archive/1970/09/homohetero/.

**255 "in *The New Yorker*":** Greenhouse, E., "Merle Miller and the Piece That Launched a Thousand 'It Gets Better' Videos," *New Yorker,* October 11, 2012, https://www.newyorker.com/books/page-turner/merle-miller-and-the-piece-that-launched-a-thousand-it-gets-better-videos.

**255 "Miller's obituary reads":** McDowell, E., "Merle Miller Is Dead at 67; A Novelist and a Biographer," *New York Times,* June 11, 1986, https://www.nytimes.com/1986/06/11/obituaries/merle-miller-is-dead-at-67-a-novelist-and-a-biographer.html.

**255 "called *On Being Different*":** Miller, M., *On Being Different: What It Means to Be Homosexual* (New York: Penguin, 2012).

**256 "'straight,' he writes":** Miller, M., "What It Means to Be a Homosexual," *New York Times,* January 17, 1971, https://www.nytimes.com/1971/01/17/archives/what-it-means-to-be-a-homosexual-a-fag-is-a-homosexual-gentleman.htm.

# Index